Solution[?]
Therapy With Families

Solution-Focused Brief Therapy With Families describes SFBT from a systemic perspective and provides students, educators, trainers, and practitioners with a clear explanation and rich examples of SFBT and systemic family therapy. Family therapists will learn how SFBT works with families, solution-focused therapists will learn how a systemic understanding of clients and their contexts can enhance their work, and all will learn how to harness the power of each to the service of their clients.

The book starts with an exploration of systems, cybernetics, and communication theory basics such as wholeness, recursion, homeostasis, and change. Following this is an introduction to five fundamental family therapy approaches and an overview of Solution-Focused Brief Therapy. Next, the author considers SFBT within a systems paradigm and provides a demonstration of SFBT with families and couples. Each step is explicated with ideas from both SFBT as well as systems. The final chapter shows how SFBT practices can be applied to a variety of family therapy approaches.

This accessible text is enhanced by descriptions, case examples, dialogue, and commentary that are both systemic and solution-focused. Readers will come away with a new appreciation for both the systemic worldview of SFBT and SFBT principles as applied to systemic work.

Thorana S. Nelson, PhD, is Professor Emerita in Family Therapy at Utah State University. She has co-written and edited numerous articles and books on Solution-Focused Brief Therapy and training, including *Handbook of Solution-Focused Brief Therapy* (with Frank N. Thomas) and *Doing Something Different: Solution-Focused Brief Therapy Practices*.

Solution-Focused Brief Therapy With Families

Thorana S. Nelson, PhD

Routledge
Taylor & Francis Group

NEW YORK AND LONDON

First published 2019
by Routledge
711 Third Avenue, New York, NY 10017

and by Routledge
2 Park Square, Milton Park, Abingdon, Oxon, OX14 4RN

Routledge is an imprint of the Taylor & Francis Group, an informa business

© 2019 Taylor & Francis

The right of Thorana S. Nelson to be identified as author of this work
has been asserted by her in accordance with sections 77 and 78 of the
Copyright, Designs and Patents Act 1988.

Library of Congress Cataloging-in-Publication Data
A catalog record for this title has been requested

ISBN: 978-1-138-54115-3 (hbk)
ISBN: 978-1-138-54116-0 (pbk)
ISBN: 978-1-351-01177-8 (ebk)

Typeset in Optima
by Apex CoVantage LLC

Contents

Foreword   viii

Preface   x

1   Systemic Thinking   1

Our Lenses   2

System Concepts   3

Cybernetics   14

Communication Theory   22

Therapy: Systems, Cybernetics, and Communication   24

And So . . .   28

2   Family Therapy Approaches   29

Structural Family Therapy   29

Strategic Family Therapy (Mental Research Institute)   35

Strategic Family Therapy (Haley and Madanes)   41

Bowen Family Therapy   44

Integrative Approaches   50

And So . . .   52

3   Solution-Focused Brief Therapy   53

Development of SFBT   53

SFBT Stance   55

Assumptions   57

General Practices   62

Specific Practices   71

Emotions		83
Changes in the Approach		83
And So . . .		84

4 SFBT Integration Within a Systemic Perspective | | **85**
Stance | | 85
Change Is Constant and Inevitable | | 88
If It Ain't Broke, Don't Fix It; Once You Know What Works,
*   Do More of It; If It Doesn't Work, Do Something Different* | | 90
Clients Have Resources; Our Job Is to Help Identify and
*   Use Them* | | 94
Relationship Between Problems and Solutions | | 94
Focus on Future and Change | | 100
Small Change Leads to Bigger Change | | 101
Clients Are Experts on Their Experiences and Lives | | 101
Therapy Is Co-constructed | | 103
Client-Therapist Relationship | | 104
Well-Formed Goals | | 104
Curious Questions | | 105
Relationship Questions | | 105
Miracle Question, Preferred Future | | 106
And So . . . | | 107

5 Solution-Focused Brief Therapy With Families | | **108**
Families | | 108
Session 1 | | 110
Session 2 | | 129
Session 3 | | 135
Session 4 | | 136
Couples | | 139
Blended Families | | 143
And So . . . | | 143

6 Using SFBT Practices With Four Family Therapy Approaches | | **145**
Structural Family Therapy | | 146
Strategic Family Therapy (Mental Research Institute) | | 151
Strategic Family Therapy (Haley and Madanes) | | 157

Bowen Family Systems Therapy   163
And So . . .   172

References   173
Bibliography   177
    Systems   177
    Solution-Focused Brief Therapy   177
Appendix: Major Marriage and Family Therapy Models Charts   179
Index   212

Foreword

Frank N. Thomas

I maintain that nothing could be more practical than to become more familiar with the patterns of movement life requires. The goal is not to crack the code, but rather to catch the rhythm.

—Nora Bateson (2016)

Solution-Focused Brief Therapy (SFBT) and family therapy models based on systems thinking have a common link: Steve de Shazer, one of the pioneering creators of the approach. While many in the SFBT world only learned more current constructions and expressions of the approach, the well-informed easily recall de Shazer's early writings across which he created the solution-focused approach. *Patterns of Brief Family Therapy* (1984a) is subtitled *An Ecosystemic Approach* and is clearly systems-oriented. The forewords were written by de Shazer's mentor John Weakland, co-creator of the interactional-strategic approach of the Mental Research Institute (MRI), and Bradford Keeney, the leading cybernetics theorist in family therapy at the time. *Keys to Solution in Brief Therapy* (1985), de Shazer's second book, radiates a systems approach throughout. And as late as 1991, de Shazer was still leaning on systems concepts and understandings as evidenced in his fourth book, *Putting Difference to Work*.

So why have I started this Foreword with a de Shazer history? The context of this book is this: systems thinking and SFBT are inextricably entwined. While some in the SFBT world may seek to leave systems thinking behind (or never acquired the perspective), Thorana S. Nelson takes us in a different direction: toward complementarity, connecting ideas of SFBT and systems thinking. Nelson is one among few scholar/practitioners who could record this beautiful harmony, creating a score that unites systemic family therapy with SFBT, an integration without forced conflation. What she places in our hands is a practical application of complex thinking about clinical work with clear applications for readers who wish to utilize the best of SFBT's practices within major family therapy models; recursively, Nelson guides readers in applying SFBT with families, keeping a systems view while outlining ways to view and do SFBT when working conjointly.

Nelson's writing is a *lingua franca* for those only acquainted with one, solution-focused or systems approaches. Using a familiar, less formal style than most academic writing, she connects us to challenging concepts and clinical models in a way I have not experienced before. Nelson successfully communicates complex ideas without diminishing their complexity. Her therapy examples demonstrate practices and ideas so readers can get a sense of possible applications. And her appendix is a gold mine for anyone wanting a concentrated yet profound overview of most major marriage and family therapy (MFT) models.

SFBT practitioners will "catch the rhythm" of systems thinking; family therapists approaching their work from systems perspectives will benefit from Nelson's thoughtful and useful integration of SFBT tenets and practices into their specific models. In a nutshell: I wish I had written this book.

Frank N. Thomas
Fort Worth, Texas, USA

Preface

In the early 1980s, I was introduced to a book called *Patterns of Brief Family Therapy*. I was a master's student in a family therapy within a counseling department at the University of Iowa. Several of us were interested in working with families, and I had heard of family therapy while I was an undergraduate at the University of Houston. I had read Virginia Satir's (1967) *Conjoint Family Therapy* and become fascinated with the idea of working with families from a holistic perspective. My family was troubled as I was growing up and I thought that if we had had something like Satir's work, life would have been different. So, I aimed to be a family therapist.

My fellow students and I learned about requirements for Clinical Membership in the American Association for Marriage and Family Therapy and worked to help faculty develop courses. Many of them were independent studies modeled after courses in accredited programs. In many ways, our faculty were learning alongside us (the main difference being that we were paying for the privilege). By focusing on family therapy approaches and systems thinking, I became even more impassioned about learning as much as I could and helped develop courses in a master's program.

During my second year, our professor introduced us to a new book he had read: *Patterns* by Steve de Shazer. In it, he described fascinating new ways of looking at the problems people bring to therapy, something he called the *binocular* view. By recognizing that looking at something from one lens only, we miss a whole other perspective, we could ask different questions, use different interventions, and help our clients reach their goals more quickly.

de Shazer was coming to Iowa from Wisconsin as the keynote speaker at a conference. The chair of that conference had to resign and I was asked to fill in. That's when I met Steve de Shazer and became fascinated with the Solution-Focused Brief Therapy approach. I continued to use the model I was trained in (Structural/Strategic/Bowen) but started adding pieces of de Shazer's work when it seemed appropriate. I met Insoo Kim Berg at another conference and became an even more interested devotee of the approach.

It became evident that SFBT was becoming an integral part of my thinking when I was working on a research grant with colleagues for substance-abusing women. We were approaching the work through a couple therapy perspective and quickly learned—all four of us—that we couldn't *not* use solution-focused ideas when things started to improve for the clients. We had to build it into our evolving manualized approach.

Even later, I was invited to attend what have become known as the "Hammond meetings." de Shazer, Berg, and colleagues Yvonne Dolan and Terry Trepper in Hammond, Illinois brought 30–35 of us together to talk about the approach, using it, and training people in it. After three meetings, we talked about how to keep things going, in part because we wanted to keep meeting and needed a good reason to do that. We hosted a conference and I edited a book on *Education and Training in Solution-Focused Brief Therapy* based, in part, on training exercises that we talked about during the Hammond meetings. We also started an association and hosted or first annual conference in 1993 in Loma Linda, California.

Through all of this, I was reading more, editing, writing, and using the SFBT approach. However, I have not been completely satisfied by the books that have been authored. It seems that new books are needed to discuss how the approach is used with different clinical problems and settings such as drinking, home-based therapy, sexual abuse, children, schools, and so forth. de Shazer and Berg had been trained at the Mental Research Institute in Palo Alto, California, steeped in systems, cybernetic, and communication theories. But I wasn't seeing that critical perspective echoed in the books I was reading. Nor were any books or articles being published on systems, SFBT, and family therapy. I heard people talking about their family therapy approaches as being solution-focused when in reality, they were borrowing some practices to enhance their work. I also heard people talking about SFBT without demonstrating a systemic sense to it. It became evident that people were thinking about SFBT as a stand-alone theory of how problems develop or of therapy, something that de Shazer was very clear about: SFBT is an approach to therapy, a description of what happens in therapy, not a theory of any sort.

Several years ago, colleague WeiSu Hsu of Taiwan invited me to do a series of two-day workshops on SFBT and families in China and Taiwan. I met with counselors, school counselors, counseling students, psychologists, and psychiatrists. The workshops were composed of lecture on the basics of system thinking and SFBT as well as exercises and practice in SFBT. Over nearly four weeks, I conducted six, two-day workshops and several short talks, all on SFBT and families. After coming home, I became determined to write a book on SFBT and families. This book would help family therapists learn more about how to use SFBT in a systemic way with families and help SFBT therapists learn about system thinking as a backbone of SFBT and how to use it with families. The book in your hands is the product of that determination.

In this book, Solution-Focused Brief Therapists will learn more about systemic ideas and how to use them in work with individuals, couples, and families. Family therapists will learn more about Solution-Focused Brief Therapy assumptions, concepts, and practices, whether adopting the approach as foundation or using aspects of it within systemic work.

The book starts with an overview of systems, cybernetics, and communication theory basics such as wholeness, recursion, homeostasis, and change. It's necessary to see systems as a worldview and this chapter provides the foundation for that.

The second chapter then introduces five basic family therapy approaches including one integrated approach: Structural, Strategic (Mental Research Institute as well as Haley and Madanes), Bowen, and Johnson's Emotionally Focused Therapy. Although not comprehensive, this chapter gives readers a sense of family therapy approaches. This chapter may be especially useful for solution-focused therapists who are not familiar with family approaches.

The third chapter is an overview of the Solution-Focused Brief Therapy approach. Beginning with a short description of the development of the approach, the concepts and practices are described in detail. Emphasis is on seeing SFBT as an approach, a description of what is done with clients rather than a theory or Theory.

The fourth chapter explicates SFBT within a systems paradigm. System concepts and ideas are used to understand SFBT concepts and practices.

The fifth chapter is a demonstration of SFBT with families and couples. Each step is explicated with ideas from both SFBT as well as systems.

The sixth and final chapter shows how SFBT can be used with the described family therapy approaches. Not all people who read SFBT literature are interested in using the approach in its more "pure" form. This chapter shows how different practices can enhance family therapy through demonstration with several family therapy approaches.

I hope that this book piques your interest in system thinking and in solution-focused ideas. It brings together my two professional passions and I am happy to offer it to you. Much of what follows is reflective of extensive reading and integrating from systems, cybernetic, solution-focused and other books, articles, and chapters as well as attendance at international conferences and conversations with solution-focused colleagues all over the world. Influences include Ludwig von Bertalanffy, Gregory Bateson, John Weakland, Paul Watzlawick, Richard Fisch, Janet Beavin Bavelas, Steve de Shazer, Insoo Kim Berg, Frank N. Thomas, and others cited in text and listed in a bibliography.

I want to thank my professors, students, clients, and colleagues who have accompanied me along this journey. Thank you to Frank N. Thomas, for many hours of discussion and emails, writing with me, and being a great colleague and friend. Thank you to my colleagues in the Solution-Focused Brief Therapy Association. Without the Association, I would have missed out on learning more about the approach as well as opportunities to meet wonderful people all over North America and the world. For my colleagues in the European Brief Therapy Association, thank you for providing a different enough perspective on SFBT to make a difference for me and my thinking as well as my practice, teaching, supervising, and writing. Thank you to Tomasz, Artur, and Jacek in Poland for opportunities to present, meet wonderful people, travel and eat together, and great conversations. I want to especially thank my solution-focused knitting friends. Thanks to Terry Trepper for getting me started on the book-publishing part of my career, and to Steve de Shazer and Insoo Kim Berg for sharing their incredible wisdom, experience, and talents, as well as good food and great conversation. I am most grateful to my friend and colleague, Dale Blumen, for reading earlier drafts of this book and giving helpful feedback. Finally, I thank my husband, Victor Nelson, who has shared this journey with me (even playing ping-pong in China!) and who has ideas that are different enough from my own to be interesting and useful.

Santa Fe, New Mexico, USA
June 2018

Systemic Thinking

Systemic thinking (von Bertalanffy, 1968) is a worldview, a lens, a paradigm. Often presented as theory, systemic thinking does not present testable hypotheses, constructs, or explanations and therefore is not a theory. The concepts lead to a way of thinking and seeing things not as isolated parts operating autonomously, but as residing in contexts and relationships with other parts, each interacting with, affecting, and being affected by all others.

Systems are groups of parts and their relationships to each other that, when viewed together, have a meaning and purpose that cannot be understood by observing the parts separately. Mechanistically, such a group might be something called a *car*. We can lay out the parts and see metal, plastic, tubes, cables, round things, square things, and so forth. However, unless and until these parts are put together and we see how they relate to each other for a purpose, they are not a car—they are just a bunch of things.

A human system is a group of individuals with a purpose related to a task. For example, we might see some people at a table listening carefully to someone at one end of the table. We might call this a *committee*, although without knowing its purpose and context, we can't really know; it might be a class. Each person has a role, each relates to all others in some way that helps describe the group as a whole, and their interactions together serve some purpose related to the aim of the group such as organizing an event or learning about something. Now, we could take the same people and put them all into a restaurant at a table with food. They are the same people, but no longer function as a committee or class. Rather, we may see them as friends at dinner with no particular hierarchy, but still relating to each other, this time around food and general conversation. The "leader" in the other setting no longer serves in that role. Members relate to each other differently than when they are interacting as a committee or a class.

This notion is called *wholeness*, sometimes described as "the sum of the parts is more than the whole," or "the sum of the parts is different from the whole." In order to understand the whole, we need to understand the purpose of the group, the roles each part plays, and the rules for the way the parts interact with each other. Each part interacts with all other parts, influencing and influenced by all other parts, by the interactions of other parts, by the meanings that arise from interactions, by the purpose of the group, and by its context.[1]

Our Lenses

When we look at parts—such as individuals—especially those that have been labeled or described as problematic in some way, we tend to see the parts through the lenses we have been taught, often in terms of psychology and biology. These lenses can lead us to logical conclusions that fit into the systems of thinking and describing that we have learned. For example, we may have been told that a child "has" Attention Deficit-Hyperactivity Disorder (ADHD; American Psychiatric Association, 2013). In our minds, we tend to see fidgeting, distracting behavior, reports of problems in school with friends and schoolwork, difficulty focusing, frustration for teachers, and worry for parents. If we watch the child in a classroom, we might see interactions with other students, concentration on a particular object, gazing out a window, and a swinging foot, as well as other children and their behaviors, the teacher and his or her behaviors, the setup of the room, the noises both inside and outside, and so forth. With the notion in our heads of ADHD, we might actually "see" the child's actions as evidence of ADHD and nothing else. Our pre-judged ideas based on our education, experience, and reports about the child make us actually, literally see things a certain way. We may automatically label something as attention deficit or hyperactivity. Without these prejudgments and labels, we may see the child very differently: social, dreaming, thinking about something, bored, interested in something in the corner or another child.

If we view the same child at home with family at dinnertime, we might see giggling with a sister, poking or arguing with another sibling, asking father questions about something, and asking for more potatoes. What judgments might we make about what we see? What explanations might we have? Further, if we have the family with us in a therapy setting, things will look different still as people take on different roles in the process called "therapy"; the child's behavior will look different to us because of our lenses, and to the family because of theirs.

One time, when I was teaching on-site practicum for a master's program, we saw a family for a fifth session. As usual, the mother took charge, complaining about one of the children and the crisis of the week. The four children operated in various ways, alternating boredom with attention to the mother and therapist, and arguing with each other. The child on the current "hot seat" tried to interrupt her mother and was shushed. The mother talked fast, scolded her daughter, and hardly let the therapist speak. The session appeared to be in chaos with other children twirling in their chairs, hiding behind drapes, and teasing each other. After the session, our practicum group went to dinner before conducting other sessions. At the restaurant, we saw the same family. The older children were helping the younger ones with their meals, the identified child during the session was talking to the mother, who was calm and listening. The family-in-therapy did not appear to be the same family-eating-in-a-restaurant.

System Concepts

Following are a number of system concepts that may be helpful at enlarging perspectives as we work with clients. For more detailed discussions, I refer you to some of the literature listed in the bibliography.

Wholeness

Wholeness is the idea that the whole is *different from* the sum of the parts—it's the parts plus the interactions and relationships among the parts plus the context of the system. It consists of many different subgroupings or subsystems and resides in a context called a macrosystem. The client family described above can be seen as two different families, each depending upon context and the ways that people interact with each other as well as their relationships. In therapy, the relationship between mother and daughter appeared to be very hierarchical; in the restaurant, it appeared to be more collaborative.

Systems are made of parts that often are organized into *subsystems*. Children in a family form a sibling group, and grownups form subsystems that may be called *couples* or *parents*, depending on the particular interactive situation and purpose. Females form one group, males another. In large families, there often are the "older ones" and the "younger ones." Within the subsystems are individuals, who also have subsystems: biological, psychological, cognitive, and behavioral. Each of these subsystems may have yet further subsystems, and so on.

The group as a whole can be seen as a subsystem within larger systems: neighborhoods; schools; work; churches, synagogues, or mosques; communities and even larger communities. Some of the subsystems are more involved in some larger systems than others. Children, for example, may be more involved as students in schools, members of peer groups, or participants in sports teams or other groups. Parents as individuals or together may be involved in politics, interest groups, hobbies, and so forth. People of similar races, ethnicities, political or interest groups, social location identities, and so forth form systems. Each of these groups may be subsystems of even larger groups such as associations, states, countries, political parties, ethnicities, races, and so on, and may overlap with other groups. The lists are nearly endless with individuals and subgroups having different identities, functions, and roles in each system or subsystem and influences on each other.

Boundaries and Rules

Each system and subsystem is defined by its *boundaries*—the invisible lines that separate groups and subgroups. The *rules* for what makes up these boundaries are often unspoken but are very powerful: Who is in a group and who is not? What may each person do within a group and what must they not do? Whom may they invite into the group and whom may they not? For how long? For what purpose? What are the rules for the person entering the group temporarily? Permanently? What are the consequences of breaking the rules? What are the mechanisms for changing the rules (metarules)?

Mechanisms or rules about changing the rules are called *metarules*—rules about rules. Metarules include things such as who can change rules and how. Rules in families may change easily but metarules tend to be less flexible. In therapy, we are tempted to help families change their rules (let children have more say in their lives; encourage parents to take more charge), which may be sufficient for resolving their difficulties. However, changing the metarules typically results in more lasting change as well as in more flexibility or adaptability of rules in the future when other changes present challenges.

For example, families may have difficulties resolving a child's school problem. Rather than focus on the child and changes he or she needs to make, a family therapist would focus on the family, not as the cause of the problem, but as perhaps maintaining the problem and certainly as involved in change. The father may have ideas about how the child could change, the mother other ideas, and the children still others. A therapist might help the parents engage in more homework time with the child or all children. In this case, the rule addressed would be "how homework gets done." And this may be sufficient. However, if the parents are in disagreement about who is going to help or enforce homework and how that help will look, and the mother refuses to participate in a discussion about this, the therapist may see a metarule that mother is in charge of this function in the family and changing who works with homework and how isn't going to change unless mother agrees. It might be different if the stated difficulty in the family is one of the children's misbehavior around family tasks or curfew.

Metarules are often unspoken but very powerful. By focusing on the metarules around how rules are made, who is in charge of what in the house, and so forth, the therapist may be able to help the parents operate more as a team so that the metarule of mother-in-charge changes to parents-as-a-team, which will change boundaries in the family and the dynamics around homework (and other things) in a dramatic way. We call this *second-order change*, discussed below. Settling for first-order change may result in short-lived changes and no overall resolution of the difficulties the family experiences, especially when those difficulties are maintained by patterns of interaction or family dynamics that have not been addressed. Second-order change results in a change in the system itself—it becomes a different system (e.g., a system where decisions around schoolwork include parents as a team rather than decisions around schoolwork being made by one parent). This altered system has different boundaries and rules about the boundaries. The parenting subsystem about schoolwork now includes both parents instead of only the mother.

Boundaries may be open, closed, or exhibit varying degrees of permeability, with rules governing their nature. Open boundaries allow information to go between subsystems or systems easily; closed boundaries allow no flow of information or so little that its almost imperceptible. In the movie *Virgin Suicides* (Soffia Coppola, 1999), the family had such closed boundaries and rigid rules that the sisters had no room to be individuals or schoolmates with other teens, to grow as children naturally do. In one scene, the parents had decided that one of the girls could "date" a boy, but it had to be in their house with the whole family. Watching a movie, the girl sits on one side of her mother and the boy on the other, with the mother sitting on the edge of the couch between them like a barrier.

In another family, the parents might not even know where the daughter is—a more open boundary with more flexible rules or perhaps no rules at all about how people are connected to each other. In this kind of situation, the saying is that the police come to the door with a child and the parents didn't even know the child was not home. These are very loose boundaries.

It would be very easy to see each of these families as dysfunctional, but we cannot be judges of that, we can only describe what we see. Each family might be quite functional in itself for many things, although perhaps with some challenges for others. Our judgments about the appropriateness of the family's way of being are typically based on our own cultural values and beliefs and may be more or less rigid or loose than the family's.

When a system enters therapy, they often describe one of the members as "the" problem or as causing problems in the family. However, by looking at the system as a whole, describing it in multifaceted ways with suspended judgment, we have choices about how we characterize the system, the members in it, their boundaries, and their system rules.

It is easy to see individuals or isolated interaction patterns as problematic or as causing problems. Problems identified this way often lead to therapy that does not include observations of their contexts, especially when the theory or approach to therapy focuses exclusively on one person's biology, thoughts, feelings, or behaviors. When we see problems in context, we see interactions among members of a family or other group and with larger systems; we see relationships; we see values, beliefs, culture, family norms and rules, family stresses, other individuals who could also be seen as problematic, resources and constraints from outside the family, and so on. We understand the complexity of the whole system of individuals and their interactions and relationships.

It also is easy to see some families as dysfunctional based on judgments of what is normal and functional from a societal or cultural view of boundaries and rules. I believe that the families we see in therapy are not so different from other families. Rather, they are the ones who choose therapy or have been referred by someone to help them resolve their difficulties. Other families, faced with similar challenges, may find other ways to resolve their problems, ones that do not include therapy. Based on our theories about how problems develop, what needs to change for them to be resolved, and how that change will occur, we often see dysfunctional boundaries (too permeable, too rigid) or skewed structures and rules (children in charge of parents, father and child in charge of mother). A common such structure is a child who has responsibility for younger siblings such that he looks like a "parentified" child. But it may be necessary for the child to care for younger children because her parent(s) are overwhelmed with other matters such as a special needs child, ailing extended family members, a financial situation that requires multiple jobs that leave little time at home, and so on.

In some cultures, it is much the norm for older children to care for younger siblings, and in others, quite the opposite. Some views of boundaries as too rigid or too loose are often based on cultural expectations. When a family's culture, values, and beliefs do not mesh well with the dominant society's or those of someone with power over them, there may be clashes. Rather than viewing these boundaries and norms as inappropriate, from a systemic perspective we may see that the family is functioning quite well within its own context and the only concern is based on the values and beliefs of a person who is observing the family.

Semipermeable boundaries allow measured amounts and kinds of information to flow through the boundaries. This is especially important in families as children grow and circumstances change. There are rules about what this information might be and with whom it is shared. In parts of our society, for the most part, children do not know much about certain aspects of their parents' lives. This may be sex, finances, or relationships with extended family or other adults. Other knowledge, however, such as what kinds of things the family likes to do together inside or outside of the house, indicate more permeable boundaries.

Further, boundaries often change when there is stress. Losses in the family, for example, may lead to a closing in of the family, a closeness among members that wasn't apparent before the loss. In other situations, such as a hurt person, the boundaries may need to be looser to allow medical professionals and other helpers access with more than usual information going in and out of the family.

Rules and Roles

We may be quick to judge through our observations but we must be careful. Judgments are made based on our own experiences, values, roles, and rules that form our ideas about what is and is not appropriate, often based on norms in the larger societal or cultural context. Certain things may not be appropriate to us, but quite acceptable to others. For example, when I was growing up, we had family dinner at 6:00 each night. We each had our usual place at the table, we ate using certain manners, and we did not leave the table unless our mother excused us. I observed other families when I visited them, families that did not seem to have "manners," who sat wherever they wanted, who reached for the salt instead of asking for it, and who left the table and came back for no clear reason or without permission. This looked like chaos and rudeness to me. I now understand that family rules and norms are different in different families and are not necessarily right or wrong.

Rules define *roles*: within each subsystem and system we have parts to play, functions to serve, things we must, may, or may never do. When is it acceptable for a child to act like a parent to other children? When is it not acceptable? Which behaviors are acceptable in this role and situation and which are not? When is it OK for people to switch or take on others' roles? Who is responsible for what functions? When? For how long? In what manner? Is there flexibility for enacting roles or must they be done the same way each time they are needed? Are they sometimes enacted even when they are not needed? Who decides what changes are acceptable, and when might those rules and roles change?

Most of these rules are unspoken and people adapt to them easily as they change. This means that there are rules about rules and change (metarules).

Metarules may be the most important kind in systems: How is change managed? Many rules and metarules just develop over time as things happen; others are brought into a nuclear family from families of origin and may need to be negotiated. People come together for a certain task or purpose, forming a system that may dissolve as soon as the task is complete or purpose is served. Two people get married and begin to "fit" with each other around roles, rules, tasks, and function; they are now less parts of their families of origin and have formed a new family or subfamily. Children are brought into the group and the original members must adapt, developing new roles, rules for those roles, norms, processes, and so on.

Homeostasis, Morphogenesis, and Change

Homeostasis is a concept that describes stability of a system—the tendency for the system to remain the same, although not necessarily static. We might think of this as limited change in motion, a dynamic that maintains the system's equilibrium, adapting to small changes that do not require change of the system as a whole. This can happen on a micro level with such things as places where people sit at the dinner table or even whether and when the family eats together. Another example might be gradual changes in children's bedtimes as they age. Or, homeostasis can be seen at a more macro level: Over generations, what constitutes a "family" or group? After several generations, none of the original members are alive, so is it the same "family" or a different one? From whose perspective?

An important understanding of families as systems includes the idea that change is happening all the time in small and large ways. How much change is acceptable within homeostatic parameters and how much is allowed for morphogenesis? With each change, the family adapts its parameters and shape or growth, termed *morphogenesis*. This process allows the function or purpose of the system to adapt to changing needs and circumstances in ways that continue to support the individuals within the system in their own changes and, at the same time, support the integrity of what is called "family." The system grows as purposes and needs evolve.

Boundaries in systems that have tight rules may be closed, or only closed or "rigid" as perceived by others, and perhaps only for some functions. Changes are not easily accomplished or adapted to. When new information comes into a system or develops from within (e.g., maturing children and their abilities to accept new roles and responsibilities), the system must adapt. For example, at some age, children begin to have more influence over their own lives, negotiating some rules instead of having them imposed. If the new information is acceptable, it may require large or small adaptations, but the system remains basically the same. If the new information is not acceptable, it may be rejected in order for the system to have stability. Some families have great difficulty accepting a grown child's partner into the family, and the partner may forever be an "out-law" with limited acceptable interaction with family members. In some families, this may even mean rejection of the child.

Boundaries that are very loose within a family may be perceived as allowing too much information in or out. Such might be the case in what some would call an "enmeshed" family—one with very loose boundaries inside the system and a more rigid one around the system. Children know a lot about what's going on in adults' lives, and parents are very involved in their children's lives.

However, in families—indeed, in most systems—boundaries are neither overly rigid nor loose, but appropriate for the system's purpose and needs for functioning. In families, this means adapting to the natural changes that occur with children's development, new jobs or lost jobs, moves, new friends, lost friends or extended family members, and so forth. Systems must have rules and processes for maintaining the integrity of the system and allowing some change but not too much or too fast. They have rules about rules and rules about change (what constitutes change or a difference, when and how rules change). How is new information adapted to the family and how does the family adapt to the new information? What constitutes acceptable change and unacceptable change? Acceptable adaptation and unacceptable adaptation? How is change managed?

One purpose of families, as perceived by anthropologists and sociologists, is the protection of children and, at the same time, the socializing of the children into the larger community. In parts of society, this is often shown through children's ages and abilities as the family adapts by gradually increasing experiences, responsibilities, and privileges that children have, starting with day-care and playdates, moving to preschool and kindergarten, then into elementary, middle, and high school. At some point, the norm may be for children to move out of the nuclear family into trade or further education, and then, perhaps, joining with others to form new families. At some point, either gradually or quickly, children's autonomy and rights to self-govern change.

Other changes may be instigated from outside the system: involvement of a school or the judicial system, health problems, a job change, a move to a new neighborhood or community, the death of an extended family member, a new member coming into the family. These changes also require adaptation and often involve a period of disruption before the system settles into a new homeostasis and set of rules.

Equifinality

For all changes and functions or purposes, the system develops processes for promoting or managing them. Groups have ways for getting things done, and there may be greater or less flexibility for *how* they get done. For example, in families, food must be provided, but there may be many ways for this to happen. This is called *equifinality* or the idea that there are many ways to accomplish a particular end. As with boundaries, roles, and rules, the processes may be more or less acceptable or even workable for a given family. Expecting a 3-year old child to fix a meal for herself may not be reasonable without help, but expecting an 11-year old to manage her own meal may be quite acceptable. In each case, the end is the same—food for the child—but the means differ.

As children grow, they typically need more time with friends and less with the family, and the family must adapt to this change. But there are many ways to do so. For example, some families prefer meeting children's new friends and their parents before allowing a child to visit a friend's home. In other families, such a visit is considered minor, and such "previewing" is necessary only if the other family is taking the child on an outing. Values, experience, many contextual variables (e.g., nature of the community), and whether others' ideas are sufficiently similar are also parts in systems and have influence over interactions and decisions.

For therapy, equifinality also is an important concept. Therapists must constantly attend to what is working toward clients' therapy goals and what is not. Therapists need important skills for adjusting to different interventions or techniques, working with different groups of family members or with individuals, inviting other people in for sessions, or changing therapy approaches altogether in order to meet therapy goals.

Process Versus Content

The reason for focusing on *hows* (process) rather than *whats* or *whys* is partly due to another concept we use in terms of focusing on *process* or *content*. *Content* refers to the topic at hand—providing food, planning an agenda, or financial problems. From a systemic perspective, we are more interested in the interactive dynamics of how things work, how people interact, how decisions are made, how purposes are served, and how ends are met rather than individual people and their behaviors or concerns. Because we understand equifinality, we believe that there are many ways for things to work and that we are not necessarily the judges of which ways are most appropriate for a given situation or family. Within certain limits, mostly related to the safety of everyone involved, we focus on processes and how they may or may not be helpful for certain purposes rather than blaming individuals for their roles in the matter. When we focus on content, we become judges of how things should work, whether the family should be focusing on that content or something else, and who should be making what kinds of changes. When we focus on process, we pay attention to how family members interact around the perceived problem and help them change their interaction so that *they* can solve their problems.

For example, as therapists, we are often faced with labels and diagnoses that have explanatory usefulness, but not necessarily usefulness for change. The "ADHD" child may live in a family where there are lots of supports or none, parents who prefer medication to those who don't, varying resources for helping the child, and so forth. Because of equifinality, we focus on how things are done and whether that works in ways that reach the desired outcome. Because of equifinality, we understand that there are many ways to reach desired ends and that processes for arriving at the ends will depend to a great extent on the values, beliefs, norms, abilities, resources, and so forth to which the family and school have access. If we get caught up in the content, on the label of ADHD, we are likely to put on our "expert" hats that suggest that certain processes are best or better than others, that we know what those are, and that the family will be able to utilize them even when they don't fit the family's values, rules, and norms. If changing the rules and norms may be useful, we will help the family more by focusing on their processes than on being experts on the topic (content) and telling them what they should be doing. As a small example, some families find that adjusting diet and paying more attention to helping their children manage their emotions and behaviors, easing parental scolding, and allowing free play in contained situations fits their values more than medication and specified parenting methods.

However, because of all these complexities we have discussed, roles and rules, boundaries, norms, and context, we are more able to see that our function with families is to help them find ways to reach their goals, and that the processes for reaching those ends must fit within acceptable limits of the family.

As a new family therapist, I learned to judge and diagnose family processes derived from their ways of doing things, as more or less functional or dysfunctional, often either good or bad. These judgments and diagnoses came from studying various family therapy theories and approaches to therapy as well as using my own values and beliefs as touchstones. By simply observing families and helping them determine processes that work and don't work for themselves, based on their ideas rather than mine, I am now being truer to the notions of equifinality and morphogenesis. Each family must find its own way of developing within acceptable limits, of developing new processes or rules and roles, and for determining for themselves both what they want (content) and how they get there. If new ideas don't work, as a therapist, I can stand by to re-examine the process without judgment and help the family work out processes that will work better for them.

By honoring the family's definitions, by not getting caught in the "shoulds" of content, I am more able to be of service. Of course, because I have education and experience, I may be able to steer them away from potentially dangerous processes and ends, and may be able to share what others in similar situations have found useful, but my expertise is more along the lines of helping them find their way than telling them which way to go (which, by the way, I have tried and has seldom worked in my practice).

Isomorphism

Isomorphism refers to the notion that patterns of interaction in families, the way they interact with each other, are reflected in several different areas of the family's functioning. That is, the way the family makes decisions—their patterns of interaction—are similar whether the topic is what to have for dinner or where to go on vacation. I describe patterns in more detail in the next section on cybernetics, but for now, suffice it to say this is important when working with systems because change in one area of interaction can easily be reflected in others. Sometimes, when parents bring children to therapy, it appears to us that the "real" problem is the way the parents interact with each other—the marriage. However, because of isomorphism, we may be able to help the parents be a better team in making decisions and enforcing rules around parenting, the topic they came to therapy for, and the changes they make in their parental teamwork may transfer to their marital teamwork. This is quite helpful, because it means we don't always need to know everything about the family's interaction patterns to be helpful to them.

Cybernetics

Cybernetics is the study of feedback mechanisms in self-regulating systems (Wiener, 1948). A self-regulating system is one that is able to maintain itself or its homeostasis. A common example of a self-regulating, homeostatic system is the temperature function in a home. A thermostat serves to govern the amount of change allowed before regulating functions kick in: When the temperature of a room (one of the parts) goes higher than the thermostatic "rule," the furnace is triggered to shut off and perhaps for an air conditioner to activate. When the temperature goes below a threshold, the air conditioner is shut off or perhaps the furnace is activated (parts are activated to interact with other parts that allow fuel to enter the system, pilot lights ignite the fuel, etc.) until the temperature again rises above the higher rule. When the temperature reaches the higher level . . . and so forth. The plus and minus allowances of the system are built in so that there is some flexibility and furnaces and air conditioners are not constantly running.

Applied to families and using a system lens, boundaries are usually less easily regulated because many more factors are at play, and change is continuous in both large and small ways. The rules that govern the family are similar to the rules that govern thermostats, although much more complex. The thresholds that trigger activation of certain rules or actions are based on many more factors than the temperature of a room and change with circumstances. For example, 2-year-old children are typically not allowed to stray as far from their parents as 12-year-old children, depending on circumstances (playgrounds and family homes are typically different from crowded amusement parks and other people's homes).

Circularity

We cannot say that the thermostat or the furnace or the air temperature cause the system to work the way it does; each fulfills its function as triggered by other parts and in combination with those parts. This is called *circularity* or *circular causality*. Similarly, in families, we see circular patterns of interaction. It's easy to say that a child's behavior is causing the disruption in the family. However, when viewed as only one part in a whole, we begin to see the context, complexity, and perhaps function of the child's behavior: it likely makes sense given its context. For example, a child may have more difficulty falling asleep when the parents are experiencing some distress, whether that is verbal or just "in the air." We can't say that what led to the parents' distress caused the child to have trouble sleeping, and it is quite possible that the child's sleep difficulty exacerbates the parents' distress, leading to even more difficulty on the child's part. We also don't know about other factors that may affect the sleep difficulty or the parents' stress: a room that is too dark and "scary," parents' distress over finances, marital problems, extended family health matters, another child's problems, and so on.

Another example in families is when a teenager takes a parent's refusal to let her do something as "control." She stomps off to her room and slams the door. The meaning *control* influences her next interaction with her parent. Further, the meaning the parent derives from the interaction (disrespectful child) also influences the next interaction. I'm sure you can picture a possible next interaction: the teen says (with attitude, which the parent expected), "I don't suppose you'll let me . . ." and the parent says, "Not as long as you take that disrespectful tone with me." Who is to blame? Neither. It's a circular interaction where meaning is one part. Each affects the other, which is called *reciprocity*, and the pattern repeats itself, which is called *recursion*.

In a linear perspective, we look for the causes of problems, believing that we must find the causes in order to resolve the problem. The medical model and our typical Western way of thinking have promoted this, and it's important in some instances (appendicitis, for example). However, when we look at the larger picture of human behavior, relationships, and context, we see many factors. Can we say that the teen in the previous example is disrespectful and that caused the mother's refusal (there could have been another reason but that didn't get into the discussion before the teen stomped off)? Can we say that the mother is stifling the daughter and that caused the daughter to stomp off? We need to know much more about the family's typical dynamics, the context of the request including what has happened in other interactions, the relationship between the mother and daughter, how the father's perspective or behavior might influence what's going on, and so on. It's just not as easy as diagnosing an inflamed appendix.

Similarly, if daughter tells her mother about something difficult that happened at school, and mother is sympathetic, daughter may feel comforted. The next time something difficult happens at school, the daughter may be even more willing to tell her mother, expecting a comforting response in return. Mother is pleased that daughter is willing to come to her and so repeats the comforting. The daughter's request for something may be met with a very different response from her mother.

Recursion

Recursion is a concept that relates to circularity. It means that A and B respond to each other in interaction in repeated ways and that responses influence the system as well as other interactions. Again, we cannot say that the interaction causes an outcome in a linear way, but we can say that the outcome and its meaning are fed back into the system, influencing ensuing interactions in patterned ways. For example, a child delays homework until bedtime, father scolds, child cries, father relents, and the whole pattern repeats itself the next night. The pattern on the first night influences the pattern on the second night. It may be replicated or change in small or large ways. We can't say that the child's crying causes the father's relenting, or that the father's relenting causes the child's delay of homework the next night, or that this pattern caused a change in either's behavior ever. However, because it is a repeating pattern, it is worth looking at. The pattern also is contained in a context of a number of other things, including the child's experiences at school, what the mother is doing, what the mother and father may have discussed about homework or the pattern itself, etc. In therapy, we are able to see the pattern differently from the family and help them see it as systemic rather than blaming the child or the father and requiring that the person at fault must change.

Feedback Loops

Feedback is a cybernetics concept that is often confusing because of its name. It is *not* referring to the colloquial use of the term, whereby we critique something and provide either praise or criticism. To further confuse things, the cybernetic term also uses adjectives of *positive* and *negative* to qualify the meaning of the term. In the colloquial sense, positive feedback is considered good and negative feedback bad or at least not-good. Not so in cybernetics.

In a cybernetics sense, feedback refers to information that is the result of an interaction being fed back into the system (the loop). This new information may affect the homeostasis of the system in terms of maintaining it or allowing change such as morphogenesis. However, the information needs to be a "difference that makes a difference" (Bateson, 1972, p. 453) in order to effect change. A child's request to change primary sports might not make much difference. A request to change to a sport the parents disapprove of might make a very big difference.

Positive feedback is the result of a change that the system is able to allow, adapt to, or even welcome; the rules of the system are flexible enough to adjust to the change, whether minor or significant. Change is OK and amplified: it's acceptable for the child to request a different sport and, in fact, may show growing maturity that the parents like. Positive feedback is not the parents' saying something like, "That's a good choice" (colloquial feedback) but the metamessage that the change (the child is making this request instead of the parents' imposing the change) is acceptable: the system is accepting the change in the rule that parents decide sports activity whether spoken or nonverbal. The positive aspect is that the change is a change in a rule and is amplified.

Negative feedback is the result of a change that the system is not able to allow or adapt to; the rules of the system are such that the change is dampened so that the system can maintain its homeostasis. Using our example of a child's request for sport choices, the child may choose something and the parents do not approve this change. This may be breaking the rule that parents choose children's sports activities, in which case whatever message or metamessage is given would dampen the change, returning the system to its most recent homeostasis. The child is not likely to make such a request later. Again, the change is not necessarily words from a parent such as, "You may not attend that sport; you must attend the ones I chose for you"; the message may come nonverbally such as raised eyebrows and the dreaded, "Do you really think that's a good idea?"

Positive feedback can result in adapted systemic change that is not good, even dangerous, such as a young child who suddenly comes and goes whenever and wherever she wants, even late at night or the parents' not knowing where she is. If the parents or other aspects of the family system do nothing to dampen this change, to send a message that this new behavior is unacceptable within family rules, the result is positive feedback that the change is acceptable.

As you can probably see by now, negative feedback in response to a change such as the one described above can be good: the child receives a message in some form that this new behavior is not acceptable. Coming and going at will is not acceptable for young children (negative feedback that is good). Understanding positive and negative feedback helps the therapist observe the family's process and stay out of content matters such as at what age children may have more control over their own lives and focuses on the family's dynamics around such issues according to its purposes and functions. When potential harm may be involved, the therapist may point this out to the family in terms of consequences of their decisions: they may be reported for child neglect or abuse. If the family accepts this, therapy may focus more on outcomes and how decisions are made that promote positive welfare of the individuals and family as a whole. If the family rejects this information, the therapist may be placed in a position of needing to report the potential neglect and/or the family does not return to therapy.

Moderate changes may go either way depending upon a variety of factors. For example, a 13-year-old child may be used to a certain bedtime, and, at the beginning of a school year, ask for a later bedtime or even a curfew. This signals at least two potentially important changes: later bedtime or curfew for the child resulting in other consequences, perhaps, for the parents such as not having as much alone time in the evenings, or for the child to take on more responsibilities in the family. It may also result in insufficient rest for the child. A second and systemically-oriented change may occur that the rules of the family change: the child may now participate in changing the rules, which is a change in the rules about who may influence the rules—a meta-rule. The parents would discuss the situation and decide that the requested new bedtime is not acceptable but that they and the child can talk about a number of things related to bedtime, responsibilities, consequences, and so on, perhaps leading to the child's earning a later bedtime or a probationary time. Prior to this, the rule was that the parents made decisions about bedtime; the new rule is that children may negotiate some rules with parents. This is a change in the metarule and signifies a fundamental change in the system—it's now a system with parents and children negotiating rules.

In this sort of case, the potential rule and metarule changes affect many aspects of the family and may call for further family negotiation, another rule, this one about *how* rule changes are made. The ripple effect can be extensive, particularly during times of big changes such as when children become teenagers or move out of the house, or when someone dies. Most families and even therapists do not pay sufficient attention to metarules, focusing instead on content issues and sometimes getting stuck in less productive cycles of first-order change (see p. 20). In addition, many of these changes in systems occur without any thought about them—they just change and life goes on in new ways without comment.

These concepts can get very confusing: rules, metarules, changes, positive and negative feedback, and so forth. And most families negotiate changes rather easily. There will be adjustments (remember that change requires adaptation, which is change) and some may be more uncomfortable than others, necessitating more discussion and negotiation. This process is called *morphogenesis* or the growth of a system as it adapts and changes its ability to adapt through many cycles of positive and negative feedback, changes in rules and metarules.

Pattern and Sequence

Pattern refers to the dynamics we see in systems that occur repeatedly over time and across content areas (recursion). Sequences are the recurring and circular actions that take place among the parts of the system and are typically predictable. For example, a child misbehaves → parents deliver consequences → the child objects → one parent responds one way to the child's objection and the other parent responds differently → later, the child misbehaves → and the dynamic repeats itself. This may look like a circle or an infinity sign:

$$A \infty B$$

I, personally, like the infinity symbol because I think it is easier to understand how communication and patterns cross each other, changing meaning and outcome, thus affecting the next occurrence of the interaction. I sometimes explain that the meeting point is usually related to meaning. A says something and it curves around to reach B, who makes meaning of it. This meaning is affected by a host of things: previous interactions between A and B, the particular topic, other aspects of the context including culture, and so forth. Therefore, B may not hear exactly what A intended to convey. B then acts not on what A intended, but what B heard and responds to that. This communication act also curves toward A, with A hearing not necessarily what B intended but what A thinks B meant and responds in kind. Remember the game of telephone where someone whispers a phrase to the next person in a circle, the next whispers to the third, and so on. And then we all laugh at what the last person claims was the phrase. Except in families, it's not always funny.

Punctuation

When a family recursively repeats patterns, there is no starting or ending point, only circularity. We have a tendency, however, to "believe" that there is a starting point: "it all started when . . ." This is called *punctuation*: We punctuate the beginning as the initial cause and the end as the result. However, if we punctuate the beginning elsewhere in the sequence, we can see that there are many ways to understand so-called cause and effect. Does a nagging parent cause a withdrawing teen? Does the teen's withdrawal cause the parent's nagging? Which comes first, the chicken or the egg?

By punctuating sequences in different places in therapy, people may be freed from their frustration about blame and become more easily able to see, admit to, and change their own parts of the sequence interaction.

First- and Second-Order Change

Change can also be seen in terms of systemic quality. First-order change is like changing from toast to bagels for breakfast. A change, perhaps even a significant one for someone (lox on bagels may taste much better than jam on toast), is still rather minor in terms of the system. One parent's making decisions about children's curfew and then switching to the other parent's making the decision is still "one parent makes decisions." These are system rule changes typically signifying first-order change.

Second-order change is a change in the rules such that the system itself changes—change in the rules about the rules, or metarules. Using the above example, at some point the parents may decide that it is necessary for them to act as a team in making certain decisions. They may decide that it is acceptable for children to negotiate their own breakfast or curfew and other rules. This is a change in rules about rules: children at a certain age or maturity may participate in making rules. This kind of change occurs as children get older and changes in the family's life cycle require changes in metarules. The system itself is different and would have great difficulty going back to old metarules.

Another example of second-order change occurs when something so significant in difference occurs from outside the system that the system's ability to adapt is challenged. If a family goes from two parents to one, or a new adult comes into the family, or even a new child or other person, the whole system must adapt with significant changes in both rules and metarules. A family's inability to adapt to such changes may present as physical, mental, behavioral, and/or emotional difficulties for one or more people in the family, or in the family as a whole. Family therapists recognize that anxiety, depression, acting out, or even violent interactional patterns are not "caused" by such changes, are not necessarily solely the problem or blame of one member or another or event, but result from systemic changes that require adaptation that the family is not able to make effectively.

Some people seem to think that first-order change is change in behavior and second-order change is change in thinking. This is a linear way of looking at first- and second-order change, although it certainly can appear this way. Rather, first-order change is change *within* a system and second-order change is a change *of* the system so that it is no longer the same system. First-order change is moving the deck chairs around on the *Titanic*, and second-order change is adding lifeboats. First-order change is helping parents develop different consequences for their rules without seeing the broader picture. Second-order change is helping the parents determine whether a child is ready to participate in making the rules and, perhaps, the consequences for breaking them. The system changes from parents' making the rules to parents and children negotiating the rules together.

Communication Theory

Axioms

There is much about communication theory (e.g., Watzlawick, Bavelas, & Jackson, 1967) that we could discuss in relation to system thinking and cybernetics. For our purposes here, it is sufficient to focus on concepts that are most directly perceivable in circularity, sequences, and patterns. These are the "tentative axioms of communication" that inform our understanding of how people communicate in systems. Axioms are "established rule[s] or principle[s] or . . . self-evident truth[s]" (Merriam-Webster, 2018). An example of an axiom is "one cannot give what one does not have." The statement does not require "proof." Therefore, the following axioms are presented not as hypotheses or theory, but as assumptions that help us understand our observations of interaction and communication among family members.

Can't Not Communicate

Couples often come to therapy claiming that their problem is that they cannot communicate. In fact, they are communicating a lot, but not effectively toward whatever ends they desire. Even when someone says nothing, she or he is communicating in a way that is a comment on the interaction: *I refuse to comment; what you say deserves no comment; I have no idea how to respond to what you just said*; and so on. The communication may be ambiguous and not easily or correctly understood, but it is communication.

Content and Relationship Properties of Communication

The content aspect of communication, sometimes referred to as "report," is the topic being discussed. The relationship aspect ("command") is a systemic understanding of the nature of the relationship among the people in the interaction as well as the particular situation, and adds information to the content. For example, the statement, "your socks are on the floor" has face-validity of socks on the floor. However, the meaning of this statement depends upon several things, including the relationship between the people, the tone of voice used, previous interactions (see the discussion of circularity above), and other nonverbal factors because there are so many things beyond words that contribute to meaning. For example, the statement may mean, simply, "your socks are on the floor" as communication to someone who is looking for socks. Or it may mean, "pick up your socks" if the relationship is one of parent and child. The relationship between the people in former may be equal in this interaction. In the latter, the speaker has authority over the other person—the relationship aspect of the communication.

Punctuation

I discussed this concept earlier in the previous section of this chapter. It connotes a circular, repeated sequence that cannot easily be described as starting at one point or another. Where we punctuate the beginning for purposes of discussion may be arbitrary and intended to help interrupt the cycle so that blame is not cast on the previously chosen beginning. Did the argument begin when he asked about her day, or did it begin the night before when they had an unresolved argument, leaving her feeling frustrated and alone?

Digital and Analogic Communication

Digital and analogic communication refer to different aspects of communication, one of which can easily be perceived (digital) and the other that may have more subtlety or nuance (analogic). Digital communication has direct referents: "chair" refers directly to something upon which one may sit. Analogic communication does not have such clear referents and requires more understanding about such things as relationship, context, and previous interactions. Analogic communication is typically nonverbal (covalizations such as "uh-huh" could be considered nonverbal) and quite open to misinterpretation. It includes posture, tone of voice, loudness, gestures, and so forth. The words themselves typically require context to convey the speaker's full meaning, and the receiver will have his or her own context that may influence meaning different from the speaker's.

Refer back to the infinity symbol earlier in this chapter. You might think of it this way: Speaker A says something with an attempted meaning attached through analog. The words, the digital aspect, can be said to be filtered through contextual factors understood by Speaker B. Speaker B does not respond to what A said directly, but to what B attaches to the words based on the filter. Then B responds, but it is clear that B responds not to what A intended to mean, but to the filtered communication. This response also has digital and analogic components and goes through another filter that is A's context. Therefore, A hears a response not necessarily related to B's intended meaning, but to what B heard as filtered, responded to, and was further filtered before it reached A. Again, remember the game of telephone? "I know you think you understand what you thought I said but I'm not sure you realize that what you heard is not what I meant" (Alan Greenspan, n.d.).

Therapy: Systems, Cybernetics, and Communication

Understanding systemic ideas permits the observance of recursive, circular patterns, wholeness, homeostasis and morphogenesis, isomorphism, feedback, and so on, helping therapists in a variety of ways. First, instead of acting as experts on a particular content or family's dynamics, we become experts on process in general. Observing the family systemically, we have a multitude of ideas that keep us from becoming stuck in the family's content areas and recurring patterns. This understanding allows us to actually "see" family dynamics in context, as wholes, as patterns, as influences rather than causes, and to help families change dynamics that prevent them from resolving their issues themselves. Equifinality encourages us to see the family's dynamics in multiple ways, each lending itself as more or less helpful to resolving the family's presenting difficulty. Getting stuck often results in trying to "fix" the content or dynamic from an expert position, often without success (the new information may not be appropriate or accepted by the family). Finally, understanding these ideas can sometimes help us to explain confusing dynamics to families without blaming anyone, which may help them feel more empowered to change their own parts.

In family therapy, we don't act as mediators, trying to determine who most needs to change their part in the process, or exactly what changes need to take place. We ask about the steps in the process around the difficulty and help the family change the pattern of the interactions and their meanings. This change needs to introduce a significant difference so that it interrupts the pattern in a way that the system cannot continue with the next predictable step, and something else must happen. This "something else" may not be strong enough to effect a large change at the moment but may lead to other changes that are more beneficial. For example, encouraging a teen to speak up for himself may not result in immediate change; however, as time goes on and the teen thinks about it more, he may try it. The "something else" may also lead to a different cycle that is not helpful but that may stir the system enough that a more beneficial change may or must take place. The teen's manner of speaking up may not be acceptable to the parents but lead to another attempt with a different tone or attitude. Finally, it may lead to something unhelpful, which must be evaluated and may result in changing to a different way of interrupting the cycle. The particular thing the teen speaks up about may be totally unacceptable to the family, or the parents may determine that the teen is not ready to have this privilege.

A common intervention with couples who argue is to change the context of the argument: sitting back to back in a bathtub, for example. Another change may be the modality of the discussion from talking to writing letters or taking a break with a set time for resuming the conversation, allowing time for cooling off and perhaps absorbing what each other are saying. Other common interventions include examining the sequential pattern and asking each partner what she or he can do differently at each step. Changing one part of the sequence requires that the ensuing responses must change.

Changing the pattern can interrupt similar patterns that are potentially very serious. This is the helpfulness of learning about *isomorphism*. I explained this kind of thinking to some clients who tended toward loud arguments about finances that each feared were getting out of hand in ways they didn't like. I asked them about arguments or differences they had in other aspects of their lives and assigned homework of making lists of differences that didn't matter much, differences that were so significant that emotions tended to run high, and differences that could be considered somewhere in between (Nelson, 1994). The next week in therapy, we compared lists and I asked them to choose a topic from the middle area. Using this content to find a way to change their pattern capitalized on isomorphism: If we could change that pattern and perhaps practice it on other moderately tough areas, they might be able to tackle difficult areas more easily or even on their own, never needing to discuss the hot topics in therapy. The content wouldn't go away, but their ability to work together to resolve it would be enhanced. If we discussed easy topics, the difference might not be different enough to make a difference. If we worked immediately and quickly on difficult or "hot topic" areas, emotions might run too high and prevent an ability to change the pattern of discussion, resulting in even more discouragement.

In another example of using sequences, the pattern went like this: She came home from work before he did and started some household chore such as laundry, he came home and asked when dinner would be ready, she would say that she would start it after she finished what she was doing, and he would say that she could do the laundry later and should start dinner earlier. She said that he could start dinner himself or get a snack, and he would say that he needed to get the children started on homework and didn't have time, irritation and discord increasing with each part of the interaction. This repeated pattern had become very frustrating for both and it escalated one evening when she slammed the dryer door, breaking it, and he left the house.

In therapy, the couple were able to describe the pattern well, and said it was similar to other argument patterns they had. I drew the pattern on a piece of paper, explained what we were doing, and asked where they thought each could do something different—themselves, not the other. I also asked about the meanings and beliefs that were parts of the pattern. She said that she could plan dinner and get ingredients ready before she started laundry because he had said that he was frustrated partly because he didn't like planning the food and finding everything. Getting things ready would mean she wouldn't be starting dinner too early, he could move into getting it started before he helped the kids, and she could take over when her tasks allowed or at least they could discuss the situation instead of arguing about it. He wasn't sure what he could do and agreed to observe the situation during the week and see what he could come up with.

The first night went smoothly (as often happens) and the husband started dinner, and so forth. The second night, however, the wife was late getting home, started the children on their homework (thinking that might be helpful), and he arrived home with no dinner ready to fix, tired and hungry, and the old pattern started. However, she did not respond to his frustration by arguing, he realized what was happening when she just looked at him without arguing, so he went to the pantry, got himself a snack, and started to simultaneously eat it and work with his wife on getting dinner things ready so she could work with the children.

In therapy with people who tend to become violent, we are careful to make determinations that some patterns not only maintain problems but can easily get out of hand, especially once violence has been used by one or both partners. In those cases, we interrupt cycles by asking people where in the cycle they might be able to do something to keep themselves and each other safe. We can give suggestions but have found that when people choose their own interruptions, they do better.

I received a call from an emergency room late one evening. The personnel had noticed a couple in an intense discussion with a baby carrier and baby sitting on the floor between them. They had determined that having disagreements in public made it easier for them to keep them reasonable, not hurting the other with words or actions, and more likely to result in good outcomes. They didn't want to do this in a restaurant where others could overhear so, its being winter and rather late, decided to try a corner of an emergency room where things were not very busy. Of course, an admitting person asked what they were doing and they said it was part of their therapy. I explained the situation to the person who called me, who thought it was creative and went on about her work without bothering them but did ask if they would like something to drink. This kindness on her part further helped the couple to find creative ways to take care of their business without escalation.

Getting away from each other—timeouts that have prescribed endings—is also helpful. One man told me he got so angry sometimes that he didn't trust himself to drive and feared that police would notice him if he walked. He feared arrest for intimate violence. So, he drove a short distance to the police department, told them he was really angry and needed to cool off, asking permission to sit in the police waiting area. Everyone appreciated this interruption in the couple's argument pattern.

Some couples become violent so easily that couple or family therapy is not likely to produce change until other things such as substance abuse or misuse have changed, including the ability of partners to take responsibility for themselves and their actions instead of blaming the other or quickly moving to violence. In those cases, individuals may benefit from separate therapy on anger management or rehabilitation from substance use. It's very important with couples who have been violent to make sure to keep both partners safe and not exacerbate violence patterns. There are many resources for working with couples experiencing intimate violence from a systemic perspective that keep the couple dynamics in mind while working with individuals to reduce violence.

And So . . .

In this chapter, I attempted to describe some elements of systemic thinking, cybernetics, and communication theory that impact therapy from a systemic perspective. By seeing wholes, interactions, patterns, and meaning instead of neurological or behavioral problems in ways that include identifying causes so that specific interventions can be applied, we operate in a way that honors each family, couple, or individual that we see—their unique contexts, understandings and meanings of their worlds, and ways that may help them with their concerns that incorporate those contexts in our interventions. For those who are interested in more in-depth descriptions, I refer to the Bibliography at the end of this book.

Note

1 Many sources were used to develop this chapter and this book. Unless specified, ideas are often found in many places. The Bibliography at the end of the book may be useful for further reading and understanding.

2 | Family Therapy Approaches

In this chapter, I describe a few foundational family therapy approaches and an integrative approach that has a research basis. In each description, I provide the basics of the approach, how change is viewed, and typical interventions. The information is gleaned from many resources and produced in common format by my Marriage and Family Therapy master's students from Utah State University. I edited the material for accuracy, comprehensiveness, and formatting. The entire document is reproduced in the appendix of this book and may be used freely as long as credit is given to my students and me. Seminal references for each approach are included in the charts.

Structural Family Therapy

Structural Family Therapy was founded by Salvador Minuchin, a psychiatrist (e.g., Minuchin, 1974). He grew up in Argentina in a neighborhood made up of family members: parents, siblings, aunts, uncles, cousins, all related to him. Through this experience, he came to believe that psychiatry was not sufficient for understanding people's problems; rather, he believed that everyone grows up in a context of relationships that affect their ability to individuate, grow, and develop lives of their own. Problems develop when the structure of the family is not sufficient to promote the growth of the individuals in the system or the system itself. His work at a New York City school for boys showed him that families are systems with subsystems and individuals, with boundaries and rules that govern how the family manages life. Charles Fishman (e.g., Fishman, 1988, 1993) also has contributed to the development and publishing of Structural Family Therapy.

A number of concepts of Minuchin's Structural Family Therapy have become almost synonymous with family therapy. Among these are family structure, boundaries, roles, and rules, described in some depth in the first chapter of this book. If you are interested in these and other concepts in more depth, I suggest family therapy texts and resources listed in the MFT Model Charts in the appendix.

Structure

Structural Family Therapy is based on the assumption that problems reside in systems' organization and in contexts of relationships, most notably family relationships. These relationships form *subsystems* and *systems* that are defined by boundaries that form structures. The structure of the family is the context within which people operate according to roles and rules. Sometimes, these structures maintain dysfunctional behaviors, inhibit the growth of individuals, and prevent the natural or morphogenic development of the family.

According to system thinking, problems do not belong only to the person perceived as carrying them (the *identified patient*); they exist in a context of people, relationships, situations, resources, and constraints. This is not to say that the family causes the problem, but that its structure needs to be sufficient so change is supported and the difficulty can be resolved. Changing the structure of the family changes the way that people in it experience themselves, others, and relationships. A clearer or rearranged system may provide better support so that problems can be resolved. Sometimes, the problem is more in the relationships among people, in which case, clarifying the relationships, boundaries, and acceptable roles may be helpful.

Changing structures drastically too soon may be met with homeostatic resistance stronger than the pull toward change. In therapy, Minuchin and colleagues who use the structural approach usually do not attempt to change a family's structure with one intervention or goal; it often is better to change one part of the structure (e.g., help parents form a bond as a team) and then work toward a structural issue that may be more directly related to the problem (e.g., reducing one parent's overinvolvement with the child or increasing another parent's involvement so that the child has more access to both parents and perhaps other resources). However, a slight change may be welcomed that will then lead to another slight change, leading to overall restructuring of the system.

Boundaries, Roles, and Rules

Boundaries are the invisible lines that define functions of systems and sub-systems. They define what information may go into or out of the system/sub-system, and what behaviors are acceptable. For example, individuals have boundaries that help define an individuated self. Couples have boundaries that define them as a couple and exclude others as not a part of the couple. The same people in a couple as intimate partners may have boundaries that define them as parents that operate in different ways from those of the inti-mate partnership.

Boundaries may be quite solid or *rigid*, disallowing much or any infor-mation into or out of the system, or they may be quite diffuse (*enmeshed*), allowing a lot of information in and out. When families are experiencing difficulties, its boundaries often are too rigid or too loose to be helpful in resolving the difficulty and maintaining optimal and appropriate functioning.

Boundaries are bound by rules that define who is in and who is not in a system/subsystem, what kinds of activities or behaviors are acceptable or unacceptable, and who may change these rules (metarules; cf. Ch. 1). Rules in families govern all aspects and are often unspoken. Things such as who sits where at a dinner table, what privacy means, or when children may leave the house or apartment are examples. Rules may be explicit, such as bedtimes or curfews, but often are implicit and people sometimes don't know a rule has been broken or challenged until something happens. For example, children may not explicitly know the limits for how far they may go from parents without going too far. Once they go too far, parents typically respond in some way that helps make the rules more explicit and brings the child back within boundaries. This can mean physical distance for a toddler or attitude and language from a teenager. Boundaries are also defined by the recursive patterns of interaction among family members. For example, repeated requests to leave a room when a parent is working emphasizes a boundary between the parent and child at certain times. However, there may also be an implicit or explicit rule about when the child can breach that boundary, such as an emergency of some sort.

Minuchin was clear that someone or subsystem needs to be in charge of the system, especially when there are children. Parents form the *executive subsystem* and are the ones who make sure that people are safe and nurtured appropriately. Often, when children are experiencing problems, a rearrangement of the executive subsystem helps support resolution of the problem. At times, this requires flexibility, for example, when parents cannot fulfill all necessary functions. At those times, another person may be charged with the care of the children temporarily: a day-care provider, older child, or grandparent. When an older child is put in charge of younger children too much, the child is termed "parentified," which may interfere with his or her growth, individuation, and independence. A rule that defines who may take these roles, under what conditions, for which activities, with how much authority, and for how long is often necessary.

The roles and rules might be quite different in families with separated parents where children are sometimes with one parent and other times with the other. In these situations, the children belong in two subsystems and the combination can still be considered one whole. It is most necessary that boundaries be flexible so that each parent has some measure of autonomy over his or her own household, but that the parents still operate as a team for the wellbeing of the child. This sometimes means that there are both differences and similarities between the two households with an understanding that this is OK, and that the parents are still in charge. A boundary that pulls children into the parenting or executive subsystem can result in a structure that supports problems. A good example of this is when one parent quizzes children about the other parent, blurring the boundary around the parents and bringing the child into the parental subsystem. This may result in the child's feeling tugged between two loyalties resulting in lies and other unacceptable behavior. A therapist might help the parents work together to firm up the boundary around them and loosen the boundary between them so that there is adequate and appropriate communication with everyone.

Goals of Therapy

The goal of therapy is not to solve the presenting problem, but to change the structure of the family so that it can support its members and resolve life difficulties, both large and small. The focus is on the boundaries, roles, and rules of the family rather than the identified patient. The therapist watches the family interact (enactment as assessment) to infer the boundaries and roles of the family. Changing these patterns realigns the boundaries to make them more appropriate for the tasks at hand. Rigid boundaries are loosened; diffuse boundaries are strengthened. Parents work as a team, and children are allowed to act appropriately for their developmental levels and family needs. Relationships that are disengaged or enmeshed are strengthened appropriately through various interventions that challenge and alter the relationships and boundaries around them. Specifics about these roles are not normative—that is, there is flexibility in the roles that each parent takes vis-à-vis the children, with one parent perhaps in charge of school and the other in charge of family life. Different cultures and family structures (e.g., ethnic norms, separated or divorced parents, families with step-parents, same-sex parents, families that involve extended family members in their functions, etc.) have diverse viewpoints about what constitutes appropriate roles, rules, and boundaries, and should be respected unless consequences might include harm to someone. Admonishing or lecturing children may be appropriate in one family and considered ineffective by another; that family may apply direct behavioral consequences such as loss of privileges when children misbehave. The "norm" is defined by the family and culture, not the therapist, although research about certain practices certainly might be suggested.

Role of the Therapist

The role of the therapist in Structural Family Therapy is to actively perturb the system (information in) so that the structure is questioned or challenged and may even become disorganized. This can look quite provocative, such as overemphasizing or challenging roles that contribute to rigid or diffuse boundaries. Therapists may encourage and coach two people to discuss something difficult beyond their typical ability or threshold for managing stress. This challenges or perturbs the boundary between them and forces them to continue talking, learning that they can do it without harm, which may enable them to more easily resolve their difficulty. The therapist facilitates the restructuring of the relationship so that the boundaries and structure support problem-solving.

Problems as Embedded in Structures

An assumption of the structural approach is that children's problems are often related to the boundary between the parents (marital vs. parental sub-system) and/or the boundary between parents and children. When boundaries are clear rather than too rigid or too diffuse, and relationships are balanced rather than disengaged or enmeshed, normal life difficulties are more likely resolved rather than becoming bigger problems. The therapist takes a directive, expert position, assigning changes within the therapy room as well as between sessions. Change must begin in the therapy session, though, and assigned tasks between sessions solidify this change. For example, a disengaged relationship between father and son may prevent the son from knowing how to grow as a man. In session, the therapist would put the son and father in direct contact with each other, with other family members physically placed away from them but observing. The therapist would then help the son and father talk about something and help them break through a hesitancy or barrier in their relationship without usual interference from other family members, who would be blocked by the therapist but complimented for their intentions of wanting to be helpful. This intervention in the session marks the boundary around the father and son as an important subsystem and is called an *enactment* (intervention rather than assessment). The therapist might then assign them the task of doing something together during the week without either the mother or siblings.

If it seems the mother or siblings are likely to interfere with this task, the therapist would assign them a task of their own that would help them stay away from the father-son subsystem boundary. Staging an enactment in the therapy session would further emphasize changed boundaries; difficulties in enacting the new interaction are helped by the therapist through reframes of attempts to help, challenging the system, and coaching members toward the new interactions so that change is evident in the therapy room. The task assigned for between-session interaction further accentuates the change.

Practices of Structural Family Therapy

Minuchin believed that therapists must be fully trusted by the family and wrote about the initial stages of therapy as entering the family system as a part of it; this is called *joining*. Many therapy approaches use this idea and research even bears out the importance of the therapist-client relationship in change. However, joining is not a technique nor an isolated intervention. It is an ongoing pattern of being part of the family so that change can be effected from within. The therapist dances a delicate choreography of being the expert needed to help the family change and, at the same time, be enough a member of the family to understand its dynamics. The therapist must then find ways to exit gracefully, leaving a more functional family structure.

Important interventions include *raising intensity* so that the family becomes disorganized (disrupting homeostasis) and the therapist can help it reorganize in a more functional manner (morphogenesis). This requires *unbalancing* the family in sometimes dramatic ways, such as requiring an overinvolved parent to leave the house for a period of time so that the other parent can take on the parenting responsibilities. The therapist also *challenges* unproductive ideas the family may hold about the problem, its causes, and necessary solutions.

A famous and important intervention that is also an assessment tool is *enactment*. As an assessment tool, the therapist asks the family to demonstrate their usual pattern, allowing the therapist to observe boundaries and roles. As an intervention, the therapist requires that family members change their pattern, often in ways beyond their usual ability to handle intensity, so that they can disrupt the usual pattern and develop a new one that is more helpful. In this way, the therapist acts as a coach to the family, helping them practice new relationships and boundaries.

As the family structure changes, the experiences of the members of the family change, allowing boundaries and relationships to settle into more functional and helpful ones that promote growth and an ability to resolve problems. It is not unusual for the therapist to never discuss the presenting problem, or to do so only in terms of relationships with people who are involved, such as teachers, police, and so forth.

Strategic Family Therapy (Mental Research Institute)

Gregory Bateson (e.g., Bateson, 1972, 1979), an anthropologist, was awarded a federal research grant to study the communication patterns of families in which one person was diagnosed with schizophrenia. Others (e.g., Don

Jackson, John Weakland, Paul Watzlawick) joined this work in Palo Alto, California, and later developed ideas for using their observations in therapy for such families. Their very large contribution to the study and treatment of schizophrenia resulted in the establishment of the Mental Research Institute, an arm of the research and therapy institution.

Prior to this time, mental health difficulties were treated as problems of neuroses or psychoses in individuals, and treatment required extensive psychodynamic analysis. Treatment at the MRI was a radical shift in this treatment thinking. Instead of extensive weeks and months of treatment, the number of sessions was kept to 10; focus of treatment was on the problem and interactions of the people involved in the problem; and the goal of therapy was the resolution of the presenting problem instead of "underlying" issues.

Assumptions of MRI Strategic Therapy

Several assumptions guide the therapy:

1. Family members often perpetuate problems by their own actions (attempted solutions)—the problem is the problem maintenance (positive feedback escalations or negative feedback inhibitions). For example, attempts to help people cheer up when they are depressed are tried over and over again, don't work, and actually make the depressed person more discouraged and depressed.
2. Problematic behaviors make sense in context. A child who avoids school may be experiencing bullying; argumentative teens are stretching their boundaries in preparation of leaving home.
3. Directives tailored to the specific needs of a particular family can sometimes bring about sudden and decisive change. Change does not need to take weeks, months, or years. Some small change may be big enough to make a big difference, getting the family on track for resolving their own difficulties.
4. People resist change. Change is hard, even when wanted; we like things to be familiar.
5. You cannot not communicate—people are *always* communicating, even when it appears they are not. Silence communicates loudly.
6. All messages have report and command functions—working with content (report) is not sufficient, you must look at the relationship (command).

7. Symptoms are messages—symptoms help the system survive (some would say they have a function).
8. It is only a problem if the family describes it as such.
9. The therapist needs to perturb the system and find a difference that makes a difference (similar enough to be accepted by the system but different enough to make a difference).
10. It is not necessary to examine psychodynamics to work on the problem.

Role of the Therapist

In MRI Strategic Therapy, strategies are devised by the therapist, who takes an expert position vis-à-vis the family, prescribing interactional changes that will interrupt the patterned sequences that maintain the problem. As with Structural Family Therapy, the therapist may ignore the presenting symptom in favor of working with the family's observed processes, particularly around the presenting problem.

Practices of MRI Strategic Therapy

Therapists assess the interactional communication patterns of the family around the presenting issue, determining what people have done to try to resolve the issue. Repeating something that has not worked is not likely to work.

Direct Interventions

Some families are more ready for change than others and respond to directives, willing to experiment with the therapist's ideas. In these cases, the therapist may simply be directive and prescribe the desired change. For example, a couple may have endless and exhaustive arguments about finances, leaving each feeling demoralized and alone. The therapist would not give them advice about finances because she or he would focus on the pattern of interaction in which each partner might attempt to outdo the other with logic and "arguing patterns" (tone of voice, pace, pitch, language, a relationship aspect that one is more in charge of finances than the other, etc.). The therapist might work to interrupt the recursive, sequential pattern that the couple's arguments typically take. This would involve getting a detailed description of the cycle, finding out where each partner attributes the "beginning" (punctuation), and choosing another step in the process to focus on potential change (the earlier, the better, before emotions are so high that the couple cannot remember what to change).

The therapist might ask the partners to each describe something different they could do early in the cycle, pointing out that the cycle will have to change to accommodate the difference. One might say that he could remember his partner's good intentions and fears about not having enough money instead of taking a remark personally. Another partner might say that instead of walking out of the room, which may be shortchanging the discussion, she will stay present and ask questions instead of assuming intent.

The MRI leaders saw that the context of a pattern often is the way a problem is viewed and the meanings that are inferred in interactions. That is, the way people frame their difficulties influences the way they attempt to resolve them. If parents think that a child is deliberately trying to drive them crazy, their responses will be different than if they believe the child is exercising normal developmental stretches to the family rules.

A strategic therapist once worked with a family with a presenting problem of sibling fighting that was driving the mother mad. She would arrive home from work, see the children playing video games instead of finishing homework, tell them to do their homework while she fixed dinner, and then tell one of them to set the table. This set up a situation of arguing in endless circles about whether homework was finished and whose turn it was to set the table. The children argued with each other and the mother yelled at all of them to be quiet and go to their rooms.

In therapy, the therapist saw the pattern as an endless, escalating cycle that needed to change early in the cycle, not at the point of the mother's exhaustion and children's confusion about whether to do homework or set the table—chaos! Since it is normal for siblings to fight with each other, the therapist saw that the context of the arguing included the mother's interference in the sibling argument as well as her exhaustion and request for two things, not just the arguing. The therapist told the mother that she thought the children were acting like normal children since siblings are always vying for power with each other, especially over a parent. She said that the problem was that the children were not given sufficient opportunities to exercise their power as fully as they would like rather than arguing because they didn't want to do the task (reframe—change in viewing). In order to have full opportunity to demonstrate their power, they should be instructed to go outside, stand at least 100 feet apart from each other, and have their argument as loudly as they could until it was resolved. They should develop a way to accurately measure the distance among them. Then, when they started arguing with each other about anything that the mother didn't want to hear about, she was simply to tell them to take it outside. After a few episodes of this (which did not require the same frustration level of the mother and, in fact, was rather amusing), all it took was a signal from the mother that they might have to "take it outside" for them to find a different way to resolve their disagreement. And then she would choose one of them to set the table.

Another time, a family presented with a 7-year-old who either had meltdowns or did nothing when asked to clean her room. After determining the specific pattern as well as patterns around other requests, the therapist instructed the little girl to ask questions of her parents. "What questions?" "Whatever comes to mind." The little girl started hesitantly and then became bolder. Her parents responded appropriately, but sometimes in silly ways to silly questions. Then the therapist instructed the parents to tell the girl to get everything ready to go home. They complied. The therapist instructed the girl to ask, "What should I get first?" This startled the parents at first, but then, after looking at the therapist and receiving a nod, they said, "Put the toys you and your brother have been playing with into the toy box." So, the therapist said to the girl, "When your parents ask you to do something and you're not sure what to do, can you ask them what to do first?" And, of course, the girl said she could. The parents canceled the next appointment. This demonstrates a way of interrupting a pattern that had turned into a mighty struggle in the family.

Indirect Interventions

Other families, however, are reluctant to give up their attempted solutions, often fearing that doing so will make things worse. An example of this may occur when parents fear a teen will leave home prematurely and have problems with drugs or not finish school if they don't give in to the teen's demands. In these cases, the therapist might use more indirect methods such as *metaphors* or *paradoxical prescriptions*.

Metaphors are indirect ways of calling attention to a family's patterns of interaction. When people are very sensitive to feeling blamed, metaphors are often very helpful. For example, the therapist might tell a story about an old lady who lived in a shoe who had so many children she didn't know what to do. So, she ended up yelling at some of her children and ignoring others. Neither of these methods worked, so the old lady consulted with a wise owl, who asked her, "What do you think each of your children is capable of?" In this case, the mother in the family is the old lady and the owl is the therapist. The therapist does not directly ask the mother what she thinks about the children as individuals but seeds a thought for her to consider each and assess their capabilities.

Paradoxical interventions rely on the confusion of logical levels that can easily happen in communication interactions. For example, it is paradoxical for me to say that all statements on this page are false. If that statement is true, the statement itself is false. If the statement is false, then all statements must be true, including "the statement." One level is the literal meaning of the message (digital, report, the words) and the other the context of the message (relationship, command, its relationship to all other statements). Telling people to not change in a context of change (therapy) is paradoxical. One such paradoxical intervention is *prescribing the symptom*.

People sometimes tell us that they have tried everything, and anything that we might suggest is met with, "we tried that and . . ." or "that won't work because . . ." A therapist might tell such a family to fully engage in their pattern exactly during the week, paying careful attention to what happens so that they can tell the therapist about it in great detail. Of course, this seems odd and is asking for no change in the context of change (with therapy as the context, which is supposed to help the family change). If the family is willing to follow the task and comes back with a detailed description of the interaction, this suggests that they are willing to follow the therapist's directives and the therapist can move to changing sequences directly. It also means that they are able to change an interaction (that is, paying attention is a change in the pattern). The therapist's next intervention might easily further interrupt the family's cycle of interaction around the presenting problem (if that didn't happen spontaneously because of the slight difference of paying attention to what happens) in a way that is more helpful.

If the family refuses to follow the therapist's directive, which is frequent in such cases because it seems silly, it usually means that they did something different, which may have resolved the problem or at least can be explored in therapy resulting in further directives from the therapist. A slight change in the pattern may make it more open for further changes. A true paradox is a win-win for the therapy: if followed, the clients are willing to do what the therapist asks; if not followed, it often means the symptom did not occur.

Another example of a paradoxical intervention is to tell the clients that change must not happen quickly, that it must *go slowly* so that it can be seen as true change, not a fluke. Of course, most clients want change to happen yesterday, so they are unwilling to follow the directive, resulting in quick changes. As you can see, the therapist is active and focuses on behavioral patterns of interaction.

Interventions in Strategic Family Therapy are designed to interrupt interactional patterns. This can happen by changing the viewing of the problem (context that leads to certain responses) or the doing of the problem—the behavioral interactions themselves. Interventions are tasks designed by the therapist to change the patterns and may be direct (do something different) or indirect (metaphor or paradox). The aim of therapy is the disappearance of the presenting problem as a problem. That is, the behavior may remain the same, but the family may not see it as problematic and therefore does not interact around it in the usual ways.

Strategic Family Therapy (Haley and Madanes)

Jay Haley (e.g., Haley, 1977) also was one of the early MRI developers of strategic therapy. Both his and the MRI approaches focus on the presenting problem rather than "underlying" issues and see the role of the therapist as active and responsible for change. When therapy is successful, credit is given to clients for their hard work; when therapy is not working, it is the therapist's responsibility to do something different. Haley's work was influenced by Minuchin, with whom he had a close relationship, and this influence can be seen in Haley's ideas about hierarchy and power. Haley and his wife, Cloé Madanes (e.g., Madanes, 1984), developed a form of strategic therapy that is slightly different from that of MRI. Rather than focus mostly on behavioral interactions around presenting issues, Haley and Madanes keyed in on a communication idea that symptoms are messages in the system. Haley saw these messages as resulting from imbalances in power, whereas Madanes saw them as messages about misplaced love in the system. They had become familiar with Minuchin's (1974) Structural

Family Therapy ideas and saw that family problems were issues of hierarchy: Symptoms had power in the family, and the family needed to get in charge of the problem instead of the other way around. Children who had problems were often perceived to be standing on the shoulders of one of the parents, giving that parent more power over the other. These are skewed hierarchies and need to be realigned.

Haley and Madanes also saw presenting issues as problems in the functioning of the family, with symptoms being metaphorical for the patterns that maintain them. For example, a father's headache may be a metaphor for his "headaches" at work that he tends to bring home. Haley thought that effective therapy sometimes works because interventions serve as ordeals that interrupt typical responses. Ordeals as interventions would include things that replaced the symptoms, so they would be given up.

I once had a client who had trouble with eating during the night. She had tried all kinds of strategies with no relief. I asked her what else was going on in her life that she would like changed and she said that she wished her closets were better organized (see Haley, 1984 for more ideas about "ordeal therapy"). I suggested that if she woke and could not get back to sleep because she wanted to eat, she get up and organize a closet, taking everything out and carefully putting it back in an organized way. If she still wanted to eat, she should repeat the task with a different closet. Regardless of the outcome, she would either be sleeping without getting up to eat, have more organized closets, or both. She complied with the request, was happy with a couple of organized closets, and decided she'd rather sleep than organize closets. She told me later that whenever she had a seemingly unresolvable issue, she thought about cleaning closets. We looked at the behaviors she wanted changed, not underlying issues that might be "causing" the eating behavior.

Haley believed that power was the motivator in symptoms and designed interventions that took the power from the symptom. Madanes saw love as the chief motivator and designed interventions that changed patterns of interaction so that needs for nurturance and love were met without unfortunate symptoms. The Mental Research Institute as well as Haley and Madanes designed interventions as strategies unique to the client system's issues and dynamics; there were no "one size fits all" interventions.

Madanes developed the art of "pretend" tasks, arguing that one cannot pretend to do something and actually do it at the same time—it's either real or a pretense, but not both. A family was suffering because one of the children had horrible nightmares, waking with screams of terror. The whole family interacted to help soothe the child. Because Madanes believed that symptoms were metaphors related to love, she framed the meaning of the symptom as related to soothing of the child—the family's typical attempt to resolve the difficulty.

In the office, Madanes directed the child to pretend to have a nightmare and the family to pretend to soothe the child. After showing Madanes that they could accurately replay the situation, she told them to go home and enact the "play" every night before the child's bedtime. This interrupted the family's usual pattern and allowed them to show love and concern without the child's nightmares. In MRI's terms, this is a paradoxical intervention with the added twist of pretense, which Madanes found less objectionable and more likely to be followed.

Haley and Madanes also reframed presenting problems so that people could not respond to them in the usual ways. An example of this is a college student who cannot get out of bed, is eating poorly and neglecting personal hygiene, skipping classes, and failing in grades. Now, many therapists would diagnose this student as depressed, which is what many parents suspect and request medication to fix the illness. Naturally, they are very worried about their child, and want to do what's best. Their frame is that the child is sick. Another frame, though, is that the child is unmotivated and does not deserve to have her life supported by parents when she is not doing what she is sup-posed to do: going to classes and passing her courses. When parents see a child as unmotivated rather than sick, they treat her differently and might tell her she has to quit school, come home, and get a job until she's ready to do what she needs to do as a college student.

Haley's notion of power would see the skewed hierarchy in the family where the parents are helpless in the face of the symptom, and therefore the hierarchy needs to be rearranged so that the parents are in charge. Madanes might say that the issue is that the child is lonely and needs more comforting from her family, is not ready to make a life on her own at college, and there-fore must remain home until the family sees her as ready to do something different about her loneliness or to find other ways to have sufficient love and caring in the family without the symptom that keeps her parents worried about her, calling frequently, and taking her emotional temperature, so to speak. Sometimes, either would frame a child's behavior as an unfortunate way of keeping the parents focused on the child and his or her problems rather than problems in the marriage. The problem is a distraction.

The point is not which frame is "correct," but which one the family is willing to "buy." By accepting a different frame, they cannot act in the same old ways and must interact in accordance with the new frame. This means disrupting the family's ways of attempting to solve the problem, which frees up strategies that have more promise for change in the family's interactions.

Regardless of the therapist's view of dynamics and motivations, strategic interventions are designed to interrupt patterns of interaction among people that maintain symptoms. Strategic approaches to therapy use interventions that are designed for specific situations and that change the viewing of problems (context) in session, which leads to changes in behavior (doing) between sessions. These changes are solidified in next sessions and therapy ends when the presenting issue is resolved.

Bowen Family Therapy

Murray Bowen (e.g., Bowen, 1978) was trained as a physician during World War II. He received further training at the Menninger Foundation in Topeka, Kansas, as a psychiatrist. There, he became interested in the dynamics of families with a person who was diagnosed with schizophrenia and followed this idea after moving to Maryland to work at the National Institute of Mental Health and later, Georgetown University.

As a pioneer in family therapy, he developed a theory of family dynamics that kept people locked into symptoms as the result of generations of unresolved family function. Bowen came to these ideas when he noticed how much more easily he could see his own family dynamics when he was not physically caught up in emotional struggles with them; when he was with them, old family patterns prevailed. He also noticed that he could more easily see dynamics of the Menninger Foundation when he was away from it, only to get reinvolved upon his return. He called this *differentiation of self*, defining it as the ability to maintain a sense of self in emotional settings while staying connected to them. When self is lost, emotionality ensues, which prevents objective thinking.

Assumptions and Concepts

Bowen assumed a number of things as he developed his theory over his lifetime. One is that the past is currently influencing the present although individuals can change and become more differentiated. Another is that a change in differentiation of self results in a different experience of the family—it feels different and therefore people respond differently to each other. A third is that differentiation is both internal and external: internal differentiation is the ability to think during a highly emotional situation; external differentiation is the ability to maintain a self and still stay connected to one's family. Anxiety is normal but can inhibit thinking and needs to be calmed in order for people to think clearly and facilitate change.

Differentiation of self is the ability to separate internal intellectual from emotional systems, to remain well connected to family members during anxious times, and to maintain ones' own sense of self, not unduly influenced by family emotionality. I think of differentiation of self as the hinge pin between individual and systemic functioning. Bowen noted that as people could increasingly separate thinking from emotions, allowing emotional influence but focusing more on thinking, they could more easily manage family anxiety without either getting caught up in the anxiety and giving in to family norms, or leaving the family altogether. Knee-jerk reactivity could change to thoughtful responsiveness. The reverse also was true: As people could manage family anxiety better, they were more able in general to use their thinking abilities without being overrun by their emotions. In therapy, both are attended to.

A large contributor to the dynamics of differentiation of self is *anxiety*. When emotions are in charge (emotionality), it is difficult to think about reasonable solutions to difficulties. We've all had the experience of later thinking of what we could have said during an argument or situation that we couldn't think at the time. We were literally unable to think of it at the time, our brains flooded by emotional reactivity.

Families develop patterns of managing anxiety that are transmitted and taken on by further generations. These patterns take the form of distance; conflict; physical, emotional, or social symptoms; or triangling. Symptoms are indications of an inability to manage anxiety, of undue influence by emotions and family patterns, of stress, and of relatively lower levels of differentiation of self. Anyone can become symptomatic with sufficiently high levels of stress. However, those with higher levels of differentiation of self are more able to manage the stress without symptoms and/or to return to baseline differentiation of self and eliminate symptoms quickly. Finally, intimate partners tend to have similar levels of differentiation of self and pass these on to their children. Some children, depending on many factors, are relieved from the family anxiety and develop higher levels of differentiation of self. Others, again depending on multiple factors, develop lower levels. Some of these factors include birth order, patterns of managing anxiety through generations, and triangling by parents. We've all wondered how it is that some children, raised in the same family, can be so different. It's actually because no two siblings are ever raised in the same family with the same circumstances. One is older, more important because of sex, or very much like another relative. Another has a different birth order, thus different experiences of negotiating with peers and parents. One may have a physical ailment or disability, another be particularly favored by grandparents. These contextual factors influence everyone's experience.

Two other important concepts are related: *fusion* and *cutoff*. Families tend to have members with similar levels of differentiation of self. In families with low levels, members can be said to be *fused*, a concept similar to Minuchin's *enmeshment*. In fused relationships, members are easily influenced by others and unable to think for themselves. In families with higher levels of differentiation, members are able to maintain their own ideas, influenced but not driven by others' opinions. *Emotional cutoff* refers to what appears to be an opposite dynamic: People do not pay any attention at all to other family members' opinions and make all decisions for themselves. We say these dynamics are similar because people caught in cutoffs typically make decisions based on doing the direct opposite of what others think. If the family says that children should live nearby, they get as far away from them as possible. This may be either physically or emotionally. Cutoff members may live in the same communities but cross the street if they see a family member approaching. Either way, their decisions are just as driven by family opinions and they lack the ability to make autonomous lives for themselves and, at the same time, stay in contact with family members.

People tend to fall along the continuum with different levels of ability to function in different kinds of situations. People may be more differentiated at work than home, or when involved in less anxiety-provoking situations.

During stress and anxiety, levels of differentiation of self tend to go down, but return to base levels or even higher levels after a situation is over. Think about how many people vow to stay in touch after coming together at funerals or weddings, but soon lose the momentum. It is natural for families to become fused when important family members die, and then to develop new levels of differentiation as emotionality subsides.

I used Bowen Family Therapy with many of my clients as they approached holidays, recognizing that they would easily fall into old patterns and allow themselves to lose sense of self. Bowen coaching helped them to plan for these times, with ideas about how they could stay connected and maintain their senses of self at the same time. I often suggested possibilities of staying in motels instead of in family homes as a way of maintaining a sense of autonomy and distance. When people described fears of falling into family patterns of arguing over certain topics or overplayed situations (e.g., a father who usually drank too much, a mother who criticized too much), I coached them to find planned ways to manage the situation. This sometimes meant taking a break such as going for a walk to get back a sense of self, changing topics, or refusing to play one's usual role. The latter plan could include not drinking even though that was the usual pattern, or complimenting mother on something rather than arguing about the criticism or giving in to hurt feelings. This involves maintaining a sense of *autonomy* without giving up *intimacy*. Of course, the best remedy is for everyone to be able to talk about the distressing dynamics, but high-stress times such as holidays often are not the best time to do that.

Engaging in the planning for such situations helps people engage their thinking as separate from their emotional processes. Behaving according (or nearly so) to plans helps maintain self in the midst of anxiety. Each reinforces the other and, with practice, the hinge becomes less rusty and squeaky and allows the gate to move freely. Planning often can involve the help of a partner who is less emotionally involved, more objective, and can send a signal about the plan sooner because she or he sees the struggles developing.

Another important concept is that of *triangulation*. I have modified my thinking about this concept over the years because so many therapists consider triangles to be bad and needing to be broken and banned. However, according to Bowen, triangles exist by nature. By themselves, as a concept, they are neutral—balanced and neither good nor bad. However, when overridden by emotions and anxiety, they contribute to poor differentiation of self. Triangles are the most stable geometric construct in nature. They are used to stabilize all sorts of things, such as walls and bridges, and are similarly used in family dynamics. Dyads may be quite stable under normal conditions but tend to need stabilizing when stressed. One of the easiest and most common such stabilizing move during stress is to triangle in another person (or topic or activity). As both people focus on the third part, the dyad restabilizes and functions better.

The third person in a triangling situation often feels special and helpful to one or both parties. However, as the original dyad stabilizes and does not need the third person as much, that person may feel pushed out and seek other ways to either re-enter the dyad as a helpful person, or find another way to triangle someone and restabilize.

When the third person can remain neutral and not overly involved with one person or the other, that person is more able to leave the triangle when the dyad restabilizes. However, if the triangling is so intense that it produces a symptom in the third person, I call that triangulation (more like strangulation) as a dysfunctional dynamic. This happens when one parent pulls in a child to take her or his side in some way, or to change the topic from a disagreement to caring for the child. Often, this can be a stabilizing thing by providing some time and space needed for the original dyad to recover their abilities to think during emotional or anxious times. After a while, calmed down, they can get back to whatever the stress was about and find solutions together that do not involve the third person.

Under stress, several dynamics can serve to relieve anxiety. These may range from temporary and almost trivial to deadly. Over time, if the dynamic is repeated or becomes more exclusive, symptoms may occur. Bowen suggested that these include distance (either a short break all the way through divorce or death), conflict (productive disagreement to murder), physical symptoms (headache or cancer), emotional symptoms (sadness or psychosis), social symptoms (shoplifting or grand larceny), or triangling (temporarily or ongoing). Thus, Bowen saw all symptoms as results of anxiety, stress, differentiation of self, patterns of managing anxiety, and triangulation. Stress reducers are not necessarily bad unless they are the only ones used, used chronically, or used to extremes, often in intergenerational patterns. Triangling is ubiquitous in families, but may not be damaging, depending on its severity.

Practices in Bowen Therapy

In Bowen Family Therapy, the therapist helps clients understand the theory's concepts and uses *genograms* (family maps like family trees) to identify triangles, patterns of managing anxiety, emotional connections, and topics that are typically either avoided or always hot. By seeing these patterns objectively using thinking abilities, people are able to practice ways of increasing thinking, avoiding patterned and dysfunctional ways of managing anxiety, and keeping senses of self during extreme family anxiety. At the same time, the therapist encourages one-on-one emotional intimacy, coaching clients to be in contact with family members without the interference of or temptation to triangle other members or avoid anxiety.

The therapist remains a nonanxious, third part of triangles, and helps clients plan strategies that will increase their autonomy and senses of self. As differentiation of self increases, people need less frequent therapy. However, because no one is ever fully differentiated or has resolved all family conflict, therapy can continue for years, although perhaps less frequently or only when stressful times are anticipated or occur.

Therapy takes the form of educating about the theory, helping to identify intergeneration patterns, and coaching change. Immediate goals include detriangling and lowering anxiety so that thinking abilities are activated. Intermediate goals are planning for intense situations, practice in separating thinking from emotions, and changing one's patterns in family of origin to enhance autonomy while staying engaged. The therapist asks *process questions*—questions that engage clients' thinking as informed but not ruled by emotions. This decreases reactivity and makes it easier to make objective decisions.

Therapy does not necessarily end when the presenting issue is resolved, although that often is when clients wish to end sessions. Because differentiation of self is an ongoing matter, therapy or coaching may be used periodically when stressful things happen or there are changes in the family requiring an adjustment of roles and interaction.

Because the therapist must take the role of a nonanxious third part of a triangle, it is important for therapists to work on unresolved issues and rigid roles in their own families of origin so that they don't get caught up in the anxiety of the dyad. Therapists can help clients differentiate only to the extent that they, themselves are differentiated, so ongoing Bowen coaching for therapists is important.

Integrative Approaches

I think it is safe to say that most of the therapy work done today is integrative. Especially in family therapy, ideas across models are viewed through systemic lenses, and combine good ideas.

There are many ways to integrate approaches. One is to have a foundational approach and "borrow" interventions from other approaches that fit the assumptions, goals, or dynamic descriptions of the approach. Another is almost the opposite: to take assumptions, concepts, and interventions from several approaches and combine them into a new, coherent whole. Others may take two approaches and combine them, although it is important to be careful that assumptions do not cancel each other (e.g., Minuchin's idea of needing to raise intensity so that families must reorganize and Bowen's opposite idea that raised anxiety [intensity] prevents the clients from finding solutions). If one wants to use both approaches in one's work, it is possible, but requires careful planning and perhaps using each for different ends or different times or situations. For example, as a therapist, I often used Structural Family Therapy to help parents reclaim their authority with respect to their children. However, with the same couple, this time addressing couple matters, I might help them see the repeated triangles and patterns of managing anxiety in their families of origin so that they can make choices for themselves about themselves and their relationship. What is generally thought of as not good is an approach that draws from many approaches upon the whim of the therapist in the moment with no clear rationale.

Examples of integrative models that have research supporting them include Functional Family Therapy (e.g., Sexton & Alexander, 2005), Multidimensional Family Therapy (Liddle, 1995), and Multisystemic Therapy (Henggeler, Schoenwald, Bourduin, Rowland, & Cunningham, 2009), each focusing on troubled adolescents and their families. Functional Family Therapy focuses on separateness and togetherness forces in the family and uses a variety of family therapy interventions to help the family develop their optimal balance of closeness and distance that does not require a symptom. Multidimensional Family Therapy uses a variety of family therapy techniques to address interactional difficulties in the family, between the family and other institutions such as schools and the justice system, and behaviors that are intended to enhance intimacy in the family but backfire. Multisystemic Therapy uses intensive in-home therapy (several times a week) to help families develop behavioral patterns that keep the parents in charge and address adolescents' antisocial behavior. Interventions are drawn from Cognitive Behavioral Therapy and Behavioral Parent Training as well as others. Each of these approaches requires intensive training after basic family therapy training, strict protocols, and intense ongoing supervision. Each is used in a number of community-based and other therapy centers and has a positive research base for effectiveness.

Emotionally Focused Therapy

Sue Johnson worked with Les Greenberg on ways of looking at interactional dynamics that stem from *attachment needs* and *styles* (Bowlby, 1979). Each of us develops in contexts of important relationships and patterns of getting needs met that develop into attachment styles that we carry throughout life. Similar to *object relations* theory (e.g., Scharff & Scharff, 2012), patterns of getting needs met are matched in relationships with complementary styles from partners. Acting on attachment styles without understanding them can easily lead to conflict, avoidance, and hurt. Greenberg and Johnson have divided interests with each going their own way: Greenberg (e.g., 2009) is more interested in attachment styles and physiological expressions, Johnson (e.g., 2008) in couple/partner interactions that maintain rather than meet partners' needs.

Johnson stated that "the inner construction of experience evokes interactional responses that organize the world in a particular way. These patterns of interaction then reflect, and in turn, shape inner experience" (Johnson, 2008, p. 109). This recursive, circular pattern is what gets couples into trouble, especially when the inner experiences polarize away from intimacy to avoid further hurt.

Therapy helps couples expand their perceptions of themselves and their partners, and the way they interact with each other as bids for closeness that go awry. There is no sense of pathologizing one partner or the other. For Johnson, the key in therapy is emotion as both the target of attachment-based needs and as the agent of change. With a skilled therapist who creates a safe place for disclosure and dialogue, couples are able to maintain contact long enough and in different ways to (a) understand themselves and their partners better, and (b) develop new patterns that will maintain intimacy.

The therapist helps the couple interrupt the negative patterns, and then to look at emotions that drive behaviors. Primary emotions (e.g., fear, loneliness, shame, joy) are expressed as secondary emotions (e.g., anger, jealousy, resentment) and behaviors (e.g., withdrawal, fight/flight, engagement). The therapist helps the couple identify their primary emotions borne of attachment needs, and to change their negative cycles that tend to push each other away rather than connect. Understanding a partner's primary emotions and attachment styles can lead to empathy, a changed perspective, and different behaviors.

The approach is nonpathologizing and creates new experiences so that partners can understand each other, develop empathy, and help their partners and themselves get needs met. This draws them together and restores their original hope and belief about having partners in satisfying and safe relationships. When there are addictions, violence, or affairs present, Emotionally Focused Therapy is contraindicated until those issues are resolved.

And So . . .

In this chapter, I described only a few family therapy approaches; there are many, many more. From a systemic perspective, each looks at how the members of families interact with each other, forming subsystems and systems, for the purpose of supporting and nurturing each other, eventually launching grown members into society to form their own families. I do not define families as white, middle class, educated, and heterosexual. There are many forms to families and, from a systemic perspective, all interact in patterned ways within their own contexts, influenced by and influencing each other and the broader communities in which they reside. This includes families with step-parents, foster families, kinship families, chosen families and many more. The next chapters in this book examines Solution-Focused Brief Therapy and its place within systemic family therapy.

3 | Solution-Focused Brief Therapy

Development of SFBT

The development of Solution-Focused Brief Therapy (SFBT) has an interesting history. I refer you to a wonderful chapter by Brian Cade (2007) in the *Handbook of Solution-Focused Brief Therapy: Clinical Applications*, edited by Frank N. Thomas and myself (Nelson &Thomas, 2007). In his review of the development of SFBT, Cade describes how several perspectives came together into the *interactional view* that was developed by colleagues at the Mental Research Institute (MRI; e.g., Watzlawick & Weakland, 1977; Watzlawick, Weakland, & Fisch, 1974), reviewed in Chapter 1 of this book. What was not reviewed in depth in that section is the tremendous influence that Milton Erickson (e.g., Erickson & Rossi, 1979) had on the development of the therapy ideas at the Brief Therapy Center (BTC), the therapy arm of the MRI. Cade (2007) reported:

> I one day asked Jay Haley what he thought was the most important contribution Bateson had made toward family therapy. He replied that it was finding the money to send John Weakland and him to spend time with Milton Erickson on a couple of occasions each year.
>
> (p. 33)

Erickson, a hypnotherapist, focused not on problems but on areas of competence and resources that people brought with them to therapy. Erickson's ideas were added to the mix of Bateson's ideas, systems theory, and cybernetics at the Brief Therapy Center to form the MRI brand of strategic therapy.

Insoo Kim Berg and Steve de Shazer trained at the MRI, meeting each other at the urging of John Weakland. They appreciated the change in views of therapy from analyzing problems and prescribing solutions for the underlying "real" problem to what clients said they wanted help with. Erickson had seen no need to search for underlying issues based in theory, but respectfully used what the clients described as problematic. The MRI adopted this stance and both de Shazer and Berg found it most promising.

After moving to Milwaukee, Wisconsin, de Shazer and Berg set up the Brief Family Therapy Center (BFTC) in 1978 with several colleagues. Using the brief approach of the MRI, de Shazer continued to consult with John Weakland. The BFTC team took to heart Weakland's admonition to listen to clients without believing that you know what the client *really* means or what the problem *really* is. This means listening to clients and their language rather than thinking under, around, and above the words to what a theory might say is going on. de Shazer, Berg, and colleagues met in de Shazer and Berg's house, seeing clients in the living room, teammates sitting on the stairs to the second floor. Similar to MRI's format, they broke midway through the session to discuss the family's situation and to send a message to the family through the therapist.

At first, the messages were similar to MRI messages that reframed the family's situation and were directive in prescribing tasks that would change the family's interactional patterns. As time went on, though, they began to hear clients talk about small things that contradicted the pervasive nature of their problems, most specifically, times when the problem did not exist, when it was less intense, when it was not problematic, or when they were coping with it better. They heard words like "almost always," "usually," "mostly," and "a little bit." When clients said the problem was 90% there, they focused on the 10% it wasn't. They asked whether "always" and "never" were actually accurate: "Are there times when it's not there?" or "Nothing is all bad all the time. When are some times when it's not so bad?"

Using the MRI's way of therapy based on an interactional view, they became more curious about what clients were telling them about their interactions with each other and others. By asking curious questions about the details of the clients' views of interactions, they learned about the wealth of information that clients already had that could be used to help them resolve their presenting problems.

SFBT Stance

de Shazer was clear in his writings, workshops, and conversations that he was not developing a theory, which is explanation. Rather, SFBT is an approach to therapy, not even a model, that describes what happens. A model might be seen as a step-by-step description of what proponents do. However, because the approach was developed by listening to clients and continuing to do what worked to help them move toward their goals, I prefer to call it an approach. An approach starts with worldview (systemic thinking) and stance.

The *stance* of SFBT is a worldview that closely attends to the clients' views of what they want and the resources they bring to therapy. According to Thomas and Nelson (2007), this stance or posture includes the following and is the fundamental way of viewing therapy and other applications of SFBT. Without this stance, SFBT is just another set of concepts and practices. With the stance, it is a worldview through which practitioners work with clients from an SFBT perspective.

Curious

We do not know or hypothesize about what might be underlying the client's perspective or description of their concerns. We are curious about clients' experiences and expressions of their experiences.

Respectful

We respect clients' ways of working with us, believing that whatever and however they tell us is important to them and therefore worthy of respect.

Tentative

We do not assume that we know what the client means, what is really going on, or what is best for them, and when we have an idea about this or anything about their lives, we present our ideas tentatively, leaving lots of room and a context that allows and encourages clients to correct us. We are *slow to know* (Thomas, 2007).

Non-Normative and Nonpathologizing

We do not see presenting concerns as symptoms of underlying pathology, problems of structure or relationships, or anything else. We take presenting concerns at face value as having importance for the family, and that the family is doing the best it can with the resources it has.

Belief in Client Competence

We do not assume that clients are less than we are in any way, or that we have expertise about their problems or about them and their lives. We believe that they tell us whatever they can to the best of their ability, have resources they know about or could become aware of, and are capable of developing solutions with the help of a curious therapist utilizing these resources. Some say that the approach is strength-based; it is more accurate to call it "resource-based" because we look for clients' resources, which may include strengths, but resources are so much more than just strengths. Further, some strengths (e.g., ability to sell drugs) are not necessarily resources for change.

Therapy Is Positive, Collegial and Collaborative, and Future- and Solution-Focused

We are not Pollyannas; it is important to acknowledge clients' pain. However, we work more toward hope than analyzing problems and their etiology. We work as non-hierarchically as we can, keeping in mind our duties regarding harm, of course. We collaborate with our clients rather than educate them and lead them through theories of how problems develop and how they should be solved. And we look to futures for clients that do not include a sense of their difficulties as problematic (perhaps they are still present but not perceived as problematic).

With these basics of the SFBT worldview or stance in mind, we can see that there are many ways to help clients. Several practices were developed at BFTC in Milwaukee, and more have developed since then in the world of SFBT practice. In this section of the book, I focus on the ones that came most directly from the work of Berg and de Shazer and their colleagues, with a few comments about more recently developed practices that fit the stance.

Assumptions

There are several assumptions in addition to the stance or posture principles that drive SFBT and its evolution. One of these is that *change is constant*; nothing stays the same in human systems. This is a useful concept because we can help clients utilize changes in ways that help them toward what they want. I have learned that a very important skill to develop is the listening ear that hears tiny things that point toward difference and change, and to become curious about how we might amplify these differences and changes toward therapy goals. The following come from Thomas and Nelson (2007, p. 10 ff).

Change Is Constant and Inevitable

In SFBT, following Erickson's ideas of *utilization*, we recognize that change is happening all the time and strive to use what is already changing to help clients toward their goals. This doesn't mean that all changes are good or wanted or necessary, only that we use this principle to help us co-construct solutions with clients.

If it ain't broke, don't fix it! Once you know what works, do more of it! If it doesn't work, don't do it again—do something different! This adage has become a *sine qua non* of SFBT. First used by the MRI, de Shazer changed the order: the last two were in reverse order in the MRI, but Steve thought this order made more sense and was simpler. He was fond of using Ockham's Razor, posed by the philosopher William of Ockham, as a basic tenet in SFBT. Following Ockham, de Shazer suggested that we look for the simplest explanation that fits a situation. Although other solutions also may fit, they may be cumbersome and time-consuming (de Shazer, 1985); if we find something that is working for the client, it only makes sense to keep doing it and perhaps amplify it. We should look for exceptions, however small, first; only if conversation reveals no exceptions, should we do something different. de Shazer once told me a story about a workshop attendee who was fascinated by de Shazer's idea of simplifying. He met de Shazer at a break, showed him a piece of paper on which he had written, "*Simplify! Simplify! Simplify!*" He was quite proud of himself that he had understood something important in SFBT. de Shazer took the paper, crossed out two of the "Simplify!"s, gave it back, and said, "There, that's better." This applies to us as well as to clients' situations: if what we are doing is working, we keep doing it; if it's not working, we do something different.

Clients Have Resources; Our Job Is to Help Identify Them and Utilize Them Toward Therapy Goals

This assumption comes from experience at fighting so-called client *resistance*. One of the biggest favors de Shazer did for us was declare the death of resistance (de Shazer, 1984b). According to this assumption, clients don't resist either us or therapy; rather, they communicate how they are cooperating in many ways. Our job is to maintain a relationship in which resources are identified and, when appropriate, used. This sometimes means identifying resources outside a current system and helping the client determine how to use them. Their capability is not necessarily already having everything they need, but the ability to use what can be found. For example, I may not know how to cook a particular dish, but I know how to use a recipe, and I may find others' suggestions about particular recipes helpful.

So-called homework or between-session tasks or experiments bring forth a good example of this assumption. Sometimes, more so when the therapist assigns a task rather than co-creating one with clients, clients do not do the task. This is information for the therapist: the wrong task, the wrong time, the wrong people, the wrong intensity—something that makes the task not a good idea for the clients. Tasks, like goals, must be important to the client, doable, realistic, and so forth. If the clients don't do it, it means it was incorrect; it does not mean that the clients are resisting therapy. Sometimes, clients don't tell us they didn't do the task, but do mention something else they did that was helpful. This shows that the clients are being cooperative and helpful by designing their own changes. However, they sometimes believe that they were doing what was asked. It was not uncommon for clients to tell me, "We did what you suggested. It was really helpful!" and when I asked what it was, not recognize it. That was OK; it meant the clients were doing what they needed to do, not what I needed them to do.

There Is No Necessarily Logical Relationship Between the Problem and Solution

In the SFBT approach to therapy, we do not assume that we need to know the problem or its details in order to be helpful. Understanding the origin of problems is not always helpful because it typically is something that happened in the past and the past cannot be changed. We have bought into the medical-model way of looking at correlations (strong relationships) as causal. For example, I was trained to believe that teenage girls who cut themselves, misuse alcohol or drugs, or engage in other self-harmful actions were likely sexually abused when they were younger. Somehow, this high correlation has translated to a need to do "trauma" work with teens who cut, which often means re-experiencing the trauma and to "work through" it. And we don't know very much about teens who were sexually abused as young children and who do not display self-harm behaviors. I don't deny the correlation—it's just not useful in SFBT. Using SFBT assumptions, we work toward finding ways for clients to obtain what they want and don't necessarily need to reprocess events to achieve therapy goals. I have worked with clients who were reluctant to tell me their problems—which was fine with me; I do not consider myself a *voyeur*—and didn't need to know the problems in order to be helpful. By focusing on what the clients wanted instead, clients found that the prior disturbing problems or events were no longer problematic. They couldn't change the past, but they could learn how to have a better present and future.

Sometimes, clients want to discuss problems, whether because of a belief that therapists need to know these things or because they want to ventilate. In those cases, it is sometimes useful to ask how talking about the problem will be helpful. They might say that talking about it will help them understand it better and what is causing it. When this happens, sometimes I will ask whether they want to focus on the problem or have it go away. If they say they want to understand how the problem developed, I'll usually ask how that would be helpful and then whether they would be willing to focus on resolving the presenting concern first, and then, if they still want to understand, we can do that later. Only once have I had a client who said she needed to understand first, and so we talked about that with my listening ear toward openings for later solution-building instead of problem talk.

I worked in a women's center when I was in graduate school, and the center had both groups and individual counseling for women who had been sexually abused. I was on reception duty one night when one of my clients came out of her group session in tears. She asked if we could talk and, because no one else was around, I asked her what was up. She said that she had been in group for six weeks while everyone talked about their abuse.

Tonight, she had told them that she didn't want to talk about the details of her abuse any more, she wanted to talk about how to have good relationships with men. The group leader's response was that this was evidence that she needed to talk about the abuse more, so she left. I learned then to honor clients' wisdom about therapy, what would be good for them, and what might be potentially harmful, believing firmly that it is not necessary to thoroughly dissect traumatic events in order to have a better life.

A Focus on What Is Possible and Changeable Is More Helpful Than Focusing on What Is Overwhelming and Intractable (Thomas, Durrant, and Metcalf, 1993)

Clients often want things to be perfect and bring things to therapy that cannot be changed. de Shazer once told me that if something cannot be resolved, it is a situation, not a problem. As therapists, we often get stuck wanting to help clients attain the impossible. We need to empathize with this desire, and then to focus on what may make it easier to cope with the situation. This may mean looking to what in the context can be different so that the situation is not experienced as a problem: "Dinnertime is fast approaching." That is a situation; it cannot be changed. "I don't know what to fix for dinner." *That* is something we can work on!

Small Changes Lead to Bigger Changes

Because we assume that change is always happening, we (our clients and us) have some influence over how to use change to the benefit of therapy goals. Often, we need only a small change to get things started and then the change can be amplified or lead to other changes that move toward the clients' desired goals. In many therapy approaches, the therapy must continue until the theoretical goals of the approach are met. These may be changed family structure, rearranged sequences of interaction, differentiation of self, and so on. In SFBT, there are no goals related to theory, only goals that the client wants. Because small changes can help people move in a direction toward their goals instead of ruminating about the problem, we can help them get started and then get out of their way. What is enough therapy? When the client says there is enough—we stay with them as long as they say therapy is needed and can identify goals.

Clients Are the Experts on Their Lives; Therapists Are Experts on Asking Questions That Help Them Reach the Lives They Want

For many therapists, this assumption takes away their purpose for being therapists. We have been taught that we must analyze problems, understand them thoroughly from the point of view of theory, and use interventions designed and tested to ameliorate problems in line with the favored approach. This is a medical model way of seeing problems and concerns that clients bring to therapy much like appendicitis or strep throat. When we are talking about concerns of mental, emotional, and relational difficulties, though, science is not as exact.

Clients know, sometimes with our help, what they want instead of the difficulties they bring to therapy. Clients are the ones who know what is going on, what the difficulties mean in their lives, and the consequences of various changes. We have our own lives to draw on and we have experience of having talked with many clients and many therapists. So, we have some ideas about what might be helpful (e.g., "This is what helped a different client in his couple relationship"), but there is no way we can *know* for certain what will be most helpful to clients. What we do know is how to ask questions about what they want, details about what that looks like, and what steps they might have already taken that move them toward what they want. That is, we believe that clients are the experts on their lives, not us, and that we are experts on solution-building conversations.

Therapy Is Co-constructed

By *co-construction*, we mean that conversation is mutual back-and-forth talk with ideas emerging from the conversation rather than mostly from our ideas related to a theory of change (e.g., structural, Bowen, psychodynamic) or what we think is a sure-fire way to make the clients' problems go away. As collaborators on this journey, we pay attention to the general formulation of conversation in therapy: as practitioners, after we carefully listen to clients' speech, we keep part of what they say (preserving language), ignore part, and add or transform something (Bavelas, McGee, Phillips, & Routledge, 2000) that helps keep the conversation in future talk and solution building. We have choices about what we ignore, keep, and add, and by carefully listening, honoring the client's words, and gently adding something solution-focused, we help clients clarify their thinking and move toward their goals.

Through these understandings of the SFBT stance and some basic assumptions and understandings of the approach, we demonstrate a fundamental difference between this approach and others that are driven by theories of pathology and what needs to change for clients to resolve their problems. We call this *leading from behind*. It means that we pay close attention to how the client is leading us and how we help by asking questions that clarify the path they are on or want to be on, not the one we think they should take. We stand behind or beside them to gently nudge them toward a future focus and what their lives look like when they are no longer focused on the problem.

General Practices

I talk about practices of SFBT because the word feels better to me than *interventions*. de Shazer (1982) called these *methods* and *procedures*. Interventions connote something we do *to* the system rather than things we do *with* the system to co-construct preferred futures. Cantwell and Holmes (1994) called this "leading from one step behind" (p. 17) and it was a favorite phrase of Insoo Kim Berg's. Berg called this "taps on the shoulder" (Berg & Dolan, 2001, p. 3). It's a gentle way of drawing the clients' attention to something present that they have not (yet) noticed.

In SFBT, using the stance, we walk beside clients in collaborative conversations in which we guide the direction much as a sheep dog guides sheep. Different from guiding sheep into a known pen, though, we are constantly changing directions as clients move along a path toward their goals. First this way a bit, then that, then a third, perhaps back to the first, and so on. Our practices help keep them from falling off the path entirely and we let them determine the path itself. And sometimes, the goals change, requiring changes in the path.

Client-Therapist Relationship

An interesting and sometimes intense debate surfaces and resurfaces occasionally in the solution-focused community about the importance of establishing a safe and trusting relationship with clients before embarking on treatment. de Shazer was fond of saying that we don't need to "establish" relationships with clients—we already have them by virtue of the fact that they have come to see us. Rather, we must simply be careful to not mess them up! Further, he believed that treatment starts with the decision to make an appointment for therapy. He believed that most people are more interested in getting on with business and chit-chatting, and that we maintain relationships with clients when we pay attention to them and listen carefully for what they want. Thus, the main practice is "a positive, collegial, solution-focused stance" (de Shazer et al., 2007, p. 4).

Well-Formed Goals

Whenever we ask questions or engage in solution-building conversations, we keep in mind the notion of *well-formed goals*. Well-formed goals include the following characteristics:

- *Important to the client*. We may have ideas based on our training in various theories about goals clients should reach. These include parents' being in charge of children, changes in communication patterns, differentiation of self, and even such specific things as gaining or losing weight, taking certain kinds of medications, or developing a stronger social network. However, if these goals are not important to the client, we're not likely to make much progress. In SFBT, it is very important to work on goals that clients state are important to them.
- *Interactional*. Because of their convictions that the MRI and Brief Therapy developers were onto something very important, de Shazer and Berg stressed that goals that include changes in the interactional life of the client were necessary. For example, how will the client be interacting with an important other in their lives when they have reached their goal? How or what will that person notice about this change and how will the client know that the person has noticed? How will that make a difference to them?
- *Specific rather than global*. It is tempting to move toward generalized goals that may include a sense of "always" or "never." Because one of the tenets of SFBT is that nothing is happening all of the time, it is much more useful to identify goals that target something specific as well

as interactional and important. If there are other situations where the change will be useful, clients will recognize this and either ask for help co-constructing similar changes or make the changes themselves.

- *Presence rather than absence of something.* It is very difficult to move toward the absence of something. "My depression will be gone." OK, but what clues does that give us about what it means to the client, how they will know it is gone, or how we can help them other than theories of what we should suggest from our expertise on "depression"? However, we can help change an absence goal to a presence one by asking questions such as, "What will be there instead?" Or, "What will you notice when it is gone that perhaps you might not be noticing now?" The "what there" and the "what noticed" may become the goals for therapy. Further, the client may be able to describe what others would notice better than what they, themselves, would see as different.

- Well-formed goals are the *beginning* rather than final step. We believe that small changes can snowball into larger changes without our expert-led help. Of course, the client will determine what is enough change but we always start with a small step after identifying a goal. This is usually done with the help of *scaling* questions such as, "Suppose you are one step or even a half step further toward your goal from where you are now, what does that look like? What's happening? What are others seeing about you that's different?" After asking detail and relationship and other questions, we might ask, "Suppose you are at that higher point. How do you think you got there?" We keep the detailed preferred future in mind but acknowledge that change starts with one small step.

- Along with being important to the client, well-formed goals include a *role for the client and for all members of systems attending therapy.* Miracles may happen but it's clients who make changes that get them to those miracle days. In an interactional way, this may mean that after responding to how an important other person would notice a change and how the client would know that person had noticed and what difference it would make, a next question might be something like, "And given this difference, how do you think that person would respond?" or "What would that person say you are doing differently?" Each person in the family may describe goals differently, and it's the job of the therapist to help co-create common goals that everyone can agree upon.

- SFBT goals are also *concrete*, *behavioral*, and *measurable* in some way. This is where asking questions to get very exact details is helpful. Vague differences such as, "I'd feel better" are not very useful for solution-building. "I would first notice that I wanted to get out of bed" is much more concrete. "I would get out of bed when the alarm goes off" is both concrete and behavioral. "I would get out of bed when the alarm goes off three days out of five" is concrete, behavioral, and measurable. It also provides a much more detailed description of an action that is different.
- *Realistic*. Clients often state goals that are not realistic: a deceased spouse would be alive, the accident wouldn't have happened, or financial difficulties would magically disappear. This is often when therapists new to SFBT get discouraged because they are not sure how to help clients turn these unrealistic goals into ones that may respond to solution-building. So, we sympathize or empathize and ask what would be different in their lives should that goal somehow be reached. This elicits the concrete differences that are more likely to be used toward well-formed goals. For example, a magically reappeared spouse may mean the client does not feel lonely. So, another vague goal; keep those curious questions going! "What would you be noticing instead of loneliness?" "Who would be there, what would they notice, what difference would that make to them and to you?" "So, you'd be OK being alone. What would you be doing? Where? What else?"

Questions

Questions are the main tool in solution-focused work. We might make suggestions, observe what others may have experienced, and so on as tentative ideas, but seldom prescribe tasks or intervene in the traditional way. When we do, these ideas arise from the conversation and clearly relate to the client's situation and language. We ask questions in terms of what clients have already said, using their language to inform our ideas and responses, and in terms that lead toward solution talk rather than problem talk as soon as possible. Questions about the past are asked to help understand exceptions to concerns and details about those situations, moving toward solution building as soon as possible.

Solution-focused therapists are not "problem phobic"; we simply have found that talking about problems easily leads to more problem talk, and talking about solutions leads to more solution building. However, we must take care that we are not so solution forced (Nylund & Corsiglia, 1994) that we "mess up" the relationship and have to backtrack or even lose the client. Rather, we have found that problem talk is not necessary and that solution building helps clients reach their goals faster. Questions rather than statements typically elicit more of the client's context and ideas and less of ours. That said, some clients feel a strong need to tell us a lot about the problem, sometimes because they have learned that it's necessary and helpful in therapy, partly because they need to express themselves. In those cases, we listen empathically and carefully, listening for openings for solution talk.

Bateson (1972) wrote about the importance of differences and differences that make a difference. This includes noticing differences, eliciting differences, finding differences, and enhancing and amplifying differences. In therapy, we need to find out about these *differences that make a difference* for clients. It does not matter whether a partner starts doing dishes before the table is cleared or after (a difference in behavior) if this does not make a difference to someone. Refer back to the system thinking section on first- and second-order change: rearranging the deck chairs on the *Titanic* made a difference while the ship was sinking, but was it a difference that made a difference? Probably not, at least not in terms of saving lives. We ask clients whether something they describe is different and, if so, how it is different and whether it makes any difference to them or to others.

Relational Questions

Relational questions are very important in SFBT. At the Mental Research Institute, systemic and interactional ideas provided an overall sense of clients, the difficulties they bring to therapy, and how changes in relationships are necessary for lasting change. Whenever possible, it is helpful for family members to attend therapy. This helps everyone to know about desired changes, to notice changes that already have happened or are happening, and to participate in the co-constructed conversations for building solutions.

However, even when important others cannot or do not attend therapy, we may keep them in mind as important aspects of the client's attending context. Therefore, we ask questions that elicit perspectives of these other people that are important to the client. This helps to make the picture circular rather than linear. It also helps to anticipate how others may respond to changes so that practitioners can help clients plan for unhelpful responses from others or to develop other changes that will meet goals without such responses. It also helps clients become better observers of themselves, which helps them assess changes they are thinking about. Further, relationship questions help identify others as resources for helping clients move toward their preferred futures.

Examples of relationship questions include such queries as, "Who will notice this small change? What difference will this make to them? What difference will their noticing make to you? What else will they notice? What difference will that make?" and so on. Even when clients claim that no person in their contexts will notice, we can elicit ideas about people who are no longer in their lives (e.g., a grandmother or teacher) and ask what they would notice if they were present. We can even ask about pets! One time, a client was struggling mightily to identify a meaningful and possible change.

TSN: That's OK. You have a dog, right? Suppose this heaviness you describe was gone and you were feeling lighter and more like doing things [using client's language]. What would your dog notice?

Client: (laughing) Well, first off, he'd notice that I go outside with him more for walks instead of just letting him out to roam the backyard on his own.

Of course, I was thinking, "Yay! Exercise! Good for depression!" But I calmed myself so as to not get ahead of the client and asked what difference the dog's noticing or the walk would make to her. She responded that she would feel better about herself as a dog parent. This is a great solution-building opening, so we explored that in detail and then I asked what else the dog would notice. And by that time, she was able to think about differences that other people would notice.

Details

Asking about details is a very important aspect of solution-focused work that many do not understand. Details, details, details! We want detailed details about who, what, when, where, and how as well as what else. We'll learn more about who in a little while, but it's worth starting here: we do not live in isolation; others notice things about us more than we realize, and it's important to find out who will notice differences, what they will notice, when they will notice them, and how they will know something, as well as what difference those noticings will make to them. Asking about details is important because it is easy for us as practitioners to believe that we know what clients are talking about, make all kinds of incorrect assumptions, and get the work, ourselves, and our clients off track. Asking about many details helps to fill in the picture for both our clients and ourselves so that we are more likely to notice differences that might make a difference for the clients.

Remember the idea of not fixing what's broken and doing more of what works? When clients come to us believing that they have tried everything and that nothing has been helpful, we search for tiny openings of things that have been helpful (exceptions and instances) a little bit and gently nudge clients toward doing more of that (de Shazer et al., 2007). This greatly helps to instill hope and a sense of competence if done gently. Asking questions about details and what clients did to make something happen helps instill new perspectives and a belief in themselves as competent.

Compliments

Compliments are important for validating clients' concerns and progress and what they are doing well. Compliments also are useful for validating difficulties by showing that the therapist cares and is listening, especially when there is a glimpse of something that is working. A client came to therapy because she was so depressed that she could hardly get out of bed in the morning. The therapist responded, "And yet, here you are, dressed, out the door, into a car, driving all this way, parking (which isn't easy around here!), coming inside, and talking to me. Well done! How did you manage all that?"

We must be careful, however, not to become too optimistic lest clients think we don't understand the gravity of their situation. Solution-focused work is often like a chess game of careful listening for clues from clients that will tell us what a next move might be that would be helpful.

It is vitally important that we not give the impression that we know what a client means. In those cases where we are so tempted, a compliment can sound hollow or as though it is forcing (Nylund & Corsiglia, 1994) a perspective rather than using clients' leads. Also, overdoing compliments may come across as patronizing. Compliments must be genuine and relate realistically to something the client does or says.

Suppositional Frame

Another basic practice in SFBT is asking *suppositional* questions. These questions assume that something already has happened or that it will happen. Think about the difference: "What will you be doing *if* you reach your goal?" or "What will you be doing *when* you reach your goal?" The second phrasing is much more likely to elicit the client's imagination and picture of something concrete and behavioral, as well as hope. There's a general idea that if we can imagine something, we are much more likely to be able to make it happen than if it is only a vague, abstract thing such as, "I'd be happier."

Timing

When to apply various practices is part of the art of solution-focused work and practitioners must learn for themselves when to use specific practices. In my own work, I prefer to find out about preferred futures rather quickly. Clients may say that in their ideal future, the problem will be gone. We follow up with a number of possibilities:

- What will be happening instead?
- What will you notice that is different?
- What will others notice that is different, and what difference will this make to them?
- What difference will that make to you?

We may then move in a couple of different directions, keeping each in mind as we explore others:

- When is some of that happening already, even a little? What are some signs that tell you that it is possible?

69

Or, when the client wants to focus more on the problem, we can encourage solution-building talk:

- You've solved many problems in your life; how did you go about doing that? (Clues for the client's usual problem-solving method that might work in this instance; exception finding for feeling stuck in making decisions.)
- Problems are usually more and less intense in our lives. When was a time in the last couple of weeks when the problem was not so present for you?

What Else?

With nearly any phase of the work, we can ask *what else* questions. These questions help to fill in details and enlarge the frame for possibilities of change. We can ask *what else* about the miracle day, about other people who would notice changes, what other differences a change would make to the client or to someone else, what else is happening when the client is one step up the scale, and so on. I have found that I typically want to stop asking what else questions sooner than the client needs me to. Clients continue to imagine and tell us about more and more when we ask them *what else*.

Situations Versus Problems

There are times when the client sees something as a problem that we would frame as a situation. Problems are things that can be solved; situations just exist. Grieving the loss of a loved one is one example of a situation. Similarly, responses to the miracle question may be unrealistic (e.g., "I would win the lottery"). In those cases, we can either wait, knowing that the client realizes the goal is impossible, or express sympathy and wait, or ask how that would make a difference for them. We would then use that information to help them formulate a reasonable, attainable goal.

For situations that present problems for the client, such inability to sleep (grief) or wanting another person to change, we can ask *coping* questions. Coping questions often open up possibilities for either finding more concrete preferred future goals or ideas for coping even better.

Specific Practices

Pre-Session Change

Fairly often, clients come to therapy already experiencing changes in their situations that led to calling for help. Of course, most therapists don't know this because we don't ask questions that might reveal these changes. It's fairly easy to ask about *pre-session changes*: Since the time you called for your appointment, what have you noticed about your situation? Clients often will tell us things that are already happening related to the problem and it's the perfect time to ask detail questions and find out how to keep these changes moving. Therapists can come back to this question later in therapy as they learn more about clients' preferred futures and ask about how changes (exceptions) they already are noticing help move them toward the preferred future.

When clients report no changes, we can simply move on to finding out what they want from their time with us. If they report things are the same or worse, we can find out how they kept them from being worse than that or how they coped. It is very interesting to note that asking clients about how they cope brings forth descriptions of changes they hadn't noticed before.

Previous Solutions

Like pre-session change, *previous solutions* questions assume that clients have solved many difficulties and problems in their lives before coming to see us. Asking about these times helps give clients and therapists ideas about how clients go about managing their lives in more and less successful ways. Clients and therapists can use ideas from these patterns for co-constructing current solutions, drawing on the clients' knowledge. I often start this part of a conversation by commenting that clients have solved many problems and difficulties in their lives, and wondering how they went about doing that. What resources did they use? What knowledge that they already had did they use? What skills did they show? Who might have been helpful?

Exceptions

Another important practice is *looking for exceptions*. Throughout all of the work with clients, practitioners listen for exceptions. In solution-focused work, we listen specifically to exceptions to the problem (when it is not happening, when it is not as intense, when it is not experienced as problematic, or what might have been helpful in the past, perhaps with different problems). Just as change is happening all the time, problems are not experienced the same all the time. Clients use words like "always" and "never," and sometimes "mostly" or "usually." When we hear "always," it's a good time to ask about exceptions. When we hear "mostly," it's a good time to ask about times when it's not happening. When clients say "sometimes," we pounce like cats on feathers and ask for details about the "sometimes."

Exceptions can also be a term used for looking for instances when parts of the miracle or preferred future already are happening. This is a specific exception to the clients' view that the problem is happening all of the time or having overall prominence in their lives. Some practitioners do not ask about exceptions to the problem (e.g., "Tell me about a time in the last couple of weeks when things were different"), preferring to stay away from "problems" as much as possible. Similarly, some practitioners prefer to not ask about "solutions" because preferred future details are not necessarily solutions to problems, but instances of when whatever was characterized as a problem is no longer problematic.

Preferred Future

We focus on a *preferred future* in some form. This might be in response to the miracle or best hopes question (see below), or it may evolve through conversation spontaneously about what clients want. This has been phrased in the past as *well-formed goals*, which took the form of being important to the client, stated in interactional terms (what others will notice), that have situational features (specific place and setting rather than global), the presence of something desirable rather than absence of problems, steps rather than final results, recognition of a role for the client, concrete, behavioral, measurable, realistic, and at least somewhat of a challenge for the client (DeJong &Berg, 2013). Often, through responses to questions about clients' preferred futures, we learn about their ideal lives. This is useful, and we use these ideas to help them get started, remembering that we must start with one step and that clients may decide they've done well enough in therapy before reaching their ultimate goals. Clients sometimes change their ideas about preferred futures as we move through therapy, recognizing limitations, values, desires, and new ideas for those futures.

Miracle Question

The *sine qua non* that many associate with the solution-focused approach is the *miracle question*. The story goes like this: Insoo was working with a client who described things such that it sounded like her whole life was falling apart. Insoo asked her what needed to happen so that their time together was useful. The woman replied, "I'm not sure. I have so many problems. Maybe only a miracle will help, but I suppose that's too much to ask" (DeJong & Berg, 2013). Insoo, ever listening to what clients tell us to ask more about, said, "OK, suppose a miracle happened, and the problem that brought you here is solved. What would be different about your life?"

The way the miracle question can be asked varies from practitioner to practitioner and situation to situation. Some believe it should be asked in the way that the BFTC team ended up with, which uses an hypnotic-like way of helping the client move into a light trance and vivid picture of the miracle. Others have said that it needs to be modified to fit the client's situation, cultural norms, and language. Regardless, the basic idea is this:

> I'd like to ask a strange question. Suppose that while you are sleeping tonight and the entire house is quiet, a miracle happens. The *miracle* is that *the problem which brought you here is solved*. However, because you are sleeping, you don't know that *the miracle has happened*. So, when you wake up tomorrow morning, *what will be different* that will tell you that a miracle has happened and the problem which brought you here is solved?
>
> (de Shazer, 1988, p. 5, italics in original
> denote hypnotic emphasis)

The question can be asked in many ways, some to deepen the trance (e.g., "Suppose, after leaving here, you go about your day, doing what you usually do, eat your dinner, finish your evening, and go to sleep. It's a very nice, deep sleep."). Some add emphasis ("The problem that brought you here is solved, just like that! [finger snap]"). Others ask about the morning a little differently ("What is the first thing you will notice that will tell you that a miracle must have happened?"). Some therapists ask about the "miracle day," imagining what a whole day would look like in detail after the miracle. We will discuss scaling in a little bit, but the scale point of reaching 10 easily can be called the miracle day. Clients know that the full miracle day may not be possible, but that noticing what's happening already or signs that parts of the miracle day could happen, and naming points on the scale is often heartening and helpful.

Now, at this point, I'd like to note that some therapists seem to think that the purpose of the miracle question is to determine goals for therapy. However, it is much more than that: it is a process, a way to help therapy move from problem solving to solution building, focusing on details of a preferred future that will then lead to questions about exceptions—what parts of the miracle that are already happening, even in small ways, or signs that the miracle is about to happen, even in small ways—or to what will be happening instead, which may not seem at all related to the presenting problem. It's about shifting conversation from problems to what happens when problems are no longer problematic, changing the whole tone of a session. It might be better called the *miracle set* or *future perfect question* or something else.

So, there is no way that the miracle question won't work if the practitioner keeps in mind that it is the first question in a series that will amplify what clients want and what is already happening toward what they want. It sometimes helps to ask detailed curious questions about the *miracle day*: what happens, and then what, and what about that is different, and so on, which helps to amplify the picture, perhaps making it more vivid, and providing more openings for asking about relationships and exceptions. This is a solution-building rather than problem-solving conversation, which distinguishes SFBT from other therapy approaches and is the keystone of SFBT.

An incredibly important and often overlooked aspect of the details of the preferred future is its interactional nature. de Shazer and Berg were trained in systemic thinking at the Mental Research Institute and were quite aware that problems (and solutions) exist in interactional, systemic contexts. This means that important others in the clients' contexts are a part of the problem picture as well as the future picture, and relationships with those people as well as the clients' views of those people hold clues to what will be different when the problem is gone.

A great example of this relates to the notion that solutions are not necessarily related to problems: A client reported that her reason for coming to therapy was because she was depressed. She went into some detail about what was happening that led her to this belief and the therapist listened respectfully. When she found an opening, the therapist asked her the miracle question. She noticed that one thing the client mentioned in her preferred future was that she would be going out more with friends. By asking *relationship questions*, the therapist found out what the friends would notice that was different, what they would be doing when they went out, what she might be wearing, where they would go, what she would see and hear, and so on—great details about the preferred future. She also asked—and this is important—what this difference would mean to her friends: what they would notice, what that would mean to them, and what difference *that* would make to the client. Having a greatly detailed though small part of the preferred future picture, the therapist then asked when some of that was happening already, even a small part.

This client was able to describe a small exception in detail, which led to a useful conversation about what she could do to keep it going and amplify it. Another client might not be able to describe such an exception, and that's OK. We have other tools in our practice box.

Scaling

Another tool that also is famous in solution-focused work is *scaling*. In this practice, the preferred future or miracle day becomes a 10 on a scale of 0 or 1 to 10, whichever you prefer. We describe this scale to the client, making 10 the preferred future or miracle day and 0 or 1 the opposite. The first question asked, then, becomes, "Where are you now on that scale?" Clients are usually quite able to provide a number that is something more than 0 or 1. We then ask about what is happening that tells them they are at that number and ask how that number is different from ones below it. This is a good way of helping to identify existing exceptions and instances, and what others notice, what difference that makes to them, and so forth.

On occasion, clients will say that they are at 0 or 1 or even worse. We can work with that! We can ask what has kept things from being even worse, or how they have *coped* with things given how difficult they have been.

After finding out what is different from where they are now and what is worse, we can now ask about a step or even one-half of a step up the scale: "You have said you are at 3; what does a 4 look like? What's different about

4?" It is amazing to me that clients almost always go along with this line of questioning—one might think that clients would find it silly, but they don't; clients begin to get into a rhythm of responding to strange questions, detail questions, relationship questions, scaling questions, and so on. And, in the process, they often realize that they are already experiencing some of what they describe as better. It seems that, when people can imagine something, they can imagine the details around it that make it more than imagining, that make it real.

In early years of SFBT, practitioners often asked people *what they would need to do to move* from where they were to that number plus 1. Somewhere along the line, it became clear that an easier question for clients to work with, one that better engaged their imaginations toward the future, was to ask *what is different at their number plus 1*, to ask detail and relationship questions, perhaps exception or instance questions, and *then* to say something like, "OK, you have described your number plus 1. How do you think you got there? What helped? What is different? What else?" At this point, clients often surprise themselves by noticing that they already are at the plus one number, or plus one-half, or are moving toward a higher number. For me, this is a clue to ask about their number plus 2, but I have to be careful to not get ahead of the client and sometimes must slow myself down. When so tempted, I usually ask detail and "what else" questions.

We also can ask scaling questions about others' scaling ideas, realizing that responses are impressions and perceptions rather than "truth." This can be quite enlightening for others as well leading to more relationship and scaling questions, and solution-building conversations. In a session with a teenager and her parents, the teen said that her parents were at 2 in terms of trusting her. She thought they should be at 7 based on her perceptions of her behavior. I asked what she thought they would be doing that would tell her they were at 3, one step up the scale. She started to describe some things, and then said she realized that they were already doing some of them. I also asked the parents where they thought they were in terms of ability to trust their daughter; they responded 5—about half and half. When I asked what they would see different when trust was at 6, they had some really good ideas that the daughter was able to understand. She also seemed more hopeful, saying that maybe it wasn't as bad as she thought.

By the way, it doesn't always go this smoothly. Although many conversations seem smooth and easily navigated, others are fraught with tension and mind-changing. The teen in the previous example could just has easily have argued with her parents that there was "no way" they could be at 5 and what their "real" position was. In these circumstances, it is important to stay focused on exceptions and perhaps back up a step. I might have said something like, "5 seems like a long way from 2 to 2.5. Parents, what else tells you that you are at 5?"

Sometimes, clients cannot imagine anything better. Their worlds are so full of problems that they just can't see any other possibilities. In those cases, we can ask about how they keep things from being worse and how they cope with such difficult situations (see the next section on coping questions). We can ask relationship questions about what others might notice about them that says they haven't given up. Responses then give us clues about their resources and abilities to use resources. For those of you wondering about safety for suicidal clients, I refer you to solution-focused authors such as Heather Fiske (2008) and John Henden (2005). As long as someone is alive in front of you, there is room for asking questions that can bring people hope for better lives.

Scaling can be done in many ways. My colleague Pamela King (2017) has written a book about working with children and their families that includes creative ways that she, her young clients, and their parents have devised to use scaling that fits a young person's world. These include abacuses, hop-scotch, lines on floors from one corner of a room to another, ladders, and many more. The aim is the same: to help people realize that change happens in increments and that they don't have to resolve their issues completely in one fell swoop. They can envision something a little better and when that's happening, something even better.

In my own work with clients, we seldom have reached 10 during therapy. Once they are started in the direction of their goals, they may decide that where they are is good enough or that they can continue on their own, calling for more appointments if they need to. When some of my clients have called, all I have needed to do sometimes is ask them what they think I would say or what they have forgotten about our work together. If that is not sufficient for them, we have an appointment and continue on from where they are and what they want. Sometimes, that's a completely different issue.

Scaling also can be used for many aspects of conversations, often using the client's language. For example, after determining a picture of one step up the scale and discussing how the client got there, the client may comment that he's not certain he has enough courage to do what he knows he needs to do. We can ask scaling questions around *courage*: "Suppose 10 is that you have all the courage you need? Where are you now?" You can then ask other questions around that: What's different from where you are now and one point lower on the scale? One point higher? Relationship questions, difference questions, and what else questions.

Or, you can ask about confidence: How confident are you that you will be able to go home and do this? Ability? Who can help you? What will they do? How will you show them you appreciate their help? These kinds of questions help with what other therapists call *motivation*. Clients are not necessarily unmotivated for change, but honestly aren't certain they have what it takes. Genuine, empathic, curious questions about what a little more courage, confidence, or ability would look like and how they got there can go a long way toward helping with solution building. If we press matters in the preferred future or goal scale, we may be forcing solution-building too soon.

Harry Korman once had a client who was paraplegic and whose mother was very worried about him. Seeing him alone, at some point in the conversation, the client admitted that he didn't want things to be better but wanted to want that. Steve de Shazer re-enacted this session, which is quite powerful (SFBT, n.d.).

One thing I hope you have noticed is that doing questions are aimed at the client: what the client can do. Clients often talk about what they would like others to do, but there are no ways that people outside the therapy room can know about this. Rather, we ask clients how they will respond when the other person does what they want. This may nudge the client to think about doing those things and see how changes in their part in systemic interactions influences changes in others.

For example, a father may wish that his son, who is not present in therapy, would "listen" more and "mind" better. First, we check to be certain we understand that "listen" and "mind" mean that the father wishes the son would obey more often. Asked how he would respond if the son "minded" more often, the father will likely give several answers, each of which may give him ideas about his part in the interaction. Asking about the last time the father did this and how the son responded helps the father move even closer toward his goal.

Situations, Coping Questions, and Interviews About Harm

Sometimes, clients are so discouraged about their situations that they are not responsive to our questions that might lead to solution-building. Of course, it is important to offer empathy and to listen, taking care to not be solution-forced. Situations are times when there's nothing that can be changed. No one can go back in time and undo an event, for example. How people respond or *cope* are things that are changeable. If they indicate that their goal is to change the way they respond or cope, we can help them with that goal in the usual solution-building ways. But sometimes, such as when things were worse during the previous week and nothing we ask helps bring about even the tiniest meaningful change, we can help them identify how they kept things from being worse, how they are coping, and what better coping would look like, who would notice, what difference that would make, and so on. Gentle compliments are very helpful at these times. Responses then give us clues about their resources and abilities to use resources.

Asking coping questions has helped me as a therapist find stronger ground for helping rather than getting as discouraged as the client. How do I cope with clients who just can't identify anything concrete? I ask myself how I have coped with that in the past.

As long as someone is alive in front of you, there is room for asking questions that can bring people hope for better lives. Insoo Kim Berg (SFBT, n.d.) interviewed a teenager who had been tasked with helping her during a workshop and who told her that he had almost killed himself the night before. She asked if it would be OK for them to talk after the workshop. He said it would be and did a good job helping her throughout the day. During the interview, Insoo elicited many ideas about how killing himself was not a good answer to his desires and helped him realize what he wanted and what was going on that supported his preferred future. She did not do a "standard" suicide risk assessment, she did not stop her preparations for the workshop, but you can be sure she kept an eye on the young man. She knew that as long as he was alive in front of her, she had room to work with him, and that did not include asking him about all the reasons for his hopeless feelings.

I just now realized that one thing that has been difficult for me is when clients identify vague rather than concrete goals and differences. At one time, de Shazer (1988) said that when clients get vague, we can get more vague. I also remember that we don't need to know the content of problems to be able to be helpful, which is hard to remember when the content of the stated problem tempts me to become the expert when I don't need to be (situations of potential harm being times I may need to be more directive). At those times, when clients are vague, I ask them to imagine what will be happening instead and about details about those imagined times. This also is helpful when clients are reluctant to talk about problems (even when we don't ask them to) because they are embarrassed, afraid, and so forth. We don't even need to know details about the scales in some cases. I once co-constructed a first session with a client by asking them only to imagine responses to my questions. I never did learn details, and the client ended the session by saying he knew what he needed to do and would call me if he needed more help.

Breaks

During sessions, many SFBT practitioners take *breaks* about midway or two-thirds of the way through to collect their thoughts and form a message. This practice was used at the Brief Therapy Center of the Mental Research Institute and has been carried out in one form or another in many other approaches, including the Milan approach to family therapy (Palazzoli, Boscolo, Cecchin, & Prata, 1978), Peggy Papp's (1983) family therapy work at the Ackerman Institute in New York City, Tom Andersen's (1991) work in Norway, and the Narrative Approach, first described by Michael White and David Epston (1990). At the Brief Family Therapy Center in Milwaukee, after the break, teams of therapists provided a summary of what they heard, complimented the clients on something, and then made a suggestion, assigned a task, or asked clients what ideas they might have about what to do next.

Many, many solution-focused therapists continue this practice, whether they can leave the room or not. Simply taking a few minutes to collect thoughts and perhaps review notes can help bring the session together as a whole and lead to either new ideas or solidifying ideas that have already been explored. Before the break, some therapists ask clients what questions the therapist didn't ask or what else the client wants the therapist to know. This further cements the idea that therapy belongs to the client and that the therapist needs to keep that in mind. Some therapists ask clients to think about next steps during the break and ask about those after the break. "Next steps" is a rather vague phrase that allows clients to think about whatever it means to them.

Directives, Tasks, and Signs

Directives, tasks, homework, or experiments may be posed when clients are unsure of clear ideas in response to questions. For example, when asked about exceptions to the current difficulty and faced with little information about what the client's preferred future or what others would notice when the problem is no longer prevalent, the therapist might ask the client to watch for exceptions, even tiny bits, or to watch for signs that the miracle or parts of it might be happening already, even a little. Other tasks (e.g., taking turns in helping children with homework) might be phrased as experiments. Because we believe that clients know what is best for themselves and their situations, we are not concerned if they don't follow the suggestion, change it, or do something else. Whatever they do is best for them and information for us. Perhaps a different experiment would be better; ask the clients what they might do that would be helpful!

Clients often surprise us when we ask them for signs that things can improve. A couple on the brink of divorce had a very difficult first session with me. They were so steeped in their pain that they did not know what anything better in their relationship would look like; they did say that they thought it was possible because they had once been happy together, just that they didn't know what it would be. They identified some things from their early days together, but these did not seem to fit the future very well. I asked them whether they wanted to come back for another session, and they did, so I asked them to watch for signs that it would be possible to work through the difficulties and stay married. The next week, I asked if they had seen any signs. I was flabbergasted when the wife said that she had told herself that if she saw a red car after leaving our session, it would be a sign that there might be hope. She saw a red car as they were leaving my office and her spirits had lifted a little. This was a sign that the husband was looking for: that his wife would be even a little more hopeful, which made him more hopeful. You might have guessed that I worked with them on scaling hope rather than the preferred future, because hope needed to come first.

What Was Helpful?

At the end of each session, I ask clients what was helpful to them. I often am surprised by their responses, because they are different from my own ideas about what was helpful. I believe that thinking about and responding to this question helps solidify changes and ideas for changes for clients and gives me clues about how to keep doing what's working in therapy. I also ask whether they might like to make another appointment; I never assume that they want one. If they hesitate, I may suggest that we make an appointment that they can cancel, or I might suggest that we have at least one more. We might space sessions out for a while or make an appointment for a month later as a booster or as a session "in the bank" that they can cancel if they want and come back for later.

Second and Further Sessions

Second and subsequent sessions look a lot like first sessions. We often say that every session should be assumed to be a first and only session. Some therapists like to ask about the previous session and what was helpful or how the homework went. Many ask about what is better and then conduct the session as though it were a first: differences, who noticed, what difference that made, scaling the miracle day or a similar scaling question, and so on. It is useful to pay attention to the unexpected. Whatever happened, clients usually mention things they would not have noticed at a lower number or something that happened that was important to them. When they say that changes have been helpful, we remember to suggest they keep doing what works: if something is working, continue doing it, if it isn't, do something different.

I do not worry if clients say things are better and then report lower numbers. Ideas about what the numbers mean are fluid and clients sometimes change ideas about what goals of therapy look like. Clients often catch on to the process of the approach and start doing the therapy themselves: "So I asked myself, look, here's where I am. How is that better than before and what would be a little better from here? What did I forget to do?"

One way to think about the process of therapy sessions is to remember the acronym EARS: elicit, amplify, reinforce, and start over. Elicit means asking about the preferred future, exceptions, or changes in scaling as well as relationships. Amplify means eliciting details about exceptions or movement on the scale. Reinforce means using the clients' language to solidify important changes. And starting over means asking what else and more detail questions. This formula can be used for all sessions as a general template, modifying as needed to fit circumstances.

Emotions

de Shazer and colleagues (2007) wrote a chapter about the myth that SFBT is not concerned with emotions. Eve Lipchik (2002) wrote a whole book on the importance of considering emotions in the context of SFBT. What I take from what I have read, learned, and discussed with others about emotions and SFBT is that they are an inner state and easily reduced to linear, non-wholistic matters residing inside a client and are to be dealt with there. In SFBT, a systemic approach that includes context, we look for the contexts in which emotions arise and are expressed, especially relational contexts. By learning more about details of preferred futures, emotions are attended to in *difference* questions. When the preferred future is happening, or parts of it, what difference does that make to clients? If we asked only about feelings, we close down rather than open up the context for noticing new or other possibilities. Rather, we can think of emotions in therapy as manifested in behaviors that can be identified and become part of the co-created conversation. Clients tell us about their emotions whether we ask or not, and we must be respectful of what they find important to tell us. However, scrutinizing or exploring emotions, especially painful ones, is more likely to reify problems and difficulties. Asking details about behaviors, relationships, contexts, and what the client is doing when problems are resolved and emotions are different is more likely to lead to resolution.

Changes in the Approach

Over time, the solution way of doing therapy has evolved in many places and many ways. Whereas at first, de Shazer's books were the manuals, we now have articles, books, workshops, and trainings all over the world that exemplify the best of solution-focused work: learning from clients in their contexts. Using the tenets of learning from clients and doing what works, this means that solution-focused therapists may develop their own ways of asking questions or conducting sessions. Steve de Shazer once asked clients how they would know that their time with him would be useful. Intrigued with this question and de Shazer's tendency to make things more and more simple as well as learning from clients, the BRIEF therapists of London, England honed the question: "What are your best hopes from our time together?" (George, Iveson, & Ratner, 1999). Other practitioners no longer give compliments or assign tasks but may ask clients after a break and summary what else they need to talk about. They may ask a question before the break such as, "Is there anything else you would like me to know?" or "What question should I have asked but didn't?" The point is to pay very close attention to what clients are telling us about their lives, not what we imagine they are telling us. Although debates are ongoing about what SFBT "is" or what we "should" or should not do as an SFB therapist, we should remember the systemic notion of equifinality: there are many ways to reach goals. There are many ways to conduct Solution-Focused Brief Therapy, and, I believe, they are all potentially useful as long as they hold true to the solution-focused stance and basic assumptions.

And So . . .

Solution-Focused Brief Therapy was developed by listening very carefully to clients. Of course, therapists from all approaches would say that they listen carefully to clients. The difference is that of perspective: instead of listening for opportunities to deconstruct the problem or for information that our theories tell us what is wrong, SFBT therapists listen for what will be different in the future when the stated problem is no longer a problem. Therapists do not assume any kind of dysfunction or pathology, instead assuming that clients have all kinds of resources available to them that will help them attain their preferred future. Therapists help them identify, utilize, and evaluate these resources instead of telling them how to fix the problem or even how to attain the preferred future.

In this chapter, I have laid out the basic assumptions, principles, and practices of SFBT. As de Shazer would say, the approach is simple but not easy. This means that in addition to understanding the approach, it is necessary to practice it with supervision in order to use it as an art of helping people obtain the lives they want.

4

SFBT Integration Within a Systemic Perspective

In this section, I will use several of the key tenets and concepts of Solution-Focused Brief Therapy and discuss my view of them from my systemic lens. The SFBT approach was developed by Steve de Shazer and Insoo Kim Berg, who had been trained in the Mental Research Institute's perspective and method. Although they upended the method by suggesting a focus on solutions rather than problems, the overall lens through which they worked was systems/cybernetics (von Bertalanffy, 1968; Watzlawick et al., 1967). Each concept below fits into the web of circularity, wholeness, and context that are the hallmarks of systemic and cybernetic thinking, and helps us understand solution building as different from problem solving.

All of these ideas work together as a whole—systems, cybernetics, and SFBT—and therefore, it's important to keep in mind a few basic ideas.

1. Clients are experts on their own experience, what works for them; therapists are experts on solution-building conversations.
2. From a systemic perspective, therapists become a part of a clinical system that is unique for each client system. Therapists are participant-observers and as such, experience the family within the clinical system rather than simply being observers.

Stance

The stance of SFBT is one of being curious, respectful, tentative, and non-pathologizing, believing in client competence, and being collaborative. The systemic lens enlarges our understanding of clients within their contexts that include us as practitioners and the context of therapy, not just clients' cognitions, behavior, and emotions. Their context includes people important to them (relatives, teachers, coworkers, justice people), circumstances of life (work, school, health, religion and religiosity or spiritual beliefs, education, neighborhood, relationships, etc.), as well as schools, probation, and any other entity, value, or belief with which they may be involved and with which they interact. Agencies and others that refer for therapy are especially important because they (a) may hold power over clients, and (b) have ideas about what needs to be different.

The stance is one of being curious about the clients' situation, ideas, relationships, preferred futures, and resources, as well as about what others' ideas are about what needs to be different. We especially are respectful of clients, not assuming that others' ideas or desires are the same as the clients' or that we know what clients' reasons for therapy or preferred futures should be; we remain curious about our clients' ideas and how they interact with others' thoughts. This sometimes means that the clients' preferred futures do not directly address the issue for which they may have been referred to therapy. For example, Lee, Sebold, and Uken (2003) refer to goals that clients develop in their solution-focused domestic violence groups. The therapists do not judge the goals or require ceasing violence for group participants. Instead, they remain curious, follow the basic tenets of the approach, and strive to help clients reach their goals within their own contexts. We believe that clients know their lives and experiences better than we do, and we respect that knowledge. Anderson and Goolishian (1992) called this "not-knowing": we do not know the clients' experience, we don't know what is best for them, we don't know what their goals "should" be, and we don't know how they are going to reach their goals. We remain curious as we journey with clients, discovering their preferred futures and how they will get there.

Being tentative, viewed systemically, assures us that we are looking broadly at clients' contexts and situations. We do not attempt to determine the "correct" hypothesis, cause of a problem, or solution, and when we have ideas about those things, we present them tentatively to clients, leaving room for them to disagree. This often leads to other ideas instead, sometimes things they had not thought of previously. We must be tentative because we can never know the fullness of clients' systems and experiences.

We do not try to diagnose our clients or try to determine what is wrong with them. Systemically, labels can foreclose our thinking, preventing us and our clients from seeing the breadth of their experiences and contexts outside diagnoses, sometimes requiring solutions that may not fit for them and preventing other possibilities. Clients do sometimes come to therapy with diagnoses that someone else gave them; however, we do not assume that diagnoses or labels encompass the wholeness of clients. We ask what the diagnoses or labels mean to clients and how they might be helpful. We tend to look at diagnoses as descriptions rather than explanations of difficulties, and, as descriptions, they cannot be complete (cf. Simon & Nelson, 2007). Descriptions of patterns of what is happening lead to cybernetic explanation rather than pathology (Papp, 1983). Meanings that are constructed around labels are fed back into the therapy system (circularity) and affect clients' interactions with us and with others.

One of my clients came to me with a diagnosis of bipolar disorder (BPD). She went through the list of descriptors from the DSM (American Psychiatric Association, 1994) and claimed that the items all fit her and her situation. As I asked curious questions, though, it became clear that some of the descriptors had not shown up until she read an article in a magazine about BPD. This did not take away from the comfort that she had from knowing that there was a word for her experience, but it did help her to see that she did not have to have *all* of the descriptors in order to keep the diagnosis. She did not need to pathologize herself, could see the list as descriptions of her experience rather than traits or symptoms of some disease, and understand that they were about behaviors that could change. We do not ignore potential biological concerns, but keep them tentative, and help clients make their own decisions about medical interventions for their situations. We consider more in clients' contexts than labels and consider other descriptions that might be appropriate, ones that are not descriptors of disease but of existing behaviors that suggest possibilities toward preferred goals. For example, this client was an avid reader and I became curious about what she had read or might read that was pertinent to her life other than her diagnosis.

The stance also includes a dearly held belief that clients are competent at working with us to resolve their difficulties. Clients do come with disabilities and limitations, and it is wise for us to understand this as part of their contexts. But we believe that no matter what their situations, if they can have conversations with us, we can co-construct better futures with them even when they have been mandated to therapy. This is especially important when viewed through a systemic lens. My husband worked with a family where the parents were quite concerned that their 19-year-old Down Syndrome son might be schizophrenic. Their presenting wish was that the clinic evaluate him for this diagnosis, which we could not do (there are no reliable tests for this disorder in developmentally delayed persons). It became apparent that their concern was easily dealt with (the "voices" he was talking to were his own self-talk so that he would get things "right," e.g., bus numbers and routes to work), but they were still concerned about his future. My husband asked the young man in a family session what more he needed from his parents that would help him reach his dreams. He replied, "Mom, Dad, you can help me more if you help me less." Although he was cognitively limited, he very well understood what kind of relationship he needed with his family, one that promoted his independence and competence.

Finally, the stance suggests that we are collaborative in therapy. From a systemic perspective, this means that we honor clients' expertise on their lives, remain curious rather than knowing about their contexts and situations, and work with them as collaborators and co-constructors to help them reach their preferred futures. Our expertise is on the kind of conversations that help build solutions rather than dissect problems, and we exercise that carefully as co-travelers with our clients on their journeys. At each step, we use feedback from successes to help guide next steps, trusting that systemically, missteps will become apparent and can be useful information for moving forward.

Change Is Constant and Inevitable

It has been said that the only things that are certain are death and taxes. And even then, there are many variables that factor into how we might die and how much and what kinds of taxes we pay. In my graduate training, I had a supervisor who described therapy as operating on the edge of a river. This spot in the river was opposite an island that acted as a divide for the water as it moved downstream. Part of the river flowed down the main channel, and our part of the river was an "oxbow" that contained only a portion of the river. That portion is what we, as therapists, can see and interact with, and what it is made of is only what clients share with us. Nonsystemically, we might see the oxbow as all we need to have in our sights, that we can tell from what we see what needs to change, that we can change that piece, and that that change will take care of everything, or it should. However, systemically, we know that there is much, much more to the wholeness of clients' lives. The river is bigger and ever-changing. We can dip our toes into it (e.g., via a conversation with a client), and that becomes part of the whole as it flows farther downstream—a change that may or may not be one that makes a difference for the client, and we cannot know exactly how it might affect the whole. What we do know is that it is moving, it is not stagnant (even stagnant water has changes occurring from biomes, evaporation, and small currents), and we can have hope that systemic changes will help clients toward their preferred futures.

I have many esteemed colleagues who use linear approaches or work with individuals as self-contained vessels upon which they act to make lives better. Their work often is useful, perhaps because the change they introduce is fitting to the situation, sufficient for lasting change for the client, and not met with resistance from others. However, they often are perplexed and frustrated that an intervention is not sufficient and may blame the client or family members for not utilizing the intervention well, perhaps even for resisting it or dismissing it. Other therapists recognize that if families do not adapt well to individual members' changes, the changes may not hold and, if they do, make things more difficult for everyone.

Many people who choose family therapy as careers do so because they recognize that helping teenagers, for example, make appropriate changes in their lives often is not helpful in the long run if the family system remains the same. The same can be said when individuals are seen in therapy, make desired changes, and then report that their partners are not happy with the changes and that their relationships are worse. By understanding wholeness and the inevitability of change, recursion and feedback, we can help clients anticipate others' changes and anticipate negative impacts. Asking for parents and partners to come to therapy may be the most efficient way of minimizing these influences; however, it is possible to work with individuals from a systemic perspective by keeping in mind others and their potential responses to change.

By understanding the systemic nature of change (think of all the things in the river that are changing at once, influencing each other in large and small ways), we can better help utilize the flows to build solutions toward preferred futures. Of course, there is no way we can know *all* the aspects of the system or the parts that are changing, but we can focus ourselves and our clients on existing changes and those parts that are most likely going to be helpful resources and upon which to build. When our efforts or those of our clients don't work, we can refocus on a different aspect of the system.

If It Ain't Broke, Don't Fix It; Once You Know What Works, Do More of It; If It Doesn't Work, Do Something Different

This adage has become such a part of SFBT that it is almost a cliché. However, it is very important to our understanding of the approach, of our clients and their desires, and the work we do. Viewed through a systemic lens, we can see that there are many parts in the system and many aspects that we know about and don't know about. Because systemically, change that is occurring has both known and unknown consequences, and we need to understand more than just what might be included in a problem description. If we allow ourselves or our clients to look only at problem descriptions, we may be joining them on a path that leads nowhere, nowhere near their preferred futures, or even into dangerous places. So, the first thing we need to think about is whether something needs to be different. If not, we don't work to change it.

A young woman came to see me because her co-workers said she was depressed. I asked her what her coworkers were seeing that led them to this description, and she replied that she was quiet at work, introspective, and had been sad about the death of her beloved cat. I asked whether she thought she was depressed and she said she didn't think so. She said she was satisfied with her life for the most part and didn't experience any of the symptoms she thought meant depression. We quickly decided she wasn't depressed but going through some normal changes and differences in relationships.

I was aware that my early graduate training would have me looking for all sorts of behaviors that would be symptomatic of depression or something else. It was my job to find something because we assumed that people came to therapy because something was wrong. We needed to find out what that was. However, as in this case, sometimes there's nothing wrong except perhaps normal adjustments to life circumstances. Systemically, when people mention "symptoms" or "problems," it is wise for us to look beyond descriptions to see *how* something is problematic or whether it even is problematic for the client.

The point is this: just because someone else says something is broken does not mean it *is*. I also worked with a client for one session because she was grieving the loss of her husband of 40 years and her friends thought she needed help with this process because it had been six months and she was still quite sad and having some difficulty focusing at work. We talked about what she thought was normal and not-normal grieving, and what she thought she wanted different. She knew what her preferred future looked like, and she knew where she was on the 10-point scale toward that future. However, she did not want yet to move up the scale because she perceived her grieving as a way to keep her husband close, not yet ready to change her relationship with him or her grief. She knew what she needed to do to reassure her friends that she was OK and said that she didn't think she needed therapy. I asked what might tell her she had become stuck in her process, and she was quite articulate about that, agreeing to call me if she wanted help at that time. I saw her about a year later and she thanked me for our time together, saying that she had become a bit stuck, but used our talk to help herself decide what to do, and was doing fine. Nothing was broken, so I saw no need to try to fix it. Her systemic context (wholeness) was such that she was drawing on previous knowledge about herself to take care of herself, and to do what she could in terms of work and social life. She realized what she appreciated about those aspects of her life and recognized what about them nurtured her and helped her with her grief. Systemically, she had no sense that something was wrong with her or that she needed to blame anyone or anything for her sadness. And she knew which friends she could rely on without burdening them.

Once You Know What Works, Do More of It

This corollary to *if it ain't broke* reminds us that some things are already working and that we need to see what we can do to become aware of them and keep them going. I saw Carol, a client who had been sexually abused by brothers and a cousin when she was quite young. She came to therapy not to process what she was told was trauma, victimization, and abuse, because

91

she didn't identify with any of them. She did want, however, to have a good relationship with a man. We talked about what a good relationship with a man would look like, and she readily noticed exceptions and men with whom she had enjoyed safe, good connections. She was able to identify things she did and was doing in those relationships that she thought were enriching and detrimental. She also recognized the circularity of her relationships, what she appreciated, and how she responded when partners said or did certain things. She easily recognized qualities of a relationship that she wanted in a long-term connection with someone. Systemically, we looked at relationships and what in them made them valuable for her as well as what she didn't want, and what would make relationships valuable in the future. Because Carol had already identified aspects of her life that she thought showed her capabilities, she was able to think about how to use them. One thing she noticed in her preferred future was that she probably would not be in the same small town in which she was living, which had limited opportunities for her. This led to conversations about what might change some of those aspects, what they would look like, what she was doing and where, who was there, what they saw as different about her, what difference that might make to them, and so on. And we also talked about what a preferred location would be like, what it would mean to move, and so on.

Through our conversations, Carol realized that she knew what she needed to do, and the steps to make that happen. This included talking with her relatives' spouses, recognizing that they might or might not be receptive, and this would likely change relationships in her family. She did not want to confront her brothers or cousin, thinking that they either knew and cared about what they had done or not; she did not think "closure" was important for her as described in some of the books she had read—she only wanted to do what she could to protect the children of her brothers and cousin, and to develop a good relationship with a man. Systemically, she had thought about the changes she was making, what they would mean in her family systems, and was ready to face consequences.

If It's Not Working, Do Something Different

One of the basic concepts of systemic thinking is *equifinality*, the property of systems that there are many ways to achieve something. For example, when I use the maps program on my phone, several possibilities are laid out. Each has pros and cons and, if I am on one and decide it's not working, I can back up or take another path to reach my destination. This hits at the heart of doing something different when something is not working. This applies to clients and their natural systems, helping them identify different kinds of exceptions and behaviors in themselves and others, and it also applies to our work with our clients. When future questions do not seem to be helpful, we can switch to exceptions, or coping, or scaling. Another client had discovered his wife was having an affair with a friend of theirs. He felt betrayed on many levels. His preferred future included his wife and marriage, but every time he tried to imagine this future, he broke down, sobbing. He said that he didn't think he could ever trust his wife again, and this was requisite for an acceptable marriage. However, neither could he allow himself to divorce her because of the vows they made when they married. He also grieved the loss and betrayal of his friend.

I understood this client's goal, and I also understood his inability to respond to a scaling question toward a preferred future, one that was slightly different from the one he was trying to imagine. I asked about aspects of the miracle day that he *could* imagine happening, and we looked for times those were already happening. I then asked scaling questions, and the immediate goal became one step or even a half step up the scale. This, he could imagine. Had this not been helpful, I could have switched to coping questions. He called several years later, asking for help with his daughters, who were now teenagers. He said that he had moved one step up the scale and realized that he would not initiate divorce and accepted his new reality of not having complete trust in his wife. He admitted that she had done what she could to help him trust her, but he remained vigilant and took what happiness he could from his life. Although this definitely was not something that I would want in my own marital relationship, I respected his choices.

On occasion, clients do not fit the solution-focused approach. Wampold (2015) is quite clear that no one therapy approach is more effective than others. We should be ready to switch to a different approach entirely, or to refer to a different therapist when we find that what we are doing is not working and decide a different approach might be more helpful.

Clients Have Resources; Our Job Is to Help Identify and Use Them

So-called individual approaches often have therapists working in very linear ways, believing quite strongly that their approaches are best for helping clients. We have learned that a solution-focused way of working encourages doing something different when necessary. This helps us understand that there are many ways to help clients, and that includes helping them to help themselves. If we believe that we truly are magicians and can wave our magic wands or peer into crystal balls to see what is truly wrong and how someone must act to effect desired changes, I believe that we are not doing our best work as therapists. Yes, we have resources, and clients come to us because they believe and hope that we can help them. However, if we forget that clients already have many resources of their own at their disposal, and that they can access them and any others we identify together, we are limiting their possibilities for better lives. A systemic approach recognizes that resources exist not only in the client and their close context, but also in all sorts of people and relationships around them. Perhaps a partner is much more willing to help with career decisions than a client believed, ready to support changes that may help lift sadness and other symptoms called depression. Perhaps a parent is willing to notice much more about a child who is struggling in school than only their failures, attributes that may help resolve the school problem, but may not, yet can be recognized as enriching a family's life. Perhaps a consultation with a different sort of professional will provide new possibilities for clients. If we stick only with what we believe we know, we may not see other possibilities.

Relationship Between Problems and Solutions

Using systemic thinking, we can understand the relationship between problems, what we do, and the outcomes of therapy better. Let's suppose we have a flat tire on our car and need to have it fixed. To get it fixed, we do not need to know how the tire got flat. There are many possibilities of cause, and it may be useful at some point to look at those causes to prevent more flat tires, but at this point, we just need the tire fixed.

In the realm of the problems and difficulties that people bring to therapy, there is even less need to know how the difficulties developed, although we have been trained to believe that we do our clients a disservice if we don't thoroughly understand the problem, its etiology, and its ramifications. In one of my therapy consultation groups, one of the therapists asked for some ideas for a client who had suffered much trauma in her childhood, most of it forgotten. As therapy progressed—the kind that examines all details of the trauma and repressed memories—the client remembered more and more details and more instances of abuse. The therapist talked about this case nearly every week in consultation for quite a while and I found myself getting more and more frustrated: first, I didn't like hearing the sordid details of the client's abuse, and second, I was frustrated that it appeared that the client was not experiencing any relief from her symptoms by discussing the details. The therapist was using a psychodynamic approach to therapy that assumed that the client could not feel relief until she had talked about everything (and I mean everything!). When I asked what the client wanted from therapy, the therapist looked at me as though I had two heads. She said that she had diagnosed the problem, knew how to help the client "work through" the issues, and that after explaining this to the client, the client agreed it was what she wanted. She thought that working with the symp-toms only would be a "Band-Aid" and that "true healing" required years of weekly or more frequent therapy, including hospitalizations during crises.

I recognized that although this was a good consultation group for the most part for me, I really did not resonate with that sort of therapy. I have worked with clients with histories of trauma and supervised therapists who were working with similar clients. Clients' expressed difficulties were indeed distressing, and it appeared to me that further discussion and unearthing of the details added to the clients' distress. I acknowledged that what had hap-pened was horrid, often expressing great empathy and anger for them about the way they had been treated. I recognized the connections between the trauma events and current distressing concerns. However, there was nothing we could do to change the past events. We could not go back and take the nail out of the road so that it didn't puncture the tire. What we could do was co-construct a preferred future with the client, one that did not include the negative effects of the trauma (e.g., flashbacks) or that included ways of managing these effects. For some, a "normal" life and preferred future was

95

not doing away with nightmares or body memories but managing them so that they did not interfere with enjoyment of other aspects of life.

Carol remembered the times she had been molested by her brothers and cousin, and she hated the memories. When she had them, she became angry and sad, and distracted from things she wanted to think about or do. So, we focused on ways she already was coping with the memories and managing to put them aside. She thought of several things: singing a favorite, upbeat song; deliberately thinking about a friend and remembering a pleasant time with that friend; focusing intentionally on something else, like work or reading or projects. She found that being more intentional about these behaviors (solutions?) was so effective that she had to consciously remember a bad incident in order to practice them!

I also asked Carol about things that would be happening on her miracle day. She mentioned that she would have a different relationship with her mother. Working with her anger about the way her mother dismissed her when she told her about the molestation was more difficult for Carol because it had more systemic facets: she cared about her relationship with her mother and wanted to be closer to her. She didn't really care much about her relationship with her brothers or cousin, so it was easier to put those relationships aside, but she knew that her mother didn't have the same feelings about her brothers. We used the same techniques we had used before—looking for existing exceptions—and scaled a miracle of what her preferred relationship with her mother would be like. She was able to picture a preferred relationship and to identify aspects that were in her current relationship with her mother. By learning details of those aspects and responding to many, many detailed relationship and difference questions about them, she began to identify things she could gradually change that brought her closer to her mother. For example, she said that her miracle picture included baking with her mother, talking about other family members and their lives, and planning a small trip together. I asked where she was on the 0–10 scale, with 10 being the miracle, and she said she was at 4 because she could picture herself baking with her mother that weekend. I actually was rather surprised by this because I had expected a much lower number. It's a good thing I didn't diagnose her low number because she might have gone along with that, assuming that I knew what was going on better than she did!

I asked Carol was about what was happening that told her she was at a 4. I also asked her relationship questions about how this affected her mother and others in the family (particularly a beloved grandmother) and what that meant to her and to them. The next step was to ask her similar questions about what 5 looked like—what was happening in her relationship with her mother, what her mother noticed, what difference that made to her, what else (about a dozen times), and so on. She realized that some of those things were already happening, so she revised her current number to 4.5.

It might have been useful or interesting to learn more about this client's relationship with her mother at the time of the molestations, perhaps using positive things from that time that were helpful to her. However, she didn't want to revisit that time, preferring to see what could change for the future, including that evening. She told me that she would be satisfied with a 7 or 8 in terms of her relationship with her mother, because she believed that there were some things that she and her mother would never be able to see eye-to-eye on or even agree to disagree. She would be happy with that because it would be much better than what she had experienced in the past, which she had believed meant the only solution was to not talk about what had happened to her.

It's easy to see how the SFBT approach might have been useful with Carol, a client who was not experiencing symptoms of Post-traumatic Stress Disorder, and who was quite adept at separating past experiences from desired future ones. Yvonne Dolan (1992), in her book on resolving sexual abuse, wrote about techniques for helping clients who experience severe flashbacks, physical symptoms, and anxiety and panic. I encourage you to review this book for yourself. Dolan acknowledges the effects of the traumatic event, but also looks for exceptions and resources that often are not noticed in trauma treatments. Her belief is that the traumatic event may have "caused" the symptoms, but that other things were happening also that can be used to help clients (personal communication). For example, disassociation is a common occurrence for trauma victims. Instead of framing this as a symptom of pathology, it is easy to comment on it as a resource, one that should be kept as long as it is useful. This means that sometimes framing parts of a self (cf. Schwartz, 1995) as useful and developing ways to manage them rather than "integrating" them into a single whole is an acceptable outcome of therapy.

Emma was referred to me by her therapist, who said that she did not have experience with sexual abuse but that her colleague (me) did. Even though the referral was because of sexual abuse, I did not assume that we would be talking about that. I was more interested in Emma's desired goals for therapy with me. She didn't mention abuse, but did talk about depression, her difficult relationship with her husband, and her upset with one of her grown daughters, who had cut off Emma's relationship with her grandchildren.

There were so many directions we could go! And many of them were quite interesting to me, especially the relationship with her daughter—I could not imagine being cut off from my grandchildren—as well as the relationship with her husband, because couple issues were a large part of my practice. But I knew that our direction needed to be where Emma wanted to go, so I asked the miracle question. She was able to identify many differences, how relationships would be different, what that would mean to her and to others, and so on. Over time, Emma reported tiny, tiny improvements toward her preferred future (we used tenths and smaller on the scale), but also many distressing and disturbing events that kept her from appreciating the positive changes that were happening. I wondered how much her unhappiness in her marriage was affecting her and tentatively asked whether her husband would come to therapy; she refused to include him.

It was at this time that Emma told me about sexual abuse from her husband during the first 15 years of their marriage. It had turned her off so much and she was so angry with him about it that she couldn't begin to imagine a better relationship with him. I asked her how she had coped with these feelings, listening for openings that might lead to solution building. I also asked her, given this very difficult situation, what her miracle might look like. She told me about her childhood abuse and how much that affected her feelings toward her husband, that her miracle would be being able to put those feelings aside so that she could care for him as much as possible. I asked her again how she had coped with her feelings for so long and she was quiet. I then noticed that she was rubbing the palm of her hand with a fingernail and was not responding to my questions; she was looking at her hand and a blister was forming in her palm. It appeared she was disassociating, so I asked if I could take her hand (she nodded), and said I was concerned she was hurting herself. I then asked if this was one of the ways she coped with her childhood abuse. She didn't look at me but nodded. This part of the session took a lot of time and I alerted my secretary to cancel my next session.[1]

Emma and I sat for some time, my asking gentle questions about coping and exceptions, her nodding or sometimes looking out the window, but letting me lightly hold her hand, which seemed to keep her from rubbing it with her fingernail. After a time, I asked her whether the part of her that wanted to go away was satisfied that she was safe, and could we find out what she (the part) wanted for Emma that would be different. I was using SFBT with an Internal Systems Therapy approach (e.g., Schwartz, 1995), careful to stay with her current state because I believed that it was important to her and was a sign that she trusted me, something that she was not experiencing in other relationships. We identified another part that could more easily picture a future without distressing feelings and behaviors, could identify current exceptions, and was willing to help the scared part feel safer. I gradually helped Emma recognize where she was and what we were doing. She was very tired and assured me she was all right and would be safe (naming some things she would be doing). We agreed to meet again the following week with a check-in from her midweek. Emma reported the following week that she had had a couple of days of being tired, but was otherwise OK, and that she actually had started to remember something about her abuser but allowed herself some distance from this memory rather than disassociating to flee it. She also reported feeling a bit calmer (what she would feel instead of anger) with her husband and mentioned some instances where she could have been reactive but stayed calm. She never experienced that state again in my office. Systemically, it seemed that something had shifted in her total context that allowed her to have a different relationship with the events, her memories of them, and her parts that had helped her survive them.

Emma said that an important part of her miracle that she thought we could work on was her relationship with her daughter. After focusing on this in a solution-building way for several sessions, she announced that she was getting a dog who would be her companion at home, because she didn't see her husband as a companion. I asked how she had made that decision and she said that she had seen a dog that she really liked and realized that her current unhappiness was loneliness, not depression or trauma, and had been asking herself how she could feel less lonely at home. Seeing the dog lifted her spirits and she was quite busy acquiring the dog and all the necessary food, toys, beds, leashes, and so on. Some time later, when she was describing all sorts of changes and differences, I asked what she thought her husband noticed and she said she wasn't sure, but she realized she was calmer (not as annoyed) with him most of the time and that they were doing things together.

Soon after, Emma told me that she and her husband would be moving away, so we would need to end therapy. As I often do, I asked her what had been helpful and she replied that the way I listened to her and helped her see "outside the box" had helped. I asked her how she had come to the realization that her unhappiness was related to loneliness. She said it was when she realized that her miracle picture didn't include a close relationship with her husband, and that if she was ever going to feel better, she'd have to start doing something herself rather than praying for a miracle in her marriage. What she intended to work on in her new home was more friendships with others. We never did talk about her childhood sexual abuse or the abuse she suffered at the hands of her husband.

Focus on Future and Change

The purpose of most approaches to therapy is to effect change for clients in some way. The SFBT approach focuses most specifically on small changes that can be amplified for the ultimate change that clients desire (see the next section for more detail). One reason I am writing this book is because I see many solution-focused practitioners focusing on individuals and the changes they want to make, sometimes asking relationship questions, but focusing mostly on the individual and changes they will make or observe. I would like to see more solution-focused practitioners working with couples and families, recognizing that including others can (a) remove the stigma of a problem from an identified client, and (b) make therapy more efficient by including others physically rather than what clients believe they would say.

Viewed through a systemic lens, solution-focused practices are interested in changes made in various parts of a client system, regardless of whether practitioners work with individuals, couples, families, or other groups. The systemic notion of wholeness emphasizes that parts are organized as systems, subsystems, and suprasystems as well as relationships among the parts. We can actually see relationships as connections among the parts, and that when something changes with one part, the other parts, including relationships, connected to it must adapt to that change. Adaptation means change. Using a mobile or a windchime as metaphors, we see that a change in one part requires changes in the other parts, some large, some small, some almost unnoticeable.

By focusing on changes that are already happening, we can amplify those that are parts of or signs of desired change. By focusing on future desires and changes clients identify, we can co-construct other changes with clients for them to become aware of in their contexts.

Small Change Leads to Bigger Change

In SFBT, we recognize that small changes can and often do lead to bigger changes, especially when they are noticed and tended—a ripple or domino effect. Ladona, a teenage client referred for poor schoolwork, noticed that her therapist used a lovely brocade appointment book to keep track of appointments, tasks, and other lists. The next week, she made a small change in her life of buying a beautiful notebook, one that she found inviting, and she started to write her school assignments in it. She then discovered that she enjoyed being able to check things off that she had accomplished, which led to her doing her homework so that she could check it off in her notebook. Her mother noticed this change that started with the pretty notebook and took Ladona shopping for another notebook she desired and lunch together. As they were shopping, Ladona's mother realized that such a strategy would be useful for her in her own busy life, but she was afraid she would misplace the notebook. Ladona suggested a whiteboard on the back of the pantry door instead, which her mother found quite interesting. This led to conversations between them about how they were similar and different in many ways. One evening, Ladona asked her father how he thought they were similar and different, and learned that her father also had had trouble keeping track of school assignments and shared some of his trials and successes. This meant a significant change in her parents' interactions with Ladona around school, changes that led to encouragement rather than expressions of anger and disappointment.

Clients Are Experts on Their Experiences and Lives

In more traditional treatment approaches, therapists are experts on the types of things hypothesized by their therapy approaches. For example, Structural Family Therapists are experts on boundaries, hierarchies, and individuation. Bowen therapists are experts on anxiety, triangles, and multigenerational transmission. Psychodynamic therapists are experts on the inner workings of clients' minds. The SFBT therapist is an expert on solution-building conversations. This requires understanding the stance and basic tenets of the approach, and much practice in listening for tiny openings that might lead to solution building rather than problem solving. We are not experts on clients' experiences, even when they give us clues such as diagnoses that others have given them or they have given themselves, details about what they see as problematic, and how others are involved with and affected by the problem. And we most certainly are not experts on either what problems or their effects mean to clients, how they and others might experience change, and whether or not certain changes are "good" for clients.

From a systemic perspective, this means that we can be free to move with clients, responding to changes in helpful ways, noticing movement that clients desire, and being vigilant about other aspects of clients' lives and contexts that might be useful to discuss as potential resources when they are introduced by clients. We do not make assumptions about clients' experiences based on theory, our own experience, or what others have told us. We do not make assumptions about how other people in clients' lives experience problems, effects, or potential solutions. And we certainly do not make assumptions about what goals clients should work toward or what ways of reaching those goals will be best for them.

Carol had been angry when her mother did not help her when her brothers and cousin molested her, but she also loved her mother and had learned many things from her mother about life. My early training had taught me that I needed to pay attention to her feelings of neglect because this surely was part of the root cause of Carol's difficulties. She did not experience either the molestation or her mother's response as problematic. It was not up to me to tell her that it was problematic and force her into talking about things that she thought were unnecessary. If she had then or later labeled the events or feelings and relationships as problematic and wanted to talk about them, I would have trusted her desire, continuing to listen for openings that might help us move toward solution-building so that the experiences did not rule her current and future lives.

Systemically, it was very important that I realize that I was part of her system and that how I initiated conversation or responded to her would feed back into the system of therapy in either helpful, neutral, or unhelpful ways. I had noticed that when she talked about the abuse as her friends thought she should, she became more sad and withdrawn. If I had continued talking about the abuse, asking for details, and so on, she likely would have complied but stayed sad and withdrawn (system maintenance, dampening change, negative feedback), perhaps becoming even more sad. After introducing questions about her future, she become more animated and engaged (amplifying change, positive feedback). At the end of one session, in response to my question about how therapy was going, what was helpful, Carol responded that she was pleased we didn't talk about what had happened with her brothers, cousin, or mother, but focused on what she wanted different. She assured me that if she had other ideas about change, she would let me know, and left the session more upbeat than when she first came in.

Carol's response to the way we worked together to co-construct her future and what steps along the way looked like suggested to me that what we were doing together was working. She was responsive to my questions that were based on responses to previous questions, did not appear to wish that we would talk about other things, and her response at the end of the session reassured me that solution-building ideas were helpful to her. So, I continued to use them. Carol returned to the next session reporting other exceptions she had noticed, signs that she was moving up the scale, and more detail about her preferred future. I had not taken an expert role of telling her what was really going on or what she should do, instead exploring details about the abuse, her mother's reaction, or anything else about her life, trusting that she knew her experience and what would be good for her to talk about and when.

I know many therapists who have good advice for their clients about what they should read, what they should do, when they should leave their partners (or not), and so on. Some of this advice is certainly helpful, there is no doubt about it. However, whether it will fit a particular client's situation or needs is something only clients can decide. Another person can give us ideas about what *might* be helpful, but we're the only ones who can evaluate and judge the advice.

Therapy Is Co-constructed

The cybernetic notions of communication suggest that communication is not a spectator sport. That is, we are involved even when we don't say anything (the axiom of "cannot not communicate"). Circularity suggests that the outcomes of our interactions with others affect future interactions. Therefore, although we certainly influence conversations with clients by the kinds of questions we ask, we cannot predict exactly how clients will respond or what that will mean for further conversation. Therapy is not a series of pre-formatted questions but uses utterances and language of clients. We construct ideas together: co-construction. The process is circular, contextual, and involves both subtle and obvious changes in thinking, talking, and acting.

Client-Therapist Relationship

Because ideas in SFBT are co-constructed, this means that the therapist and client are in a relationship. We don't need to "make" a relationship or "join" with clients because we already have a relationship by virtue of the fact that we now know each other and have specific roles as client and therapist. When asked about this in workshops or presentations, Steve de Shazer often said that we already had relationships with clients and it was our jobs to not mess them up. When we listen carefully to what clients are saying and what they want rather than interjecting our own hypotheses, solutions, or advice, we are following their leads, being respectful, and honoring their expertise. They are more likely to trust us, let us know when roads are not right, and tell us the things we need to hear to help them determine and work toward their preferred futures.

Well-Formed Goals

When we help clients with goals that we have determined for them, usually in well-intentioned ways and based on our training in certain approaches, the goals are less likely to be formed well enough for clients and us to know when they have been reached or whether our process is helping them with changes toward those goals. Systemically, aspects of SFBT well-formed goals work together to assure they fit clients, their contexts, and others in their systems. Think of "well-formed goals" as a system itself. Changes in some parts effect changes in others. Any system is a subsystem of larger systems, and changes affect other subsystems and systems, and are, in turn, affected by them. Well-formed goals will help make differences that make differences to clients and other parts of their systems that are important to them.

One of my training supervisors was also a psychoanalyst. I was learning systemic therapy from him and asked how these two seemingly antithetical approaches could work together. He said that they were like two sides of the same coin, one side the individual and the other, the family. He said that he had worked for many years in analysis with a patient and near the end, the patient had said, "Now I know why I'm a jerk; but what am I going to do with that?" The patient had come to my supervisor saying he needed analysis because of his neuroses and so my supervisor had complied. He never asked what the person wanted out of therapy. I realized some time later after learning about SFBT that if the person had come to me, I would think of him as a client (less hierarchical than the medical model, enhancing the collaborative relationship), and that asking him about what he wanted out of therapy might have cost me a lot of lost fees, but a greater likelihood that the client would reach meaningful goals for himself.

Curious Questions

Therapy approaches tend to dictate the kinds of questions and interventions we use. Sometimes, therapists seem to "know" the "right" answers to these questions. Genuine curiosity means that we not only don't know the answers but that we're not even sure what the next question is going to be or in what direction it might take us. We take "not-knowing" or "slow-to-know" (Thomas, 2007) stances so that we can be open to whatever the client says. From a cybernetic perspective, this means that we recognize that whatever the client says or does is communication and we must consider the words, nonverbal behaviors, and our relationship with the client to make sense of the conversation and keep it moving in solution-building ways. Genuinely curious questions keep us in a mindset of clients as experts on their own lives and our jobs as leading from behind to help them formulate and move toward their goals. I believe this communicates to clients that they are trustworthy and capable of what is best for themselves.

Relationship Questions

As you may have learned by now, other people in clients' lives are incredibly important in Solution-Focused Brief Therapy, not as the people or relationships that cause clients' distress, but as resources, as observers, as walking with clients whether they attend therapy or not, as part of the clients' systems. Asking clients what they think others will observe about them at different points along the way toward reaching goals helps them think about relationships and what they mean to clients. It also helps clients position themselves as observers of themselves and their relationships. What do I want my relationships to look like? What will I be doing? Will that be helpful? What does that say about my relationship with my future self? What will others notice? What difference will that make to them? What difference will their noticing make to me and to our relationship? This way of thinking is at the heart of a systemic approach.

Relationship questions can be especially useful when clients are having difficulty thinking about preferred futures. de Shazer sometimes used a "best friend" question: What would your best friend say would be different about you? Clients' responses to questions say something about them and what they think their best friends think about them, and strengthen relationships between them whether the answers are accurate or not. What would your best friend say about your miracle day? What tells your best friend that you are capable of making a small change toward the person you want to be? This question requires that clients look at past behaviors or attributes in themselves that they might be able to use toward desired change, and also encourages them to look at themselves as someone whose friends respect and care about them. Recognizing such positives about oneself, attaching change to what others might experience about oneself, encourages further change (positive feedback).

Miracle Question, Preferred Future

Regardless of how a preferred future question is phrased, the goal is to understand in detail how a person's or family's system will be operating when the problem is gone or is no longer problematic. Responses to future and follow-up questions provide great information for clients and therapists about how to proceed to amplify existing exceptions, co-create new ideas, and amplify changes that clients make, either in observing themselves or in doing something different outside of therapy.

When working with couples or families, we ask the same question of everyone, and also ask circular questions (e.g., Fleuridas, Nelson, & Rosenthal,

1986). When partners or family members respond to future, exception or instance, scaling, or other questions, we can connect those responses to the family system by finding out who shares the ideas, who experiences things differently, what difference those differences make to everyone, and so on. This helps the therapist and family see the system as a whole—the individuals and their relationships with each other. It also becomes information that is fed back into the system, helping people understand each other in different ways, requiring changes in the ways they respond to each other.

Finding agreed-on preferred futures for couples and families can be challenging. However, when we remember that goals in systemic solution-focused therapy must be relational and co-constructed, we can help clients talk about what their lives in the context of relationships will be like.

And So . . .

Although Solution-Focused Brief Therapy is often practiced and useful for work with individuals, it is enhanced when used within a systemic understanding of people's lives. Because relationships and interactions were so important to de Shazer and Berg, keeping systemic ideas in mind enhances the work, whether with individuals, couples, families, or other groups.

Note

1 What I have written is only a small part of my work with Emma. I know that there is much that can be critiqued, including my use of coping questions when I did, which resulted in her showing me her coping instead of telling me about it.

5 Solution-Focused Brief Therapy With Families

I was fortunate that my initial training in counseling and therapy was systemic. Although I learned about so-called individual approaches such as those of Freud, Adler, Jung, Ellis, and Perls, among others, the courses that resonated most with me and matched what I wanted to do were the family and interaction courses. In these courses, I learned about systemic and cybernetic ideas, as well as several family therapy approaches that were current at that time. Since then, I have learned about other approaches, including integrative ones, and taught both general family therapy courses and several specific ones, including one that included Solution-Focused Brief Therapy. What appealed to me most was the way that each of the approaches could be adapted to different family systems, subsystems, and individuals. In this chapter, I will present ideas about using SFBT systemically with these various client systems.

Families

Several of my colleagues who were trained to work with individuals have commented that they find couple and family therapy difficult because they are unable to keep track of all that is going on with the individuals and communication in the therapy room. When working with couples and families, the most important skill is one of being able to see the family as a whole and to track patterns of interaction, not individuals or their behaviors per se.

M'Lin and Janine, a lesbian couple in their 30s, came to therapy with their three children, two of whom were M'Lin's from a previous relationship, and one that they had together, with Janine as the biological mother. The donor father was anonymous to them. Jamel, 12, and Cora, 10, were M'Lin's biological children from a previous relationship, and Fancy, 6, was theirs together, adopted by M'Lin. The presenting complaint was Cora's acting out in school by hitting other children and refusing or ignoring requests from the teacher. M'Lin had visited the school unannounced and watched Cora in her classroom with her teacher. She observed Cora's talking with other children and getting out of her seat while the teacher was talking. M'Lin and Janine agreed that Cora's schoolwork was acceptable, although not as good as they thought she could do. They had asked Cora what was going on and received little information and many tears, accompanied by, "you don't get it!" Further queries about what this might mean produced no ideas about what was going on with Cora.

M'Lin and Janine reported that Jamel was doing well at school and at home, beginning to spend more time with friends playing sports. Fancy was the family darling, had recently lost her two front teeth and delighted in making family members (except Cora) laugh by purposely lisping.

There are a number of things about this family that are worth noting, but not necessarily pertinent to solution-focused therapy. It would be easy to hypothesize about Cora's behavior as part of her sibling position, and as having many features (skin color, hair, eyes) that were very different from her younger sister's. We might want to know more about hers and Jamel's father and other family members, what contact Cora and Jamel had with their father, and what those relationships were like. We might want to know more about cultural and ethnic heritage and experiences of the family. We might want to know how M'Lin and Janine were doing as a couple and how their sexual orientations were viewed in their families of origin and their communities. We might even wonder whether Cora had been abused or been tested for Attention Deficit Hyperactivity Disorder or any other learning or physical disabilities such as hearing loss. As you can see, depending on our training and experience, there are many things we could wonder about.

Solution-focused therapists are sometimes accused of not being concerned about contextual factors that affect families such as race, sexual orientation, economic resources, and family constellation. Berg, who was Korean, once said that it is sometimes useful to have a general idea of the kinds of resources that families have, but that people will tell us what we need to know about their circumstances (personal communication). Therefore, the therapist in this case did not start therapy by gathering information that might or might not be useful in solution building.

Session 1

Th: Hello everyone. I am so pleased to meet you! Please tell me your name and kids, I'd like to know how old you are and what grades you are in.

Fancy: I'm Fancy and I'm 6. I just had a birthday and lost a tooth!

Th: Fancy. I'm pleased to meet you. May I see where you lost your tooth?

Fancy: Here! See? [sticks tongue through hole where tooth used to be]

Th: Wow. Did it hurt?

Fancy: Nah. I'm a big girl. Jamel helped, and it bled. I got a dollar from the tooth fairy.

Th: A dollar? Do you know what you are going to do with it?

Fancy: Yes. I'm going to put it in my house bank and save it so I can buy a bike.

Th: House bank?

M'Lin: She has a bank shaped like a house.

Th: Ah. Sounds like a good idea, Fancy. What grade are you in?

Fancy: Kiddygarten. It's fun.

    [therapist looks at Jamel]

Jamel: I'm Jamel and I'm 12.

Th: What grade are you in, Jamel?

Jamel: Sixth. At Highlands Middle School.

Th: Middle school. What are you best at?

Jamel: In school?

Th: Or anything else!

Jamel: I play pretty good soccer, forward.

Th: You enjoy soccer? Yes? That's really good. What else do you like at Highlands?

Jamel: Not much. It's OK, I guess. I do OK because I have to get OK grades to play soccer.

Th: That's very forward-thinking of you, Jamel, pun intended. It's good you know what you need to do to keep doing something you like. What's your best subject?

Jamel:	Art.
Th:	Art? That's amazing! May I see some of your art sometime, maybe?
Jamel:	[ducking his head] I guess so.
Th:	And you must be. . .
Cora:	Cora.
Th:	Hi Cora. How old are you?
Cora:	10.
Th:	So, is that . . . fourth grade?
Cora:	Yes.
Th:	And what do you like best?
Cora:	Playing four-square with my friends.
Th:	Four-square. You know, my friends and I didn't play four-square when I was your age, so I never really understood it. Could you show me sometime?
Cora:	[looking up for the first time with a quizzical expression] I guess so?
Th:	I'd like that.

Children are generally doers. Their experience with adults is mostly about talking, not doing, so I think it's helpful to connect with what they do.

Th:	M'Lin and Janine, I'm not going to ask your ages, but which of you is which? What would you like me to call you?
M'Lin:	I'm M'Lin.
Janine:	I'm Janine.
Th:	What would you like me to know about you?
	[M'Lin and Janine look at each other]
M'Lin:	Um, I guess that we're a blended family, that I stay home most of the time with the kids, and I do some home-based work as a financial consultant.
Janine:	I work at a bakery making specialty cakes and other stuff.
Th:	Finances? Bakery? Do you like your jobs?
Both:	Yes.
M'Lin:	Sometimes, I wish I could go to an office, and Janine works odd hours, so sometimes I wish she had a more regular job.
Janine:	I get up at 3:00 am, so go to bed 8:00, which is hard on M'Lin because she has to do all the bedtime stuff with the kids.

As I write this, I find myself wondering as a Solution-Focused Brief Therapist about the purpose of all these questions. Some therapists would start by simply introducing themselves and asking about the family's best hopes for the session, and moving to the next question from there, making sure that they heard from all family members. Personally, I like a little bit of getting-to-know-you time because it helps me settle down a bit and learn what is important to the family members. Structural Family Therapy (Minuchin, 1974) would call this joining. This sounds too much to me like a technique for getting the family to accept me. I think it's useful for clients also to have some settling-in time and to have a chance to get to know me a little. I think of this as reinforcing a relationship and limit the time we take. Clients usually are eager to get to business. However, when children are present, parents typically enjoy hearing good things. That said, therapy can start by asking about their best hopes from the session, what would tell them that the session was useful, just their names and what they would like to be called, or something else. What is not considered useful in SFBT is to ask them about the problem that brought them to therapy. If they feel a strong need to talk about the problem, they will.

Th: Yes, I can see how that would be tough. I'm sure you're eager to tell me what's going on in your family, but first, I'd like to find out where we're going. Is it OK if I ask a strange question and then get ideas from each of you? [everyone nods or otherwise indicates assent] OK. Now, this strange question: Suppose that tonight, after we're finished with our time together, you go home, do your usual things, and go to bed. You sleep really, really well and, while you are asleep a miracle happens. Fancy, do you know what a miracle is?
[Fancy looks at Janine with a puzzled face]

Janine: It's when something wonderful and unexpected happens and everything is perfect.

Fancy: Ohhh . . .

Th: So, this miracle happens, and all the things that brought you here today are gone. Just like that! But you don't know the miracle happened because you were asleep. What's the first thing you would notice that would tell you that a miracle must have happened?
[family members are quiet]

M'Lin: Well, I guess I'll start. Cora has been a problem at school. She doesn't listen to her teacher and has been hitting other kids.

Th: OK. Suppose the miracle happened, how will you know?

M'Lin: Oh. [looks at Cora] I guess the first thing I'd notice is that I would wake up without dread. Cora's teacher has been calling again and I dread the calls.

Th: You'd wake up without dread. What will you feel instead?

The formulation idea of communication helps us make choices about what we say: we keep something, ignore something, and add something. In this case, ignoring the comment about the teacher's phone calls helps move the conversation from problems to solution building, yet we keep it in mind for later in case we might need it. We trust that if there's anything else we need to know, we'll hear about it.

The therapist also could have asked what would tell family members that their time with the therapist was useful. This would have brought more short-term responses that could have provided information about exceptions and small changes that would be helpful.

M'Lin: I'd feel relaxed, looking forward to the day. Fancy would come into my room and I wouldn't snarl at her, I'd be happy to see her.

Th: Relaxed, looking forward to the day. Smiling?

M'Lin: Yes.

It's very helpful to repeat clients' words; I write them down so that I can be sure to use their exact words later. I think it also helps to show that I think the words are important and to solidify them in everyone's minds, being as concrete and behavioral as possible; in this case, smiling is connected to relaxed but was added tentatively as the opposite of "snarl."

Th: Who will notice that you are relaxed? Fancy? What would she notice?

M'Lin: She'd notice that I stayed in bed for a few minutes to snuggle instead of getting up right away.

Fancy: She'd tickle me!!

Th: You like tickling? Who else would notice, what would they notice?

113

M'Lin:	Well, Janine would be gone, so she wouldn't notice, although she might notice that I wouldn't call or text her about Cora.
Th:	What would she notice instead?

Using the same pattern of speech, I believe, helps clients begin moving toward a solution-building rather than problem-solving ways of talking about things. Instead of the problem thing, what would there be?

M'Lin:	[looking at Janine] I'm not sure she would although she might notice at some point that I hadn't called or texted her. Or maybe I would text something nice like, "We're up. Hope your day is going OK." Something like that. Or maybe later, after the kids are off to school, I might text to see if we could maybe have lunch when she gets off work.
Th:	So, you might have something to talk with Janine about that's nice, maybe suggest lunch together.
M'Lin:	Yes. That would be nice.
Janine:	That would be very nice. I would like that. We used to do that sort of thing a lot.
Th:	So, you used to do things like that together? That would mean something to you? That *is* nice. OK, so who else would notice. What would Cora notice?
M'Lin:	I guess she might notice that I wake her up with smiles and a nice voice instead of all tired like and snarly.
Cora:	That would really be a miracle.
Th:	What else would you notice, M'Lin?
M'Lin:	I'd get up and fix a regular breakfast for the kids instead of just throwing cereal on the table.
Jamel and Fancy:	Yeah! We'd like that! Pancakes!
Th:	Pancakes? Wow.
Th:	Cora, what's the first thing you would notice that would tell you that a miracle happened?

Systemic and solution-focused therapists time their questions to family members for many reasons. Usually, it's better not to start with the person identified as a problem. Starting with others allows everyone to get a sense of how the therapist works. In this case, the therapist moved to Cora after M'Lin instead of to Janine, which would be logical: to start with the parents. However, because Cora spoke up, the therapist wanted to capitalize on her participation.

Cora: [with some welling tears] Mama wouldn't be yelling at me to get up. I get stomachaches when she yells at me.

Th: That doesn't sound like fun. I don't like stomachaches at all.

Solution-focused therapy isn't all fun and positivity. It's not problem-phobic. Solution-focused therapists have empathy and compassion for clients and acknowledge problems and pain when appropriate.

Cora: Sometimes I don't want to eat breakfast and she yells at me even more, and then I get hungry at school. When I told my teacher I was hungry, she asked why my mothers don't feed me, so I quit telling her. I just keep it to myself until lunchtime.

Th: You keep it to yourself. That you feel hungry.

Cora: Yes. I don't want Mama and Mommy to get into trouble.

As a systemic therapist, I might be wondering about the connections among M'Lin's yelling, Cora's stomachaches, and the complaints from school as well as other things that may be going on in the family. As a solution-focused therapist, I want to be careful to not move toward linear cause-and-effect thinking or thinking that *this* is what we need to focus on in therapy. It's hard for Cora and M'Lin, but I want to stay confident and broad in my thinking, focusing on exceptions and what can be better, using the whole family as a resource. I want to trust the approach.

Th: That's very thoughtful of you Cora. When the miracle happens, and your mama is no longer yelling at you, and you don't have a stomach ache, is fixing a nice breakfast . . . pancakes?

Cora: [looking up] Yes.

Th: Something else?

Cora: Maybe waffles or fixing Fruit Loops for me?

Th: OK. What else will you notice that's different?

It's OK to incorporate others' miracles at times as long as we are tentative and check them out.

Cora: [more tears] Mommy [Janine] might call and tell me she hopes I have a good day.

Th: That would be really nice, I bet. Has she done that before?

It would make sense to assume that this has happened before, but the therapist wants Cora to paint pictures as vividly as she can and to begin hunting for exceptions. It appears that tension has been demoralizing this family for some time and we want to start bringing more hope to them as soon as possible.

Cora: Yes, she used to call us every morning when she could. 7:45.

Cora was certain of the time, indicating that it was important to her. In SFBT, we are always on the watch for what's important to clients.

Janine: I'd like that, too Cora.

Th: What else would you notice, Cora, that the miracle happened?

Cora: No more stomachaches.

Th: Of course. How else would you feel in the morning?

Cora: Hungry. Like on weekends.

Th: Yeah! Hungry. What would you be looking forward to?

Cora: Maybe seeing my friends?

Th: Sure. That would be great. Playing four-square?

Cora: [looking up at the therapist] Yes.

Th: Thanks, Cora. That was very helpful.

Clients like it when we remember things they have said, especially children. They often are not used to adults remembering "little" things. I think that children are more likely to trust us when they think we listen to them.

Th: Janine, what's the first thing you would notice that would tell you a miracle must have happened?

We certainly could stay with Cora, asking more questions, getting more details, but sometimes it's best to keep things moving. Timing is an art and asking "what else" is seldom a poor move.

Janine: I'd call at 7:45 and hear happy sounds. It's been a while.

Th: So, you still call?

Janine: Oh, yes, I like talking with them in the morning since I can't be there.

Th: Makes sense. What else would you notice?

Janine: [laughing] If M'Lin called me and it wasn't about a call from the teacher. That would be terrific!

Th: Yeah, I guess that really would be terrific. What might she call about?

Janine: Well, like she said, maybe to see if we could have lunch or something. Or maybe something about the kids that was fun.

Th: Something fun about the kids, invitation to lunch. Sure, it's your way of staying in touch?

Janine: Right.

Th: OK. M'Lin would be happy, Janine would get a nice phone call. Cora would be looking forward to seeing her friends at school. What else might you two notice?

M'Lin: I think I'd notice that Janine seemed like she wanted to come home instead of avoiding us.

Janine: Yeah, that makes sense. I would look forward to coming home.

Th: OK. Kids [meaning Jamel and Fancy], what's the first thing you would notice?

Jamel: Mama [M'Lin] wouldn't be yelling at Cora to get up. It would more quiet, like [soft voice], "It's time to get up, kids."

Fancy: Yeah! Not, "Cora, Cora, you gotta get up! You gotta get up for school!" [bouncing on her chair, clearly having fun]

Th: What else would you notice, Fancy? What might you notice about Jamel?

When someone has been named as the problem in the family, it's very easy for everyone to point to that person for both problems and not-problems. In systemic family therapy, we view the named client within the context of the whole family. The therapist wanted to spread the focus around, including all family members.

Fancy: [looking at Jamel] I don't know. Maybe he wouldn't be complaining about the yelling. He doesn't like yelling.

Th: What do you think he'd be doing instead?

Fancy: Helping me get my backpack ready?

Th: Helping you. Would you like that?

Fancy: Yes. I like it when he helps me. I don't like it when he's cranky with me. [cranky voice] "Fancy, get your backpack."

Th: Jamel, would that be part of your miracle?

Jamel: [a bit grudgingly, but mostly in an embarrassed big-brother sort of way] I guess.

Th: What would you notice instead of yelling?

Jamel: I guess I'd notice the quiet. Or Mama in the kitchen fixing breakfast. Cora would be up, so I wouldn't be thinking I should get her up, or if she wasn't, I could just shake her and tell her it's time to get up.

Th: Cora, what would you notice about others the day after the miracle?

Cora: I don't know.

This response may have been a signal to the therapist that she had allowed too much attention on Cora's behavior and M'Lin's yelling. However, "I don't know" also may simply means the person is thinking. People often say "I don't know" because, in the moment, they really don't know.

Th: [waiting to give Cora time to think]

Th: [after some time, but not so much that it becomes an uncomfortable silence] That's OK. When you think of something, you can tell me, OK?

Cora: OK.

Cora has already mentioned a few things, so it might be best to move on to other things. The therapist can always come back to Cora's ideas.

Th: Janine, suppose the miracle happened. What do you think your employer might notice? What would she. . .

Janine: He.

Th: He. What would he notice?

Janine: I think he would notice that I'm not worried and quiet. I'd be talking with everyone, participating in the conversation.

Th: Participating in the conversation. What difference do you think that might make to everyone?

Janine: I don't know that they'd all notice, but when we're all in a good mood, everything goes better. We work as a team, get things done and then the shop has a good atmosphere when we open.

Th: Wow. That sounds good. What would that mean to you?

Janine: That things are better, that I don't have to worry about home, or Cora, or the phone calls, or anything.

Th: M'Lin, who else would notice that something has happened, that things are better?

M'Lin: Well, Cora's teacher would notice right away. Cora wouldn't be such a problem. She'd be nice to the other kids, listening to the teacher, maybe getting better scores.

Th: What difference would that make to you? What would that mean?

M'Lin: It would mean that I don't have to worry about Cora, that she's unhappy or something. I don't know why she hits and doesn't listen, but I worry it means something is wrong with her or something bad is happening.

Th: And if that were so, if worry continued, what do you think would happen?

M'Lin: I worry that she'll always have a hard time in life, that other kids won't like her, that she won't have opportunities for a happy life.

The therapist wants Cora to hear what she (the therapist) thinks she's hearing: that Cora's parents don't see her as a bad person, but that they're worried.

Th: Do you agree with that, Janine?

Janine: Yes. We worry that what we see as a sweet girl will not be seen by others, and it could get worse.

Th: You want to keep things from getting worse, you want everyone to see the sweet girl.

Janine and M'Lin:	Yes.
Th:	OK. And you see the sweet girl she is.
Both:	Yes.
Th:	What do you see in Jamel and Cora and Fancy that makes you smile, that tells you they are sweet, good kids?

The therapist wanted to spread focus to all of the children, and also noticed that Cora had been paying close attention to the conversation.

Janine:	When I come home, and everyone is in a good mood, I see lots of things. I see Fancy helping M'Lin in the kitchen, I see Jamel helping Cora with homework. I might see Jamel teasing Fancy in a fun way or playing with Cora. Fancy might bring me a picture she drew.
Th:	So, you see three kids who like to work together, to play together, to be helpful.
Janine:	Yes. And they're just sweet. They make us happy. When we're out, they have fun, behave themselves, listen to us.
M'Lin:	[smiling] I couldn't have said it better and can't really add anything. Cora helps with Fancy sometimes and I think after the miracle, I'll see her helping get Fancy ready for school while I fix breakfast. She sometimes helps on weekends.
Th:	I can tell you both love your children very much and I'm glad you came here today to see what we can do to get you back on track with a happy family. Not perfect, of course . . .
M'Lin and Janine:	Of course.
Th:	. . . but more happy than worried.
	M'Lin and Janine: [smiling] Yes.
Th:	OK. Kids, are you good with numbers?
All:	Yes!
Th:	I want to do some number games with you, but there's no math involved—no adding or subtracting or anything. Would that be OK?
All:	[sure, head nod, etc. from kids, smiles from mothers]

Th: OK. First, I want all of you to imagine that the things that are going on the day after the miracle are a 10. And we'll draw it here [drawing a vertical line on a piece of paper, writing "10" at the top and "0" at the bottom]. Now. Ten means the day after the miracle and all the things you want to happen are happening. Zero means the opposite. Where are you now?

[M'Lin and Janine look at each other]

M'Lin: I guess I'm at a 3. I'm pretty discouraged with all the phone calls from Cora's teacher.

Th: 3? What's the difference between 2 and 3?

M'Lin: Well, there are some days when the teacher doesn't call, and we do have fun as a family on weekends. Cora doesn't complain about stomachaches as much.

Th: I'm sure you both prefer days when people are having fun. What else do you see at 3?

M'Lin: Um, we're taking care of things without fussing?

Th: I'm not sure I know what you mean. What kind of things?

M'Lin: Oh, like homework, house things, bedtime routine—necessary things.

Th: OK, getting things done, going more smoothly. And that's happening now? Better than 2?

M'Lin: Yes, somewhat. Not too much fussing.

Th: That seems pretty good to me. How do you think the others notice you're at 3 instead of lower?

M'Lin: I probably don't yell as much.

Th: What do you do instead?

M'Lin: I'm more likely to ask what they want for breakfast, make some fun plans for the day. Laugh. If there's work to do, ask instead of grouch about it like I used to.

Th: OK, thanks. Before I ask the others about their numbers, could you tell me what 4 looks like for you?

M'Lin: 4. Well, 4 includes some days where Janine and I get to have coffee or lunch together without talking about Cora's problems.

Th: What do you talk about instead?

M'Lin: Oh, normal things. Like Jamel's soccer game, or a birthday party Cora's been invited to. What might be coming up on the weekend. What Fancy is up to.

Th: That sounds really pleasant. When was the last time something like that happened?

M'Lin: It's been a while. Not this week, but the week before, we did have lunch after I took Fancy to school and talked about some things that are happening with her brother.

Th: Janine's brother?

M'Lin: Yes. He started a new business and we're hoping it goes well.

Th: It was nice to talk about something pleasant. What else will be different? How will you know you are at 4?

M'Lin: Um. I'll feel more like doing things in the apartment. Like clean up the kitchen, start some laundry.

Th: Get some things done in the house. That sounds good. What do you think the others will notice?

M'Lin: [laughing] They'll see me fixing dinner without cleaning the kitchen first?

Th: What difference will that make to them?

M'Lin: Probably not much. Except I'll be in a better mood because I don't have to clean the kitchen.

Th: Who will notice first?

M'Lin: Janine will see it first. She might even help with dinner.

Th: OK, so you will have lunch with Janine and talk about something pleasant, get some things done around the house. Are you sure that's 4? That sounds a bit better than that to me.

M'Lin: You're probably right. That's probably 6; it's a pretty big step.

Th: Yes. Is some of that happening now?

M'Lin: Hmmm . . . I see more energy around the house—maybe getting the kitchen cleaned up and straightening the living room.

Th: Janine, what difference will it make to you when M'Lin is at 4?

Janine: Seeing the kitchen cleaned up when I get home from work would be really nice. It would make a difference.

Th: How so?

Janine: It will mean she's doing better.

Th: How do you think you will respond?

Janine: I'll probably ask how I can help with other stuff, maybe homework.

Th: So, M'Lin's energy might help you with some of your own?

Janine: Yeah.

Th: What difference do you think that might make to M'Lin?

Janine: I think she'd like it a lot. We used to work more together in the house.

Th: What else would it mean to you that M'Lin's feeling a bit better?

Janine: I'd have more hope that we can pull this off together, not have to worry about Cora, feel more like we can handle things as they come.

M'Lin: Actually, I already have more hope, coming here and talking. And Janine called me one day instead of waiting for me to text her. So, maybe I'm on my way to a 4 already.

Th: So, you're already making progress? Three and a half, maybe? [M'Lin nods] More hope. And Janine called. Is that different?

M'Lin: Yes; usually I'm the one to call, which I don't mind.

Th: Janine, did you know this made a difference to M'Lin?

M'Lin: Yes, but not that much.

Th: Wow. So, it made a difference to both of you. And there's more hope. Janine, do you like that? Do you agree?

Janine: Yes, I agree that we're a little more hopeful.

Th: What number do you think you are at, Janine?

Janine: I think I'm at 5. I've seen kids have problems like these and families figure out how to help them. I think we can do it. I think M'Lin is more worried than I am.

Th: 5. More hopeful than M'Lin?

Janine: Yes.

Th: So, what does 6 look like for you?

Janine: M'Lin has even more hope, is not as discouraged, talks with me more about other things. Is more confident we can figure this out?

Notice that the therapist is not asking about Cora and her problems, how they started, details about what happens at school, in the phone calls, or the conversations about how to "fix" Cora. Also, the therapist noticed that Janine was tentative and already getting into the pattern of SFBT with scaling and presumed future focus.

Th: And that would make some difference to you?

Janine: Yes, it's hard enough to be worried about Cora, but it's worse when I have to worry about M'Lin, too.

Th: OK. So, M'Lin is 3 plus, maybe 3.5 and moving toward 4. Janine is 5 and knows what 6 looks like. Jamel, where are you? Where are you toward your miracle day?

Jamel:	Oh, I'm OK. Most of the time, it doesn't bother me. I'd say I'm at 7.
Th:	And what tells you that you are at 7, not 6? What's different?
Jamel:	Well, weekends are nice, everyone gets along pretty well. Mama doesn't yell much.
Th:	OK, weekends are nice. What else tells you that you are at 7?
Jamel:	When we come home from school, Mom [Janine] tries to make a better mood. She says hi and gives us hugs.
Th:	Wow, that's a lot. You notice that? That means something to you?
Jamel:	Yeah, that's what normal families do. If Mama is working, Mom tries to talk to Cora about school and stuff because when Mama talks with Cora, it gets nasty sometimes.
Th:	So, it's better when Mom talks with Cora? What does that mean to you?
Jamel:	It means she cares about her even if everyone's kinda mad and all.
Th:	Your moms show they care when they talk with you? Even about tough stuff?
Jamel:	Yeah. But I don't think Cora sees it that way.
Th:	OK. So, you're at 7. What does 7 and a half or 8 look like?
Jamel:	Yeah. What does better look like? Hmm . . . Maybe more days like that? Mama and Mom both seeing us when we come home?
Th:	OK. You think about that. Cora, where are you on this scale toward the miracle day?
Cora:	2.
Th:	2. How come not 1? What's different?
Cora:	I know Mama and Mommy care about me. I just don't like yelling and talking when the teacher calls.
Th:	You know that your moms really care. That's good, because I think so, too. I think they care a lot or they wouldn't have brought all of you here to help make things better. What does a little better look like for you? Just a little.
Cora:	[silent, looking down] I guess if Mama didn't act so mad at me.
Th:	What would she do instead?
Cora:	Help me with my reading. Or just give me a hug when I get home instead of "talking" to me or telling Mommy to "talk" to me.
Th:	That would make a difference to you? How would they know it matters?
Cora:	I'd stick around in the living room instead of going to my room.

Th: What would you be doing in the living room?

Cora: I don't know. Maybe watching TV or playing with Fancy. Reading. I like to read.

Th: So, tell me, Cora: when does a little bit of your miracle day happen, even a little?

Cora: [quiet for a bit] I don't know. Maybe when Ms. Ackle hasn't called Mama?

Th: What does that mean? That Ms. Ackle didn't call?

Cora: It means she's not so mad at me.

Th: And what happens at home when Ms. Ackle doesn't call?

Cora: Mama's in a better mood, not stuck off working in her room. Mommy doesn't "talk" to me.

Th: What does she do instead?

Cora: I guess she's watching TV or cleaning the kitchen. Maybe playing with us or asking for help with laundry or something.

Th: And what are you like when it's like that? What are you doing?

Cora: I kinda wait to see if it's going to stick, see if they're waiting before "talking" to me.

Th: And if you wait long enough. . .

Cora: If nothing happens, I sorta relax a bit, start teasing Fancy or playing dolls with her.

Th: That sounds like fun. And that happens sometimes?

Cora: Yeah, sometimes.

Th: So, you're at 2 and not 1 because you know your moms care about you, and you see that they're just doing regular things. What does 3 look like?

Cora: Hmmm. . . [brightening a little] When I'm at 3, I'll think maybe I'm not going to get into trouble.

Th: Really? What will that look like? If I were to see you going into your apartment building, how would I know you are at 3?

Cora: [looking up] I don't know. This is hard. I'd just feel better. [therapist waits] Well, if you knew me better, maybe you'd see me swinging my backpack. If I knew Ms. Ackle probably hadn't called so I wouldn't get into trouble.

Th: Wow. Does that happen sometimes now?

Cora: Yes. When I know she hasn't called.

Th: M'Lin, Janine: did you know that Cora sees that sometimes?

Janine: No, I didn't know that. I guess I've been paying more attention to when the teacher calls and M'Lin is unhappy than when she doesn't call.

M'Lin: I had no idea Cora saw that. I had no idea she sees the difference.

Th: Hmmm. . .

Th: [after letting this sit for a while] Where do you think you two will be when Cora is closer to 3?
[M'Lin and Janine talk over each other] Better. Things will be better. I'll feel better. I feel better already.

Janine: Cora, do you think you know what you need to do so Ms. Ackle isn't mad at you?

Cora: [quietly] Yes. I need to sit in my seat and not talk to others when she's talking.

The therapist could have followed up on this but decided not to at this time because she wanted to focus more on the miracle day and small signs of progress toward that. She also did not want the mothers to start telling Cora how to fix the problem.

Th: M'Lin, Janine, what will you be doing when Cora comes home swinging her backpack?

M'Lin: Well, I wouldn't need to talk to her about a phone call.

Th: What would you do instead?

M'Lin: Just give her a hug, ask if she wants a snack, tell her to go play with Fancy?

Janine: That sounds good to me.

Th: What will you be doing, Janine?

Janine: Oh, I'm not sure. Maybe ask her how her day was.

Th: What might she say?

Janine: If it was a good day, she'd tell me about her friends, maybe what lunchtime was like.

Th: When was the last time something like that happened?

M'Lin: Hmm. About 6 months ago. Ms. Ackle called to tell us that Cora had been advanced in reading.

Th: Really? What did you do?

M'Lin: Well, I told Janine, of course, and asked Cora about it when she got home.

Th: So, the teacher called and it was good news.

M'Lin: Yes. I guess the she doesn't always call with bad news.

Th: Cora, do you remember that?

Cora: I remember getting advanced, but I don't remember what happened when I got home.

Janine: Don't you remember? We had special dessert at dinner. Strawberry shortcake.

Cora: Oh. Yeah. Now I remember.

Th: Is special dessert part of your miracle?

Cora: Yes! Every day! [moms and therapist laugh; therapist notes that Cora is more animated than when the family first came in]

Th: OK. Fancy, I haven't asked you yet: What number do you think you are at on this scale from zero to 10? [showing her the paper] 10 is the miracle day, which, if I remember right, means pancakes.

Fancy: Pancakes! Yeah, but I think I'm at 7 because we usually get pancakes on weekends. But I want them more!

Th: [laughing; moms are laughing] OK, OK. You're at 7. How will you know you're at 8? Almost to the miracle day?

Fancy: I'll be bouncing on the bed, waiting for Mama to tell me that the pancakes are ready!

Th: That sounds really great! Maybe I'll come and get some, too!

Fancy: Yeah!

One of my rules as a therapist is to do my best to help therapy end on a good note. Watching the family's reactions, seeing some lightness, could help a therapist gauge how to end a session. Solution-Focused Brief Therapy makes this easy. In this case, M'Lin and Janine seemed to gain some understanding of what things were meaning to Cora and what would be different on the miracle day as well as signs that some of that already was happening. From a systemic perspective, the envisioned different behavior, well within capabilities, could mean that the cycle of Cora's behavior → teacher's phone call → yelling or "talking" to Cora → Cora's behavior can change, replaced with a different cycle. Without explicitly pointing it out, the parents seemed to understand without feeling blamed.

Th: We're nearly out of time. I'd like to take a few minutes to think about what we've talked about and then give you my thoughts. I'll want to hear yours, too. OK?

Th: [after a few minutes] OK, everyone, what are your thoughts? What are you thinking about helping your family reach everyone's miracles? Maybe what's already happening, perhaps a little bit, that you can do more of.

M'Lin: I think that there's more that Janine and I can do to help Cora besides just talking to her. We've been assuming she's mad about something or has some sort of problem that makes her act like she does at school. And maybe there is, but we need to do something different. Cora, I don't like giving you lectures or cross-examining you any more than you do. I'll try to change that. And when Ms. Ackle calls, I'll just thank her for calling and see what we can do next. It's worth a try.

Janine: I'll try, too.

Th: [waits to see if any of the children have anything to say] Well, it's clear to me that all of you care about each other a great deal. You enjoy doing things together, you like to laugh together. I'm not sure what's going to make a difference yet, but I'm wondering whether you'd be willing to do an experiment for me if you want to come back. Do you want to come back?

Parents: Yes.

Th: OK. When would that work for you? [they schedule another appointment]

Th: OK. Here's the experiment: Would each of you please watch what's going on in the family that tells you that things are moving toward the miracle day—for yourself and for others? You don't have to talk about it, just watch for it so we can talk about it.

There are a number of tasks or suggestions or experiments that the therapist could have mentioned, including asking the family what they thought might be a good thing to try. When there are many people, finding a common idea about a task or experiment can be demoralizing if some come up with unrealistic ideas. In this case, the therapist wanted to let the new information settle and see how it informed the systemic dynamics.

Of course, it's not likely that there will be a quick miracle, and that's all right. We're not looking for 10s and whatever happens will be information for the family and for the therapist if they come for a second interview.

Session 2

All troop into the therapy room. Fancy seems a bit subdued and Janine explains that she's had a cold and still isn't feeling great. The others seem a bit bouncier than the previous week.

Th: Hi everyone. Hi Fancy, I'm sorry you're not feeling well. I hope you get better soon.

Fancy: Thanks.

Th: So, what's better?

[M'Lin and Janine look at each other and Janine indicates that M'Lin should go first]

M'Lin: Well, we got a phone call from Ms. Ackle only twice. Janine didn't ask about specifics when I told her. I did call her after Ms. Ackle called the first time and we had lunch and decided what we'd do when Cora came home: no yelling, no lectures, no quizzing about what she did or why or anything. Just standard operating procedure. Except we asked her where she thought she was on the scale and she said 3 because she really tried, she just couldn't help herself that day. So Janine asked her what 3 and a half would look like.

Th: Wow. That seems like a big change. Cora, did you notice something different one day?

Cora: Yeah. I'd been trying real hard but I knew I messed up at school and thought they'd be mad, but I hoped they wouldn't be. They weren't. It was just like the day before.

Th: So where are you now on your scale, Cora?

Cora: 4.

Th: 4? Wow! That's a big change! How did that happen?

Cora: I tried really hard to be good at school. Mommies didn't yell at me. And the second day I knew I was in trouble, so I told them I tried really hard to be 3.5.

Th: You tried hard? How did you do that?

Cora: When I started to talk out of turn, I pinched my mouth. Ms. Ackle didn't like that, though. She told me to quit showing off.

Janine: Cora, I don't think that was showing off. I think it was trying hard and that when you're more used to not talking, you won't have to pinch your mouth.

Th: That's a very clever idea, Cora. How did you think of that?

Cora: Well, I started to open my mouth and thought, "I better shut it" but it was staying open, so I pinched it shut.

Th: Amazing! It worked?

Cora: Yeah, I did that every day.

Th: Your mom seems to think that was a good idea, too. And you thought of it yourself?

Cora: Yeah.

M'Lin: Ms. Ackle called another day because Cora was doing that and it was disrupting the class; the kids were laughing at her. Janine and I talked over lunch before Cora got home and decided not to say anything because we didn't want to make things worse, and we could talk about it here. We thought you might have some ideas for Cora. But then she told us about it on her own.

Th: It sounds like it might have been easy to fall back into old patterns but you didn't. How did you do that?

M'Lin: Well, I decided to not call Janine about the phone call and wait until we were together later. That way, it wouldn't ruin the mood of the day. Besides, I thought it was a little funny, in a way, and a good sign. [to Cora] But not so funny it's OK to keep doing it. We'll find another way, OK?

Cora: Oh-kay. . .

Janine: So, she told me over lunch so we could discuss it instead of calling me right away or texting.

Th: So, instead of texting or calling Janine, you decided to wait. And the two of you talked and made a plan to leave it alone until you could talk more. Do I have that right?

M'Lin: Yes. So, when Cora got home, we didn't say anything.

Th: Cora. Do you know what day that was? Did you notice any differences when you got home?

Cora: Well, I was expecting trouble, but it didn't happen. I wondered if maybe Ms. Ackle hadn't called like she usually does when I've been bad. But I wanted to tell them anyway.

Th: It was just normal at home this week?

Cora: Yes, except Jamel didn't get home 'til later most days. He has soccer practice.

Th: So, something changed, it was good, and things are better. Is that right? [all nod their heads]. Do you think your moms knew you'd say 4?

Cora: [looking at M'Lin and Janine] I don't know. Did you?

M'Lin: [looking at Cora] I knew things were better for us, and I thought they'd be better for you, but I didn't think you'd feel this much better.

Th: M'Lin, what told you that things were better?

M'Lin: Things were more peaceful around the house. I felt more like getting up in the morning and even fixed breakfast once instead of just throwing cereal on the table.

Th: So, where are you on your scale?

M'Lin: Solid 4, moving toward 5.

Th: Solid 4, moving toward 5. That's great. I want to come back to that, but I'd first like to talk some more with Cora. Would that be all right?

M'Lin: Sure.

Th: OK. Cora, what told you that things were better, so much better that you now are at 4?

Cora: Well, Ms. Ackle was nicer to me.

Th: She was? How so?

Cora: She didn't tell me to sit down and be quiet, and she didn't do that heavy sigh thing she does [demonstrates].

Th: What did she do instead?

Cora: She just went on with the lesson. Once she looked at me and pointed to her lips, so I quit pinching my mouth. But she didn't look mad.

Th: She didn't look mad? And she noticed you were behaving better? How do you think she figured that out?

Cora: The other kids weren't laughing at me so much or frowning and looking away.

Th: Yes, you are a clever girl. What else told you that you are at 4?

Cora: That's about it. Oh, Mommy gave me a special hug one day when I got home from school. I could tell that Ms. Ackle had called because both Mama and Mommy were looking at me when I came in. But they didn't yell or anything and Mommy gave me a hug and was smiling.

Th: [noting that M'Lin and Janine are smiling now] Oh, what was that about?

Janine: Well, Ms. Ackle had called about the mouth pinching and we weren't sure what to do. We wanted to wait to talk about it until we were here. But we did think it was clever and *so* like Cora. Like the Cora we used to have. So, we were smiling a little.

M'Lin: She's quite an imp and good at making people laugh. Too good. So even though things are better, we need to help her find a way to keep it up without making the other kids laugh and disrupting the class.

Th: Hmm. M'Lin, you said that you are a solid 4 moving toward 5.

M'Lin: Yes. Cora's impishness is something we really love about her except when it gets out of hand. I think that's normal because she's smart, and we just need to help her learn when it's OK and when it's not. And that just will happen over time; she's only 10.

Th: Keep her impish self, learn to control it. That's how much better. . . ?

M'Lin: Oh, I think that's part of 10. I don't think we need to have that completely now. Just a little better. Maybe 5 is she's coming up with ideas that aren't disruptive instead of pinching her mouth.

Note that the conversation has shifted to talk about what Cora needs to do instead of not do. This process needed to shift to the whole family for systemic purposes.

Th: And when you are 5 [noting that Janine seems to have been completely engaged and in agreement], and you, Janine, you're at. . . ?

Janine: 7.

Th: And you're at 7, Janine, what will you notice? What will be different for you two?

Janine: We'll be talking about the kids in terms of normal ups and downs, helping them with whatever comes up.

M'Lin: I think that sounds more like 10. I think we have some things to learn about how to do that, first.

Th: How do you do that? How do you do that now? Suppose Jamel has some difficulty with something. How do you help him?
            [after a pause in which Janine and M'Lin look at each other]

M'Lin:	[to Janine] I don't know. How do we do that?
Janine:	I don't know.
Th:	I don't want Jamel to think we're looking for problems, but when was a recent time when you two or one of you had to help him with something?
Jamel:	When I got mad about math and broke Fancy's tower.
Janine:	[to therapist] He was having trouble with his homework, got started late, had come home in a bad mood, and when he threw his book, it took down a tower Fancy had been building with her blocks.
Th:	Oh. Thanks. Sorry about your tower, Fancy.
Fancy:	It's OK. He apologized later and helped me build another one.
Th:	So, Janine, M'Lin. What did you do to help Jamel? Something other than yelling and "talking" maybe?
Janine:	Well, we were both in the kitchen, so we talked for a minute about what to do, then decided M'Lin would go and talk with Jamel about what was going on with his day to put him in such a mood.
Th:	And that helped?
Janine:	I think so. Do you think so, M'Lin? [M'Lin nods yes]
M'Lin:	He apologized to Fancy and then went into his room for a while. When he came out for dinner, he was in a better mood. Sometimes, he just needs space. And he might have been hungry, too.
Th:	Jamel, does it help for one of your moms to talk to you when a day's been hard?
Jamel:	Yeah. I'm glad they don't yell at me. They listen and try to understand. They just can't always.
Th:	No, I don't suppose so. They've never been a middle-school-aged boy. But they listen? You're willing to tell them what's happened?
Jamel:	Not always, but if they give me some space, I usually can tell them.

M'Lin and Janine realized that they talked about what to do together and a few things they did that were helpful to Jamel instead of yelling and "talking." The therapist complimented them on being able to stay calm and work together. This is what she saw as how they were helpful when Ms. Ackle called about Cora—they stayed calm and worked together to develop a plan. This is isomorphism: seeing that patterns in one area can be and are replicated in others.

Th: Do you think there's something there that might be helpful with Cora?

M'Lin: Maybe. Cora's a different child, though.

Th: Sure. It sounds a lot like what you did after Ms. Ackle called, though.

Janine: Yes, it does. Maybe we can use that.

Th: We have a few minutes left. So, I'm curious: Jamel, what did you notice this week?

Jamel: I was busy this week with soccer, so I didn't really notice much. I guess things were quieter and dinnertime was nicer. Cora wasn't all quiet and such.

Th: So, where do you think you are on your scale toward the miracle? You were at 7 last week.

Jamel: 8, I guess. I don't know. If things keep up like this, I don't know why we would need to be here.

Th: OK. Thanks. Fancy, are things better for you at home except for your cold?

Fancy: I guess. Mama's not yelling in the mornings and she fixed me some medicine for my cough.

Th: That was a good thing for her to do. I hope you'll feel better soon.

M'Lin: I hope so, too.

Th: So, M'Lin and Janine, what difference did all these changes this week make to you?

Janine: Well, it meant a lot to me. It felt like M'Lin and I could work together again, you know, to help Cora.

M'Lin: I agree, although I'm not sure what we'll come up with.

Th: Do you think this clever, smart Cora of yours can help with that?

Janine: [laughs] Oh, I'll bet she can!

Th: OK. Let me take a few minutes to think and then we'll wrap things up.

Th: [after a break] Do any of you have anything else you want to add? [they shake their heads] Well, first, I'd like to say how impressed I am with all of you. Cora came up with a clever idea for staying quiet at school, M'Lin and Janine worked together to decide how to handle some things. It seems you're going in the right direction. Is that correct?

M'Lin: Yes. I think so. But I don't want them to go backwards.

Th:	Of course not. But if there's a bit of kerfuffle, you can learn from that. Ups and downs are normal. Do you want to come back?
Jamel:	Do we have to? I'm missing soccer.
Th:	That's up to your moms.
M'Lin:	Can we come back without Jamel?
Th:	Sure, if that's what you two decide will be helpful.
	[the mothers look at each other]
Janine:	I think I'd like to come back at least one more time. I'm worried that Cora doesn't quite understand.
M'Lin:	Me, too, but I think we'll be able to handle it if we remember to talk with each other. I think that's on me.
Janine:	Only partly; I need to let you know if you're getting ahead of us.
M'Lin:	Yeah. [to therapist] We want to come back.

Note that the therapist did not ask about the experiment. This is a matter of debate and preference. Some think that if it's not discussed, the therapist loses credibility and the experiment was not necessary. Others, including myself, think that it depends on a number of factors. In this case, the family was doing better, didn't bring it up themselves, and the therapist knew that she or the family could bring it up later if anyone thought it would be useful.

Session 3

The next session was very similar to the second. Things were a bit better, no big leaps up the scale. M'Lin and Janine had talked and decided to just chat with Cora about some things. They told her that they thought she was clever and smart but that she needed to learn to not disrupt class. They realized that this was hard for her and before they could talk about what she would do, she said she had an idea. She would write her thoughts on paper and if she thought they were really important, she would raise her hand. They asked her how she came up with that (quick learners) and she said that she needed to do something with her mind and find a better way to use her hands that the other kids wouldn't laugh about. The therapist complimented all of them, asked detail questions about their scale, exceptions, and their future, then asked if they wanted to come back. They did, but not right away, so they set an appointment for a month.

Session 4

When the family came to the next session, they said that there had been a setback: Jamel had gotten into trouble in soccer for throwing the ball at another child's head. They said that at first, they were really mad and M'Lin started to yell at him. Janine reminded her that they needed to talk, so they sent Jamel to his room so they could talk. Janine reminded M'Lin that they needed to remain calm and not yell or lecture. When Jamel came out of his room, they asked him what had happened and what he thought would have been a better move. He responded well so they thought they were back on track for parenting. They each said they were at 8 or 9 on their scales and thought they could continue without therapy.

This looks like a wonder case because there were so few sessions and the changes were so dramatic. It demonstrates the approach as rather simple. However, it's not always that easy. For example, kids are often quite sullen in therapy, refusing to talk. I believe that's OK. I tell them they can listen and, if they want to say something, we'd like to hear it, so they should let us know. We don't need kids to "open up" in order to be helpful to them and their families.

Systemically, what we notice about this case is what de Shazer pointed out some time ago:

> People come to therapy wanting to change their situation, but whatever they have attempted to do to change has not worked. They have been getting in their own way, perhaps have accidentally made their own situation worse, and have developed unfortunate habit patterns.
>
> (de Shazer et al., 1986, p. 208)

The authors go on to say that when we try to force our position, we are likely to be met with so-called resistance. Structural Family Therapy (e.g., Minuchin, 1974), for example, might see that the parents are not working well together and intervene to help them become more of a team. Notice that by following what the clients want and how they have managed similar situations in the past, M'Lin and Janine discovered for themselves that teamwork was helpful. Although yelling and lecturing were not helpful and thus they needed to do something different, their perspective on what needed to change was Cora. Looking at the circularity of the family, the mothers' parenting was not "causing" Cora's distressing behavior, yet changing their parenting became part of a solution. There may have been other solutions as well. For example, helping Cora change her behavior separately may have affected how M'Lin and Janine interacted with her, and lessened the tension between them. Talking with M'Lin and Janine without the children would have left Cora out of the spotlight and might have led to some good ideas. Systemically, I believe that by seeing the whole family, parents are better able to understand their children, and are left with ideas about how to manage on their own better and how to come up with other ideas when necessary.

People come to therapy wanting change. They usually see the needed change as someone else's behavior. A systemic SFBT therapist sees the needed change as understanding resources and helping the family access those resources (such as ability to work as a team) and change their process. We are culturally conditioned to believe that we have to dissect the problem in order to understand it thoroughly. Only then can we, as experts, diagnose and intervene correctly. Often, people come to therapy saying they need to understand what's wrong. At that point, I ask them, "What if we work on changing things first, and then, if you still want, we can talk about what went wrong." They usually agree to this. If clients say they really need to understand, I say something like, "OK, let's look at this a bit." Then, after hearing about the problem (some people really need to tell us something of their problems and that's OK), I'll say something like, "I see. [reflect some understanding] What if I told you I thought the problem is 'x.' What would you say we need to do?" Getting the client's ideas may help move more quickly into solution-building by avoiding what may look like resistance. Then, "So, we could do . . . Suppose that's successful, what will be different? What will you see that will tell you that things are better? Suppose the problem is 'y.' Then what would we do and how would that be helpful?" And proceed from there.

In the case we just reviewed, the parents may have said that Cora needed to learn how to behave better at school. The therapist could have indicated understanding, perhaps by asking what "behave better" looks like and reiterating some details. So many people think that things like Cora's behavior are symptoms of an underlying problem. In fact, as therapists, we tend to talk this way: "What are the presenting symptoms?"—symptoms being signs of something "deeper." Cora's behavior could be a symptom of or distraction from tension between M'Lin and Janine. Or just the behaviors of a creative and active child. If Cora's behavior at school reflected something such as abuse, I think she would have said something like, "I wouldn't have to visit my dad anymore."

Th: What difference would that make to you, Cora? Staying with your moms?

Cora: [looking at mothers] Sometimes he hurts me or Fancy. Jamel gets mad at him.

Somehow, details about what would be different in a preferred future help bring forth information about abuse when it's present. In those cases, therapists must follow their jurisdictional requirements for reporting to authorities or keeping the child safe, and do their best to not let this be the final or only intervention. If the therapy has been mandated for abuse reports, it's very important to follow required guidelines and, at the same time, help the system work together so that everyone is safe and doing well. Andrew Turnell and Steve Edwards (1999) have written an excellent book on *Signs of Safety* for therapists working with family abuse matters using solution-focused ideas. Two questions in such instances are "What will you do to keep your children safe?" and "How will you do that?," which provide needed safety information that can be used for solution-building.

You may be asking yourself about other "what ifs": "What if the presenting problem is a teenager and his/her acting out?" Jamel easily could have been labeled as troubled at some point. He might begin coming home later than he is supposed to, or acting secretively, or, later, showing signs of drug abuse or other problems evidenced by problems at school and mood at home. He might not want to come to therapy, but it's a good idea to start there. Some therapists prefer to have the parents come first because they don't want the teen to hear all the bad things about them. The fact is, the teen probably already knows this and, besides, a solution-focused therapist is likely to cut short any litanies of bad behavior. Instead, the therapist can do the same thing as we saw with Cora and her family: find out what is important to them, what they want, exceptions to the problem, evidence that what they want is possible (i.e., signs it has happened in the past or is happening a little now or can happen in the future), making sure to get each person's ideas, scaling, asking relationship questions to help bring desires together, and so on. It's my experience that kids know what needs to change in order for them to reach their goals. One of my early supervisors used to see teens alone for a session in these situations. He would say, "Your parents are on the ceiling. What are we going to do to bring them down?" Also, it's sometimes helpful to ask parents how much they see their children's behavior as developmentally normal: "Is it normal or just frustrating and annoying? What will be different when you are not frustrated and annoyed?"

For example, asking Jamel about what he would like for himself for the future might reveal he would like to go to college or other training, a decent job, marriage and family, and so on. I've never heard a teen say that she or he wanted to go to jail, really drive parents crazy, or die young. Their impulsivity might get in the way of what they want and finding out what happens when things are a little better usually gets the ball rolling. I've also found that it is helpful to ask parents what they want for their teens and then compliment them on how much they love and care. There's a story about how Insoo Kim Berg was called in the night to attend a domestic call with police officers. The situation they found was a woman holding her very large teenager at bay against a wall by holding a frying pan as though she were ready to hit him with it. She was yelling and cursing. Insoo said to the woman, "You must care a great deal to be willing to hit your son with that thing." The woman replied something like, "You bet. If he's gonna go out, it's not going to be by gangs and getting shot or overdose or something. It's going to be by me!" I have never seen that complimenting parents on how much they love and care about their children resulted in more damage. Indeed, parents are likely to appreciate recognition of their efforts, even the ones that look bad. At least as important, systemically, is that this may be the first time the kid really hears how the parents' behavior is about love and care, not control.

Couples

Brad and Janet came to therapy because, as they said, they were on the brink of divorce. Janet was an attorney and Brad was a middle-school teacher. Both were very busy with their jobs and their two young children. Finding time for themselves or each other was a challenge. Brad had begun to suspect that Janet was a little too friendly with a coworker, which she denied. His second suspicion was that she was stopping for drinks after work often; she smelled of alcohol and cigarettes when she came home late.

The beginning of therapy is the same as with families: settling in, getting to know the couple as individuals and as a whole. I often ask if there's anything they would like to know about me, reserving the right to not answer. After getting to know each other a bit and how I work, we'll work on finding out what's important to them and what they want.

Brad said that he wanted the marriage to work but was tired of the way things were. The therapist asked about how things would be when the marriage is working the way he would like.

Brad: We'd be working together more. She'd be coming home earlier more often or at least calling when she's going to be late like she used to.

Th: She used to call when she was going to be late?

Brad: Yes, she used to call or text fairly often, even knowing I couldn't respond when I was at school.

This clearly is an invitation for solution-building, and the therapist writes it down and marks it, so he can come back to it later.

Th: OK. You'll be working together, Janet will call when she's going to be late, maybe more calling and texting in general?

Brad: Yes.

Th: And what about you? If I were a fly on the wall, watching you, how would I know that things are better, the way you'd like them to be?

Brad: [pause] I think you'd see me smiling more, being more affectionate toward Janet. [turning to Janet] I just don't feel much like being with you right now.

Janet: I know.

The therapist asks more questions about Brad's preferred future. Notice that the therapist did not ask the miracle question; he would have if necessary. The point is to find out what the client wants, not a particular way of getting there. After learning more about Brad's future, scaling can proceed as usual: 10 is the preferred future, who notices, what they will notice, what that will mean to them, and so on.

The therapist asks similar questions of Janet and learns that she would feel more like coming home instead of staying at the office so much. She also says that Brad would not be complaining about their kids or the kids and teachers at school so much. "He's a complainer," she said. The therapist asks what Brad would be doing instead, and then what she would be doing. The pattern for working with complainers is to not get hooked into their complaining and to keep "instead" as well as "what will you be doing when he is doing that more?" in mind as mantras. Another mantra is "what else" and relationship questions. I like to get good pictures of details, then move to exceptions (when was it like this before, even a little) and scaling.

A good experiment for couples is to notice what they want to keep in the relationship without talking with each other. They often come back to therapy reporting that things are better, which wasn't the task, but is such a good response! The therapist can ask whether they found the experiment useful and follow up with their response, asking for details, other exceptions, scaling toward the miracle day or preferred future, etc. If they say they didn't do it, or one of them didn't do it, the therapist can ask them to list some things now as they look back at the week.

Couples come in expecting us to ask about their latest fight. Interactionally, we can do that, asking about sequences and patterns, for example. From a solution-focused perspective, this would look more like learning details of sequences and patterns that are different, or how they would be different in the preferred future. When couples get stuck, we can still draw the patterned sequence, point to a place on it, and ask what either of them could do differently at this point. Compliments, exceptions, and scaling are logical follow-ups along with, of course, relationship questions.

Relationship questions can involve any number of other people, including each of the partners. Children, parents, friends, coworkers, pets, and so forth are potentially going to notice something that's a little different, at least in the imagination of the couple.

When couples work hard and still decide that they want to divorce, we do what we can to help them make that as amicable as possible. Sometimes, their final decisions don't work out very well and neither does therapy. I worked with one couple where the wife had had an affair with the husband's best friend, so he felt twice betrayed. We worked and worked on trust on both sides, how he would know he could trust her, what she would be doing to earn the trust, how she would know she could trust him to keep moving forward, what she would be doing, and so forth. I realized that we were talking about trust too much and switched to "what difference will that make" and "what else will be happening," remembering that solutions don't always look like they are related to problems.

Whenever I tried to get away from the affair into their preferred future, it seemed to always fail. It could only look like what he thought they had before but he was wrong, he didn't want a divorce, it was against their religion, he thought they needed time, and back to trust—trusting her or trusting himself. She definitely didn't want the divorce and wanted to keep working on the marriage, professing many times that the affair was over, she wasn't seeing him, she didn't respond to his calls or texts, had told him she was done, and so on. She asked for a private session and wanted my help in letting go of the affair, so we worked on that for a few sessions, helping her figure out how to resist temptation to text him, how to reinforce to him that she wanted to work on the marriage, what her preferred future would look like. We also talked about how she was coping with what seemed to be an impossible situation (therefore, not a problem that could be resolved).

I saw the wife about a year later in a store parking lot. She came up to me and said that she'd been thinking about calling me for a follow up, that things were pretty much the same, they continued to argue about the affair, but that they were able to get along decently enough because they still had one child at home, the others being grown and on their own. She said she didn't think they'd be able to divorce because the kids wouldn't allow it and she would be excommunicated from her church if he didn't agree to the divorce.

This case was very sad for me. I consulted with solution-focused colleagues and they didn't have any other ideas for me. I encouraged the wife to take care of herself and to feel free to call me for an appointment. I did not want to talk further in the parking lot, and don't think that would have been wise for her, either. I offered to refer them to a different therapist.

Another difficult situation is when working with divorcing or divorced parents who insist on blaming each other and can't get past their own personal hurts and anger. There are many ways of working with difficult clients, and sometimes it's best to refer to other therapists whom we trust and who work from different perspectives.

Blended Families

On a happier note, it is a joy to work with so-called blended families when they are struggling so much to make things work and are willing to do almost anything. Kids are bound to be jealous of step-siblings (Brady Bunch not withstanding) and parents are bound to resent step-parents' interference in parenting. Using literature and systemic ideas can be quite helpful at understanding what seems to work well in such families. For example, a general idea is that until and unless the kids accept their step-parents as legitimate parent-figures, it's best for the biological parents to enforce discipline with the support of step-parents. It's also good for parents to be sure to make time to discuss what's going on and make decisions together, even about the other's children. My daughter-in-law, step-parent to two, said that her job as a step-parent wasn't to set rules or enforce them unless requested to do so; her job was to be awesome. I sort of like that.

A final thing to keep in mind, in general, about blended families is the myriad ways that ex-spouses interact and are involved. Because the complications of some of these scenarios are plentiful, it's good to make decisions about which systems and subsystems to see based on the particulars of the situation and the preferred futures that emerge. In these cases, it's important to stay on top of what's realistic because often a preferred future is for someone else to be doing something that the speaker has no control over. Even then, ideas about how one would act if the other did change can be helpful at managing and coping.

And So . . .

Working with families from a systemically informed, solution-focused perspective is very gratifying. An extensive overview of working with various kinds of difficulties is beyond the scope of this book. What's most important is keeping in mind the basics of each lens. From systemic ideas, think about wholeness, relationships, interactions, and patterns. The process of how people interact is what maintains both problems and solutions. From solution-focused ideas, keep in mind preferred futures, solutions are not always clearly connected to problems, exceptions, scaling, and "what else?" When using SFBT as the primary lens and stance, systemic ideas fall easily into place. The next section of this book looks at somewhat the opposite: when you want to keep your primary approach and use solution-focused practices also.

Using SFBT Practices With Four Family Therapy Approaches

In this section, I will recap basics of four family therapy approaches and show how you might use solution-focused practices with them. My best hope is that these demonstrations will help readers use SFBT with their own therapy approaches. Solution-Focused Brief Therapy as a basic approach assumes a paradigm shift of looking at therapy through a lens that incorporates a future focus, privileges clients in terms of what is important to them and what they want, and is collaborative rather than expert-based. It is not primarily a set of practices, although several are identified in this book and elsewhere. Instead, it is a way of thinking that does not assess for underlying pathology or disease, that assumes that clients have ideas about what they want, and that assumes that clients are the experts on their own experiences and what works or will work for them. We may provide ideas about resources for clients, but they are the ones who will access such resources and use them in ways that are best for them. Therapists are experts on solution-focused conversations, but not on what might be best for clients.

An appendix in this book includes a set of systemic models that are presented in a common format. The model charts were developed by myself and students and are free to use as long as we are given credit. Each chart includes areas or cells that include prominent leaders, assumptions, concepts, goals of therapy, role of the therapist, assessment for the approach, interventions, how change is viewed, how termination is determined, matters related to the self of the therapist, any evaluation of the approach existing at the time the charts were developed, and main resources for the approach. The information is not exhaustive and has not been updated to account for more recent research. Seminal literature is listed; each approach has many other uses than those listed and many resources describing the approach and its uses. When used in a word-processing document, a chart can have its cell data removed and the chart becomes a template for an individual practitioner's own approach to therapy.

Although I name and illustrate some ways to use SFBT with four approaches in this chapter, descriptions are not exhaustive and other SFBT practitioners may not agree with my way of thinking. Many are concerned that simply using a few solution-focused techniques as part of other approaches dilutes the solution-focused approach and should not be encouraged. Based on my experience, using solution-focused practices in family therapy helps to make therapy richer and sometimes faster. Clients seem to appreciate developing their own goals and recognition for their hard work.

Solution-focused practices also can be used by therapists to gauge how well they think they did in sessions or cases. They can evaluate sessions, cases, their own use of preferred or SFBT practices, and so on. Further, solution-focused scales can be used to ask families to evaluate their therapy on different dimensions: toward goals, how well they think they cooperated, how motivated they were at the beginning of therapy and at the end, how well the therapist listened and understood, and so forth.

At its core, solution-focused approaches aim at doing more of what works toward clients' goals rather than deconstructing problems or assuming underlying structures or problems that require close examination. What I am suggesting is a way of getting things started in therapy and, when progress toward goals is noticed, to get out of the client's way and help them continue toward their goals. In SFBT lingo, you are the expert on your work and this chapter only provides some ideas to get you thinking about how solution-focused ideas can be used with other therapy approaches.

Structural Family Therapy

Salvador Minuchin's first book, *Families of the Slums*, was published in 1967 (Minuchin, Montalvo, Guerney, Rosman, & Schumer, F., 1967). It was followed by articles on working with families and then by the book *Families and Family Therapy* in 1974. These and other books discussed practices of Structural Family Therapy in more detail (e.g., Minuchin & Fishman, 1981). After many articles, books, workshops, and published video examples,

Structural Family Therapy continues to be popular in family therapy training programs and practice.

The main premise of Structural Family Therapy is that families are systems that are organized to support growth of the system, individuation of family members, and patterns that maintain problematic and helpful behaviors. Tenets of Structural Family Therapy do not support a notion of family or organization causation of troubling behavior, but suggest that reorganizing the family structure provides a better context for resolving the concerns. Unfortunately, the approach often is used as a way of blaming families for their members' woes, which may lead to "rescuing" the identified patient from the family. In appropriate Structural Family Therapy, no one is blamed and all members participate in making changes.

Concepts of Structural Family Therapy

Important concepts of Structural Family Therapy include *boundaries, subsystems*, and *roles and rules*. Boundaries mark the margins of systems and subsystems, distinguishing them from other systems and subsystems. Minuchin was particularly noted for placing the parents or parent and support system at the head of the family as the *executive system*. He believed that every system needs to have someone who is in charge, aware of what is happening with members, serving to reinforce the often-unspoken rules that define boundaries, and encouraging the growth of individuals in the family as well as maintaining the integrity of the family.

Practices of Structural Family Therapy

Therapy practices in Structural Family Therapy flow from assessments of the family structure. This is best accomplished by first *joining* the system: entering and becoming a part of a newly formed therapy system so that the family dynamics can be experienced first-hand by the therapist. After assessing by experience and by staging an *enactment* (asking the family to demonstrate their dynamics through an in-session assignment such as discussing the problem or planning a family event), the therapist works to first disrupt the family's structure by increasing intensity so that the normal structure is challenged and stressed, and then helping the family reorganize into a structure that supports new behaviors that do not support the problem behavior. The person defined as the problem is called the *identified patient*, a term that spreads the difficulty from the individual to the family and perhaps to others in the family.

Challenging and realigning boundaries is accomplished by challenging family beliefs and current dynamics, sometimes by simply requesting that people talk about them. This will uncover different views and encourage the people involved to resolve them or agree to disagree and move on. Boundaries can be marked and changed by intensifying conversations between people, which often is accomplished by rearranging people in the therapy room, putting two people together to talk or marking boundaries by separating a person or subsystem from another. For example, a therapist might seat parents together instead of with a child between them, then asking them to talk directly with each other rather than using the child to buffer their conversations. Rearranging can also include separating different subsystems and asking them to discuss something, allowing others to observe but to keep out of that conversation. For example, if a father is discussing his concerns with a son, the therapist would not allow other children or the mother to interrupt, perhaps even blocking eye contact with his own body. Therapists support conversations by coaching, aligning themselves with first one then another person, and encouraging family members to continue talking when they reach their usual point of stopping. They may find out that the sky does not fall if they deepen their conversation.

Therapists are very active, leaning in to increase discussion of intense topics, settling back as people discuss and talk in ways that indicate a realigned boundary, or moving their own chairs to support or challenge one family member and then another. Minuchin much preferred to have all family members present in therapy because even the youngest ones are part of family dynamics. I was quite taken when observing a therapist's work with a couple who had been unable to secure a babysitter and so brought their infant to therapy. They took turns holding the baby, especially when one or the other was tense and discussion was heating up. At one point, the father even stood with the baby, rocking it back and forth, but expressing himself clearly to his wife. I believe he could not have talked to her so clearly without both the support of the therapist to not give up and the comfort of having the baby in his arms. This *enactment* of helping people interact in a new way led to the parents' calmer discussion of their situation with the baby in her seat.

Examples of Solution-Focused Practices
With Structural Family Therapy

Solution-focused practices can be used at any point in the therapy. During assessment, families can be asked what they would like out of therapy or what they think their family life will look like when the problem is gone. They can be asked about times some of those behaviors are present. Just as Structural Family Therapists might ask the family about the last time the problem happened and to show the therapist what that looked like (assessment enactment), the therapist also can ask the family about the last time one of the future-preferred behaviors was present and what that looked like (exception finding).

Structural Family Therapists often prescribe homework that consists of continuing some change that occurred in therapy. For example, after having a mother and daughter discuss their relationship and helping them to first tolerate increased intensity by supporting them and blocking other family members, and then helping them to discuss the topic in a different way, the therapist might assign them the task of getting together during the week for ten-minute discussions, practicing the new way of talking. Alternatively, the therapist might assign them the task of a mother-daughter date without any other family members present. At the next session, the therapist could ask about the homework. When there are signs that the mother and daughter were more able to talk with each other in a calmer and more productive manner, the therapist could use SFBT practices by complimenting them, asking how well they thought they were doing on a scale, and asking other family members how well they thought the mother and daughter did and how well they thought *they* had done at staying out of the discussion. If the family reports that things did not go well, using solution-focused ideas, the therapist would assume that at least some small part was better and ask about that. It's also possible that some other thing, not already discussed, went better that might be part of a better pattern. The therapist would use whatever the family brings up in therapy as potentially important and useful.

As the family progresses, the therapist can use exceptions, future focus, and scaling to help therapy continue moving toward goals. Instead of revisiting the presenting problem in a way that might reinforce it, the therapist can compliment the family on their progress, assign tasks that use behaviors that are working for the family, and assign new tasks that align with stated goals and progress.

Th: [to family] How did the homework go?

Mo: I think it went fairly well. Sherri mouthed off a couple times and I was able to calmly ask her to talk with me about it.

Fa: I knew it was happening, so Geri and I went into another room so I wouldn't interfere [it was common for him to tell the girls, "listen to your mother," thereby undermining his wife's parenting].

Mo: Yeah, he did stay out of it pretty good. He came into the kitchen once but left when he saw that we were talking in loud voices but not as loud or as intense as usual.

Th: That's impressive. Dad, how did you manage to stay out of it [exception]? Mom, how did he do that?

Fa: I just remembered what you said, and I knew I needed to not get into it, to let them deal with it. I stayed in the other room.

Th: I'm really impressed. Mom, on a scale of 1–10, 10 being the absolute best you could have done, where do you put yourself?

Mo: 5. I was pretty upset, especially the first time, so I think I was louder than I needed to be.

Sherri: Yeah. And I tried to keep it going, but when I saw that you weren't going to give in, I got mad. But I didn't leave. I stayed and tried to talk with you.

Mo: And I think I listened fairly well.

Sherri: Yeah.

Th: And the second time, when you were less upset, where were you on the scale?

Mo: Oh, well, I guess I was at 6.

Th: 6. How did you do that? How did you get there or what was different?

Mo: Well, I think I must have remembered from the first time that I didn't give in, so I wasn't as scared about it.

Th: That's impressive. And it sounds like Sherri figured that out, too.

Mo: Yes. I think she did. Then, the next time, she wasn't as loud and didn't stomp out when I held firm.

Th: So, Sherri, scale of 1–10, where do you think you and your mom were on that one, the better one?

Sherri: Ummm . . . Maybe 4. I think we can do better.

Th: 4? Hm. Not 3?

Sherri: No, 3 would be my staying in the room, but Mom getting worked up.

Th: And what does 5 look like for you?

Sherri: Getting what I want without having to yell!

Th: [laughs] OK. Do you want to show me? Dad, you and Geri can sit over there. Sherri and mom, show us what 5 or 6 looks like.

In Structural Family Therapy, therapy is designed to be complete when the so-called symptom is gone. However, if the structure of the family has not changed, the therapist may advise that the family continue in therapy until the executive subsystem or other system boundaries are clearly different from when the family first came to therapy. Without structural change, the family may find that another symptom develops that requires a similar change as the earlier one, substituting the identified patient or problem with another family member or situation. Using SFBT practices, the therapist may be able to determine the degree of change more easily. For example, if a family says that they are at 8 toward their goals and that's good enough, the therapist may still ask what 9 looks like. In the above example, one of the parents may state something like, "when something else happens and we remember to use our new skills."

Strategic Family Therapy (Mental Research Institute)

There are two versions of Strategic Family Therapy in the model charts: Mental Research Institute (MRI; Watzlawick et al., 1974) and Haley and Madanes' version (e.g., Haley, 1977; Madanes, 1984). As discussed in Chapter 1 of this book, Gregory Bateson formed a group of professionals to help him with a grant on communication patterns of families with a member who had been diagnosed as schizophrenic. Out of these studies came a way of looking at communication as *interactional* (Watzlawick & Weakland, 1977), that is, between and among people, and that symptoms are communication acts. They determined that so-called symptoms were not evidence of underlying problems or pathology but made sense within the context of the individual. An arm of the project is the Brief Therapy Center, a therapy-focused center that uses systemic and cybernetic ideas to explain and intervene with problematic behaviors. Seminal therapy books include Watzlawick, Bavelas, and Jackson's (1967) *Pragmatics of Human Communication* and Watzlawick, Weakland, and Fisch's (1974) *Change*. Strategic Family Therapy continues to be popular in educational programs, therapy clinics, and as part of integrative approaches.

Concepts of Strategic Family Therapy (MRI)

At its core, this Strategic Family Therapy approach focuses on presenting problems as attempts to solve problems that have themselves become problematic. Prior to this way of viewing human difficulties, mental and behavioral problems were viewed as evidence of underlying pathology related to psychodynamics. The MRI way of looking at such matters was quite revolutionary: troubling behaviors make sense within their contexts; such behaviors have become habits as attempts to fix something else and have become problematic themselves. Instead of hypothesizing and looking at those possible difficulties through pathological theoretical lenses, MRI Strategic Family Therapists work directly with the family on their presenting issue. If the family were able to work on another issue directly, their attempts would have been successful, and they would not have presented to therapy with something else. The approach is called *strategic* because interventions are designed uniquely for each family and situation. Therapists take expert roles in devising interventions and expect family members to follow their directives.

Practices of Strategic Family Therapy (MRI)

In the MRI Strategic approach, it is not necessary for all family members to attend therapy. Helping one person to successfully change their own behavior necessitates other members' changes to adapt to the initial change. In general, there are three types of interventions: *reframes* that change the viewing of the problem, *interrupting sequences* that help change interactional patterns that support the problem, and *paradoxical* interventions that are used when reframes and interrupting sequences directly are not possible or helpful.

An important aspect of strategic approaches to family therapy is the *reframe*. Because behaviors are based on people's *views* of what's going on—their own logic or reasoning—the frame that is used during problematic times is considered to lead to logical but ineffective ways to solve the problems. When a person's behavior is perceived as sickness, others tend to use care-taking roles and behaviors. When the same behavior is perceived as rebellious, others tend to set limits on behaviors. Reframes are stated in such a way as to try to "sell" them to the family so that they make sense and clients are then willing to follow the therapist's directives. This idea is based on the concept of *constructivism*—the notion that reality is constructed from views (contexts and perspectives) and the process of constructing meaning. This is especially important in interactions because each person has his or her own view; in fact, we might say there is no observable reality of meanings that influence interactions, there only are views.

Interrupting sequences has become an intervention in many forms of therapy and focuses on the patterns that develop over time and are repeated in such a way that they support the identified concerns rather than changing them. Because changes in one part of a system or pattern require that others adapt to those changes, helping families change even small parts of interactions can lead to completely different interactional patterns and dissolution of presenting concerns. For example, if a spouse comes home from work and asks when dinner will be ready, thereby setting off a pattern of arguing about household contributions, that person may change one small thing when coming home: asking about another person's day, or folding laundry, or something. At another point in the sequence, one of the family members might agree with something rather than becoming defensive.

Paradoxical interventions can be used when families seem resistant to suggestions. These interventions utilize the clients' energy in a different way and therapists should be well-schooled in them before attempting them. One example of paradoxical interventions includes clients' continuing to do or doing more of what they're doing that is problematic so that the therapist can see how it works. A symptom or behavior cannot be spontaneous and uncontrollable if the clients are able to make it happen. This directive can change a part of the pattern such as the place, time, or length of the behavior as well as one's sense of control over it. Another example of a paradoxical intervention is the "go slowly" message. In essence, it suggests that change takes a long time and it is important that it not happen so quickly that unexpected and negative consequences aren't prevented. If the family slows down, they are following the directive and the therapist can better understand subtleties of the family's patterns of interaction. If the family does not slow down, but does something to make the presenting concern dissolve, their problem is solved.

Much attention has been given to strategic approaches' use of paradox, which often is misunderstood but appears clever. The misunderstanding comes when therapists prescribe behaviors with a belief that clients will resist the prescription and do the opposite—reverse psychology so to speak. However, a true paradox is a prescription that is a win-win for therapy: if the clients don't follow the prescription, they don't make the symptom appear on purpose, and the symptom disappears. If they do follow the prescription (somehow make the symptom happen), they are not resisting therapy or therapist and thus will cooperate with directives that will interrupt problematic sequences of behavior that support the problem, and thus the problem behavior will disappear. Many therapists, especially those who are influenced by feminist approaches, do not like paradoxical interventions because they seem excessively manipulative and "tricky" or "clever," which can be quite detrimental for people who have grown up in contexts that are paradoxical (such as having parents who act like children rather than parents or abusive homes where caretakers are supposed to protect children, not harm them). Further, paradoxical interventions that prescribe the symptom as a way of gaining control over it should never be used when clients may actually follow through with harmful intentions or behaviors such as homicide, suicide, or self-harm.

Centered more appropriately in the tenets of the MRI approach are reframes and interventions that interrupt sequences of behavior. Because troubling behaviors are supported by failed attempts to change them, MRI therapists examine sequences by asking about these failed attempts to change things, and then helping family members interrupt sequences by changing at least one part. When two or more people attend therapy, each person's parts in the sequence are targets for change, increasing the chances that something different will happen.

Examples of Solution-Focused Practices
With Strategic Family Therapy (MRI)

Developing joint goals for therapy can include clear pictures of what will be different and how that will make a difference to the family. During assessment, as therapists interview clients for their perspectives on the presenting problem and strive to determine sequences of behavior that support the problem, solution-focused practices that can be helpful may include complimenting family members on their cooperation or looking for exceptions in the failed attempts (how the attempts helped even a little or changed things into a slightly different pattern). For example, therapists and clients can look for times when the problem was either not present or could have been present but was not as problematic. Interactional behavior of family members at those times can be built upon or used to help interrupt sequences when the problem is present or more severe.

A family comes to therapy complaining about their 18-year-old daughter's "rebellious" behavior. After discussion about each person's goals for therapy and determining joint goals, the therapist speaks.

Th: Tell me about the last fight the three of you had about this.

The family describes the situation, mostly agreeing except when each characterizes another's intention. Emily frames her parents' behavior as controlling; the parents describe Emily's behavior as irresponsible.

Th: Thanks. I think I have a picture of what happens, although there are different beliefs about why people do certain things or what things mean. Does this sketch show it? [shows a drawing of the sequence, bringing the last action around to show its lead-in to the first] Emily does something that breaks a rule, Sarah [the mom] calls her on it, Emily says something that makes sense to her about how unfair the situation is, but that Sarah finds disrespectful, Phil interjects that Emily needs to be more responsible and respectful, Emily says that the parents need to be more respectful of her, stomps off, and later breaks a rule. Do I have it?

And so it goes. The "starting point" is where the family punctuates the beginning; the start could be labeled as any of the behaviors and meanings of the family members. For example, Sarah and Emily would have to have a different pattern if Phil didn't interject. Perhaps that is the "start" of the problematic interaction. In systemic terms, it doesn't matter: the "start" can be described as any place in the sequence. One of my brothers once said, "It all started when he hit me back!"

Fam: Yep [head nods].

Th: Well, it looks to me like you are all correct: Emily is working to be ready to be independent and on her own, practicing, so to speak, and parents are doing their best to help her do that by protecting her while she's at home. In this way, she can learn skills with a safety net [positive reframe]. So, you, Phil and Sarah, try to hold her back from doing too much before she's ready, and Emily helps you by showing what she needs help with and what she wants: more space and control over her life. This tells you what you need to work on: appropriate space and degree of self-control for Emily. But you get into fights about what that means and that's what you really don't like.

Fam: Yes.

Th: It strikes me that you started to tell me about a time when you were able to talk about one of the house rules that Emily doesn't like, but you talked with much less heat. Using a scale of 0–10, where 10 represents the ideal way of talking about house rules and potential changes, where would you place that conversation?

Phil: [after a pause] 6. We were angry, but we didn't get so argumentative. No one stomped out, slamming doors.

Many therapists have a hard time believing that clients are so compliant with scaling questions. It amazes me, too, that it happens nearly all the time. Once in a while, a client may ask for clarification.

Th: Sarah?

Sarah: 10 is everything is perfect? OK: 5. It really hurts that she wants to grow up so fast. She's only 18. I left home when I was 18 and really wish I had stuck around a while longer.

Emily: 4. I thought they were trying to understand where I was coming from, but they wanted me to change my thinking, to agree that I'm not ready to be on my own. I know that, but sometimes, they are *so* unreasonable about things!

Th: OK. You were angry, hurt, trying to understand, but not quite there. Emily, suppose during this next week, for one of the arguments, you were at 5. What would be different?

Emily: They'd try harder to understand me.

Sarah: Maybe you'd try harder to understand us.

Th: Emily, suppose you saw them trying harder. What would be different about what you would do?

Emily: [pause] I guess it wouldn't be so loud and intense.

Th: Sarah, suppose you and Phil were showing Emily that you were trying harder to understand her, and she was quieter and calmer, what would you do?

Sarah: I'd probably calm down, too.

The therapist goes on with this exception to the problem behavior. Solution-focused practices such as scaling can be very helpful when working to change sequences of behavior. In ensuing sessions, as clients describe and show changes, they can be complimented and scales can be further used to gauge progress. Therapists can use relationship and future-oriented questions to further understand, reframe, and interrupt sequences, especially to reframe meanings that family members are using to justify their behaviors.

Strategic Family Therapy (Haley and Madanes)

In addition to the MRI version of Strategic Family Therapy, Jay Haley, who was involved in the early years of developing the therapy, and his wife, Cloé Madanes, moved to Philadelphia. Both were quite steeped in the MRI approach to therapy using systemic and cybernetic ideas. Haley commuted to work with Salvador Minuchin (Structural Family Therapy) and each influenced the other during their long talks.

Concepts of Strategic Family Therapy (Haley and Madanes)

Haley and Madanes developed a version of Strategic Family Therapy that used different frames for behavior and emphasized hierarchical structures, particularly skewed structures when children had power over their parents with their behaviors and symptoms. In fact, they suggested, when children were displaying troubling behavior that was not successfully corrected by the parents, they (the children) were "standing on the shoulders" of one of the parents relative to the other, thus caught in a triangle between them. The behavior served to exacerbate the parents' marital difficulties. Once the child's behavior was no longer viewed as problematic, the parents either resolved their marital difficulties via isomorphism (using a team-parenting metaphor that was successful as a template for marital communication) or were willing to use therapy to help with the marriage. Problematic behaviors were viewed as messages in the system, communicating something that could not be discussed directly. Resolving the "something" could isomorphically resolve the presenting concern.

Practices of Strategic Family Therapy (Haley and Madanes)

Therapists help families develop better boundaries and communication patterns that do not support the problematic behavior, resulting in either the disappearance of the problem or a view that the behavior is not problematic. Haley believed that the motivator of behavior was control and thus used metaphors and reframes that reflected this belief. Madanes, on the other hand, saw behaviors as motivated by love and used metaphors and reframes that reflected this belief. Other reframes are used in ways that are similar to those in the MRI version of Strategic Family Therapy. Reframes help family members view the problem behavior from a different perspective, which requires different responses, responses that support more effective structures and communication. This form of therapy is not as likely to work with communication sequences per se; instead, interventions rely on reframes and directives that support behaviors consistent with the reframe.

Because Haley saw presenting concerns as related to control, his prescribed homework was designed to realign the hierarchy in the family. The college student described earlier was first framed as depressed (thus sick) by the parents. This meant that the symptom had control of the parents. A reframe from a Haley strategic perspective would put the parents back in charge by labeling the situation as the child's being irresponsible. The parents' behavior vis-à-vis an irresponsible child would be very different from their behavior vis-à-vis a sick child.

Haley (1984) saw therapy as influential because clients didn't really want to be in therapy and would do whatever was necessary to get out of it. This included doing things that appeared nonsensical or paradoxical. Clients would typically give up the problematic behavior because continuing the contradictory, prescribed behavior was worse. For example, a person who cannot sleep might be directed to get up and clean the kitchen floor (a second wanted outcome) for an hour and then go back to bed. The ordeal is worse than the problem (not sleeping) and the client would fall asleep rather than get up again and clean the floor.

Madanes, on the other hand, saw metaphors as communicating something related to care and concern, and would describe them as beneficial to the family in some way, a positive reframe. The unwanted behavior was described as an unfortunate way of resolving a family difficulty. This allowed the problematic behavior to be set aside so that the corresponding concern could be resolved. For example, the college student who was not going to class, ignoring her hygiene, and so forth might be praised for helping her parents. The frame for this help might be that the child was really very concerned that her parents would be lonely without her or that without her to moderate their arguments, they might divorce. The prescription might be, then, that she needed to go home and stay with her parents, perhaps until they died and she was an old lady, having never been able to leave. This, of course, is a paradoxical prescription because the child was being asked to do something contrary to what her stage of life dictated: she was directed to stay home at a time when she should be leaving. If the girl rebelled against the prescription, her behavior at college would change, and her parents likely would be helping her grow up in different ways, such as setting new rules around grades. If the girl followed the prescription, the parents would attend therapy to address their loneliness or arguments until the girl was satisfied that they could be all right without her.

Madanes liked pretense directives. A real behavior and a pretense could not co-exist. If one is pretending something, that something is not real. If it's real, it's not a pretense. Instructing a father to pretend to have headaches in the session, the therapist would instruct the other family members to act as though the headache were real, bringing him a pretend cool cloth, settling him in his pretend recliner, putting on pretend soothing music, and so forth. The therapist would instruct the family members to practice the pretense in great detail during the session and then prescribe the pretense at home every night during the week. This could be seen as improving the nurturing communications of the family so that the father did not need to have a real headache to receive family care. At some point, the family would give up the pretense because they tired of it and would develop more nurturing behaviors at home, or find avenues for discussing troubling things outside the home.

Examples of Solution-Focused Practices With Strategic Family Therapy (Haley and Madanes)

Examples of SFBT practices with the Haley and Madanes approach to Strategic Family Therapy are similar to those of the MRI approach. The first thing that happens after introductions and getting to know each other is to develop clear understandings of the goals for therapy, which may need to be negotiated among family members with the therapist. In this phase, therapists may use SFBT practices to help them get very clear and detailed pictures of what will be different when goals are reached for the family, both for individuals as well as the family system. The therapist would attempt to get pictures of changes in both the stated problem and in the suspected issue that requires the stated problem. Further, during assessment, it is common in strategic work to find out what clients have done to try to resolve their difficulty. This information gives clues to the underlying behavior that the attempted solution is matching and the family may like to change. There may be times when the attempted solutions worked in the past, perhaps a little. These are not necessarily occasions that "prove the rule," but could provide clues to clients and therapists about some differences that might make a difference. For example, the spouse and children of the father who comes home from work with a headache may give him lots of attention, rub his shoulders, and so forth, which helps relieve the pain for a time. With this information, the parents and therapist may be able to learn more about what helps and find a way to have the family do it more (if it's working, keep doing it). The family may not realize that the attempted solution to the headache is helpful, but not different enough to make a difference. Doing more soothing and interpersonal caring may provide support to the father that he needs in order to resolve the "headache" at work.

A Haley-type directive may instruct the father to deliberately develop a headache so that the family can soothe him. Since it's nearly impossible to force a physical symptom, the father may give it up, especially if the family's nurturing interactions continue without it. Madanes might ask the father to pretend headaches when he doesn't have them and instruct the family to pretend to soothe him. This behavior may morph into family members' soothing and caring for each other without requiring the actual headache. The father cannot have a real headache if he's pretending and the intervention may include telling the therapist at the next session when the headache was real and when it was pretend, but the family didn't know the difference.

At this point, the therapist might use scaling to gauge the various members and the family as a whole in terms of progress toward the goal. Other scales also could be used, such as asking people on a scale of 0–10, 10 being no need for real headaches in order to receive family support, where they consider the current situation on the scale. Further questions could ask about differences between family members in numbers and meaning, and what numbers up the scale might look like. This especially might be useful if it seems difficult for the family to move toward their ultimate goals. They may need to work on scales about family support in order to help understand better what each number on the scale means to them, or to increase motivation or hope.

Th: So, how did the homework go? Were you able to pretend the terrors, Korley?

The family had come to therapy because 6-year-old Korley was suffering from night terrors, which had been clearly distinguished from bad dreams because Korley could not be calmed, didn't recognize her parents, and didn't remember them the next morning. She had been examined by the family physician and a psychologist, who could find nothing wrong. The parents had described to Korley what usually happened so that she could pretend to have the night terrors and they could pretend their usual attempts to comfort her.

K: Yes [giggles].
Th: And did everyone else remember to pretend their parts?
K: Yes [more giggles].
Th: Great. Let's find out what everyone else thinks. Mom, Dad, when did Korley pretend?
Mom: Tuesday. She couldn't help giggling. But she did pretty well.
Dad: Yep—Tuesday.
Th: Is that right, Korley? Was it Tuesday?
K: Yes. And Saturday.
Dad: Saturday, too? We thought that was real!

A therapist not using SFBT might ask for details about what happened, how the others did their parts, etc. A therapist using some SFBT practices might ask other questions, such as questions about exceptions.

Th: Korley. Were there other times when it didn't happen?

K: I don't know. Mommy?

Mom: She didn't wake us after that for three nights. And then she did, but I thought it was real. I was hoping they had gone.

Th: We have to go slowly so we can see what's working. How confident are you that we'll be able to work on this so that Korley doesn't have such a hard time? Maybe she'll have regular bad dreams, but not the night terrors where she doesn't know what's happening and you can't wake her? Scale of 0–10, 10 being all the confidence in the world?

Mom: 4. If she hadn't had one on Saturday, I'd have said 6. And maybe since she said it was a pretend one, 5. I thought maybe it was something she ate. Maybe she's allergic to something, although the doctor said not.

Th: 5, higher during the week. What does 6 look like?

Dad: I think she'd feel more confident that things are changing for Korley.

Mom: 6. Well, I guess 6 would be more confident and fewer nights. Three nights was awfully good, though, so maybe I'm closer to 6 than I realized.

Th: OK, so maybe you're closer to 6. Suppose that's happening. What's different? Besides fewer nights, that is.

Mom: Well, I'd be getting more sleep, wouldn't be as worried for Korley. It really takes a lot out of her and I worry that she'll always have to deal with them.

Th: Of course. You'd sleep better. What would you be doing other than worrying about Korley and her sleeping?

Mom: I'd be more relaxed. I'd be able to go to bed without wondering if she's going to have another bad dream and wake us up.

Th: You'd be more relaxed, perhaps enjoy bedtime more?

Mom: Yes.

Th: And if you were enjoying bedtime more?

Mom: Her dad and I could enjoy some time together without worrying. We could talk about other things. Do other things.

Th: Do other things. And what difference do you think that would make to your husband?

The therapist might or might not have been thinking that the night terrors and waking her parents were connected to the parents' general relationship or sex life, as Madanes might think. The mother brought it up and the therapist saw it as an exception that could be explored further. However, before going into details about those exceptions as goals, the therapist wanted to help the family be relieved of the symptom.

Th: [later] So, you both agree that people would be more relaxed in the family, more enjoyment, confident that Korley would be OK. Tell me more about what will be different [more future-focused discussion].

Because Strategic Family Therapy of any version was developed as completely different from standard therapy at the time, therapy is focused on goals and getting rid of symptoms, rather than discovering underlying pathology. We would not say that the cause of Korley's night terrors was the parents' relationship. However, it is likely that improving the symptom (problem-focused therapy) through strategic means (directives aimed at changing interactions) can certainly include solution-focused practices of asking about details of what's happening in various relationships when the preferred future is reached. Therapists can then use this information to either help develop reframes and directives, use more SFBT practices, or determine when therapy is no longer necessary.

Bowen Family Systems Therapy

Murray Bowen (1978) is famous in the family therapy field for developing what some consider to be one of the very few actual theories of families and change in families, most of which are often called "theory" but actually are models or approaches to therapy. A theory is explanatory of why something works the way it does, not only descriptive of how therapy is conducted. Bowen theory is nearly the opposite: it provides a comprehensive explanation for how so-called symptoms develop from a family systems point of view and what constitutes change. However, it provides little in terms of how therapy is conducted. Others (e.g., McGoldrick & Gerson, 2008; Kerr with Bowen, 1988; Lerner, 1989) have written about Bowen coaching and how ideas in the theory can be used in therapy and coaching. Intergenerational approaches are not popular at this time, generally because they take more time than therapists and clients want to spend, focus on change is slow, and insurance is less likely to reimburse for it. However, Bowen's theory has informed many therapists who find family dynamics across generations to be both interesting and useful in helping people change and reach goals.

Concepts of Bowen Family Therapy

The main premise of the Bowen theory is that patterns of interacting are transmitted across generations of families. Patterns that are important include how people manage stress, emotional processes, and differentiation of self. Bowen hypothesized that patterns used in nuclear families are projected to ensuing generations. When these patterns become fixed or exaggerated, symptoms are likely to occur (distance; conflict; mental, physical, or social dysfunction in one person; and triangulation). Differentiation of self-connects internal functioning (emotions and thinking) with external relationships (reactions to others and maintaining a sense of self) and is the keystone of Bowen's theory. People with low differentiation of self are easily swayed by family members and reactive to them, and more prone to symptoms, including schizophrenia, than those with higher levels of differentiation of self; people with higher levels of differentiation of self are more able to maintain a sense of self, remain close to family members, and to manage and recover from stress more easily with fewer and less intense symptoms.

Practices of Bowen Family Therapy

Therapy consists of examining multiple generations of family, looking for patterns of emotional responses, especially during stressful times; triangles; anxiety; and both overly close relationships (fusion) and overly distant ones (emotional cutoff), and discussing them with the clients. By recognizing such patterns, clients are able to re-pattern themselves in terms of their responses in their families, detriangling (removing oneself from others' anxious relationships but staying in contact with family members), and making attempts to reconnect with distant family members. By changing oneself and one's interactions in one's family of origin, one is more able to separate emotions from thinking and change responses in relationships other than extended family, primarily with spouses and children. Changing emotional reactivity and thinking helps to change responses in families of origin, which then circles back to current nuclear family functioning. Therapy, or coaching, as Bowen theorists prefer, does not have a clear ending because no one can ever experience complete differentiation of self. Rather, there may be times for sessions as well as periods of fewer sessions or none throughout life.

Genograms are the basis for Bowen therapy. A minimum of three generations is mapped like a family tree, with the current client as the latest generation of focus, although a fourth generation of the client's children might be added. Emotional relationships among the client, siblings, parents, parents' siblings, parents and their parents, client and grandparents, and grandparents and their siblings are mapped according to levels of emotional closeness or distance, patterns of managing stress, and topics that were or are particularly important (either because they are constantly discussed or avoided). Births, deaths, marriages, illnesses, addictions, moves, and losses are noted as important stressors. The client's role in the family and relationships with others are noted, particularly in triangles where stress has pulled the client into a position of importance as a confidante or caretaker.

Process questions help clients think about the patterns and interactions in their families of origin and nuclear family relationships. First by noting such patterns, and then by asking clients where else they might notice them, the therapist encourages thinking about the patterns rather than experiencing strong feelings (which are the labels we give to physiological phenomena called emotions in Bowen theory). When clients report current experiences, the therapist helps the client connect them to family patterns of one's role in the family, how anxiety is typically managed, and how the client is triangled in relationships. These questions are designed to engage clients' thinking ability and awareness of their roles in the family interactions from a more objective rather than experiential position. Clients are then encouraged and coached to think of different stances and responses, ones that maintain their senses of themselves while also maintaining connections in their relationships.

Examples of Solution-Focused Practices With Bowen Therapy

Solution-focused ideas can be used throughout Bowen therapy. Because assessment and therapy are continuous, solution-focused questions can be asked that help continue a path of differentiation of self from family of origin. Differentiation of self is not separating oneself away from family but staying emotionally close and maintaining self at the same time. As patterns and roles are identified, ones that suggest differentiation of self, the therapist can focus on those instead of the ones that point more toward fusion or cut-off, toward problems instead of development of self.

Scott and Bry Johnson came to therapy because they were arguing about her family. They had a similar argument every year around the holidays in terms of whose family they would spend time with: Bry preferred to spend time with his family, not hers. Bry had left home at 17, graduating from high school early so she could leave. She had an older brother and two younger sisters, all about 2 years apart. She had experienced her family as stifling with her parents' constant arguments, a mother with a drinking problem, and a lot of responsibility placed on Bry for taking care of the younger siblings as well as the cooking and laundry. She was embarrassed to bring friends home because her mother, when she wasn't working, lounged around the house with a drink in one hand and a cigarette in the other. Since Bry married Scott, her parents had been demanding that she spend holidays with them because they missed her. However, she felt more accepted by Scott's family and preferred spending time with them, particularly his mother.

Scott's family of origin was different. His parents were separated and had divorced when Scott was 7. He had an older sister and a younger brother, all of whom lived with their mother as they grew up, seeing their father frequently on weekdays and for overnights on weekends, as well as for vacations with their dad's family. Even though they were divorced, Scott's parents did not attempt to pull their children into their relationship business and got along fairly well with each other, attending weddings and birthdays mostly without incident. Each had a new partner: Scott's dad had remarried; his mom had a "boyfriend." Scott, however, identified that the standard pattern of managing stress in his family was conflict, and he often argued rather heatedly with his father, who would give up and separate before an issue was resolved. This had been the pattern in his family and between him and Scott's mother.

The difficulty was that Scott thought Bry should be more interested in maintaining contact with her family. He was willing to help in whatever way he could because "family is important." Bry agreed to therapy to see what might be accomplished but wasn't promising anything.

After learning some basic information about their reason for coming to therapy, the first thing the therapist—or "coach," as referred to in Bowen therapy—did was draw three-generation genograms of Scott's and Bry's families. During this phase, the therapist learns about clients' siblings and birth order, geographical distance between clients and their siblings, emotional distance patterns, information about siblings' lives including whether they are in relationships and have children, and emotional connections among nuclear family members. The therapist might also ask questions about work and education, and about basic health or patterns of dysfunction such as trouble with drugs or alcohol. Similar information is gathered about the parents' generation and family relationships.

During the assessment phase, a therapist learns how people managed basic family interactions and events, along with identifying difficulties and strained relationships. The therapist looks for triangles and how they have been managed over time, and asks about fused or cutoff relationships, keeping in mind patterns of managing stress: distance (or cutoff), conflict, triangling, and symptomatic people (physical, mental, or social). Solution-focused questions can be used to look for exceptions in intergenerational patterns.

When people are reticent or seem overly emotional when talking about family members and relationships, it sometimes is better to start with another member or a generation removed. It often is easier for people to talk about grandparents and aunts/uncles than about parents and siblings. In Bowen work, we want to focus on thinking, on helping clients be observers of themselves and their positions in their families of origin, so we avoid discussions that evoke strong feelings.

In what follows, I will focus on Bry's family. Bry had a hard time talking about her parents, so the therapist switched to her grandparents and aunts/uncles. Solution-oriented thinking at this point can be used to note exact language that clients use, listening for exceptions, asking how different people might have preferred their lives and relationships, how much those preferences are shared by the client, and what all of that might mean to different people. The therapist learned that Bry's grandfather on her mother's side was a shopkeeper and seldom home. Her grandmother was a bookkeeper and managed the finances for the shop, which kept her quite busy. Bry reported that her mother had said that she usually went home to an empty house. She wasn't sure about her grandparents' relationship because her grandfather had died when she was young, and her grandmother and mother never talked about him. This indicated distance in the grandparents' marriage and between Bry's mother and her parents. In this case, the therapist explores relationships among the women in the family and notes the distance between Bry and her mother.

Th: Hmm. It seems your grandparents were both quite busy keeping the family going financially. What do you think they enjoyed together? [focusing on connections in family as well as distance]

Bry: I'm not sure. I didn't see Grandma very often because Mom wasn't too keen on that. [indicates distance or conflict between Bry's mother and grandmother]

Th: Would you describe their relationship as distant or conflictual?

Bry: Mom and Grandma or Grandma and my grandfather?

Th: Oh, I'm sorry. Your mom and grandma. [Bry seemed able to talk now about "nearer" relationships, but still not between her and her mother]

Bry: It was OK, no fighting that I know of, just not close. Grandma was closer to my Aunt Sylvie.

Th: [therapist makes notes on genogram as she is drawing it] Is Sylvie younger or older than your mom? [younger] Was she your mom's only sibling?

Bry: Yes. And she and Mom are pretty close. Not on the phone all the time, but they talk and visit at least every other month.

Th: OK. I would like to come back to that later because it might be helpful. What's your relationship with your Aunt Sylvie like?

Bry: I'd say it's good. She's my favorite aunt. She's my only biological aunt; my dad has a brother and he's married. But I don't see them very often, maybe every few years or so.

Th: So, you're pretty close to your Aunt Sylvie. You can talk with her about things? Things you're going through, family, school, etc.? Scott? [getting even closer to emotional relationships]

Bry: Yes, to a certain extent. I wouldn't call her up, but when we're together, she asks questions and I like talking with her. More than with Mom.

Th: So, how would you describe your relationship with your mom?

Bry: Not very good. I mean, it's not like we fight or anything, but we don't have anything in common and I don't like being around her with the smoking and drinking. She's always asking about school and stuff but it's not like she really listens or cares.

Th: [solution-focused exception question] What's the best thing about your relationship?

The therapist is getting a picture of Bry's family and some of the difficult relationships she has been in or witnessed. A problem-focused way of looking at her family would be to find out where the triangles and anxiety have been, events that have precipitated distance or conflict, and perhaps how the other people might describe the same relationships. The therapist might be thinking about those as frames, context, or causes for the conflictual relationship between Bry and her mother. In a solution-focused way, the therapist can also look at the good parts of even distant relationships, or potentially good aspects as exceptions.

Bry: [quiet for a moment] Not much. I can't really think of anything. We weren't close when I was home, we're not close now. I guess one thing I can think of is that she likes Scott. She thinks he's good for me. In some ways, they're closer than Mom and I are.

Th: Do you agree with that, Scott? Do you have a good relationship with your mother-in-law?

Scott: I wouldn't say it's good, but it is better than Bry's and hers is. I think I try harder than Bry does. Bry doesn't understand that her mom cares about her, worries about her.

Th: What would you say are some of the ways Bry tries, perhaps a little? [exceptions, also looking for patterns to amplify]

Scott: Well, she's learned that when things get tense on the phone, it's better to end the conversation than get confrontational.

Th: Yeah? How does she do that?

Scott: She'll say something like, "Well, I gotta go fix dinner" or something. "I'll talk to you later."

Th: Bry? How do you do that? It seems that could be hard, but you do it?

Bry: Well, we got into a big fight one time and Scott said, "Why don't you just tell her the conversation is over and hang up?"

Th: Did you do that?

Bry: No. That would have fueled the fire and would have made things worse next time. [Note: circularity and feedback: Bry notices that the outcome of an interaction would be fed back into the system.] But I knew he was right about ending the conversation, so I decided to do it differently. Making something up about why I had to leave seemed better than fighting.

Th: What happened the next time you talked?

Bry: Actually, it wasn't as bad. We talked for quite a while.

Th: You know, sometimes, when people are having such problems with family members, we ask whether something else might be helpful: talking with them about the pattern during a calm time—not during a heated discussion, but a calm time—and telling them you don't like the pattern and will end the conversation rather than continue it and make things worse. Do you think you could do something like that?

This is a condensed version of a conversation that would last longer over several sessions after learning more about the family's interaction patterns. For example, in this instance, the therapist was thinking that a pattern between Bry's mother and Bry was similar (isomorphism) to one between her mother and her grandmother. This transmission of patterns is something that occurs frequently in families, that is not the fault of or caused by one person or another but just the way families operate. Helping clients break these patterns can take time and be difficult, but is possible. It might take several ideas, attempts, learning, and revising.

Bry: I'm not sure. I think she'd feel hurt and fight back.

Th: Sure. And we would have to plan for that. I was just wondering if the pattern between you and your mom is similar to that between her and your grandma.

Bry: Oh. Yeah, I'll bet. Aunt Sylvie told me that they would fight and Mom would stomp out of the house.

Th: OK. So, do you see that there might be a triangle between your mom, your grandma, and your grandfather? Was your mom caught in some way, perhaps? [tentative language rather than expert pronouncement; therapist had talked with Scott and Bry about triangles]

Bry: Umm. Could be. They didn't see each other much and Grandma might have fought with Mom rather than with Grandpa. It sounds like Mom made that pretty easy, gave them things to fight about.

Th: And could you be caught in a triangle with your mom and grandma?

Bry: Oh. Actually, I don't think that's it. See, Aunt Sylvie and I get along better than Mom and her. I think it might be easier for Mom to fight with me than for her to talk with Sylvie. Aunt Sylvie said they used to be close before I was born.

Th: Ah. So, the triangle might be between you, your mom, and your Aunt Sylvie?

Bry: Yeah.

Th: So, when was the most recent time you and your mom talked without a fight?

Bry: Gosh . . . I don't know.

Scott: Two weeks ago, when you first started talking with her about going home for the holidays. You said you didn't want to fight and you didn't.

Bry: Yes, that's when I said I had to fix dinner and got off the phone.

Th: What had you been talking about? [taking advantage of a thinking moment; emotional content is a trigger for old patterns]

Bry: I had said that I hoped Aunt Sylvie and her family might be there.

Th: Did you realize that might trigger a reaction from your mom?

Bry: No. But I do now!

Th: So, you managed to keep the reaction from escalating. You didn't allow yourself to get into it because you had thought about what you wanted to do different. Yes?

Bry: Yes! I didn't even realize what was happening except I didn't want it to continue.

Th: But you did it. So, on a scale of 1–10, 10 being you and your mom having the best relationship possible, where were you when you first called me for an appointment?

Bry: Negative 10. I just hated it but couldn't see any way to make things better. But I knew I didn't want to just leave the family.

Th: OK. And where do you think you are now?

Bry: 2, maybe 3.

Th: Wow. And what's different from negative 10? That's a huge difference.

A Bowen therapist or coach would continue asking about relationships and triangles, helping clients think and act differently. Using solution-focused practices helps by noticing what is working rather than what's not, or in addition to what's not. I believe that these practices help to calm anxiety, increasing thinking, which leads to more thoughtful responses when possible. When the responses work, the work continues. When the responses don't seem to have been helpful ("we did what we planned, but nothing changed"), a solution-focused question about coping can help backtrack a step and calm things again.

And So . . .

We end this chapter and the book on this note. I have enjoyed thinking about systems and Solution-Focused Brief Therapy. I hope that by learning more about system thinking, SFBT, and how they integrate, your work is enriched. Whether you think about systems in a different way as you use SFBT practices or think about how you can use SFBT practices in systemic work with families, I believe that what is important is to think about our clients: what is important to them, what they want, and how we can help them, however we do that. What is most important is that we continue to learn from our clients about their unique situations and about helping people in general. Obviously, I have a passion for both system and solution-focused work and hope that a little of that has rubbed off on you.

References

American Psychiatric Association. (1994). *Diagnostic and statistical manual of mental disorders* (4th ed.). Washington, DC: Author.

American Psychiatric Association. (2013). *Diagnostic and statistical manual of mental disorders* (5th ed.). Washington, DC: Author.

Andersen, T. (1991). *The reflecting team*. New York, NY: W. W. Norton & Company.

Anderson, H., & Goolishian, H. (1992). The client is the expert: A not-knowing approach to therapy. In S. McNamee & K. J. Gergen (Eds.), *Therapy as social construction* (pp. 25–39). London, UK: Sage.

Axiom. 2018. In *Merriam-Webster.com*. Retrieved May 21, 2018, from www.merriam-webster.com/dictionary/axiom

Bateson, G. (1972). *Steps to an ecology of mind*. New York, NY: Ballantine Books.

Bateson, G. (1979). *Mind and nature*. New York, NY: Dutton.

Bateson, N. (2016, January 2). *Practicality in complexity*. Retrieved June 1, 2018 from https://norabateson.wordpress.com/2016/01/02/practicality-in-complexity/

Bavelas, J. B., McGee, D., Phillips, B., & Routledge, R. (2000). Microanalysis of communication in psychotherapy. *Human Systems: The Journal of Systemic Consultation & Management, 11*(1), 3–22.

Bowen, M. (1978). *Family therapy in clinical practice*. New York, NY: Jason Aaronson.

Bowlby, J. (1979). *The making and breaking of affectional bonds*. London, UK: Tavistock.

Cade, B. (2007). Springs, streams, and tributaries: A history of the brief, solution-focused approach. In T. S. Nelson & F. N. Thomas (Eds.), *Handbook of solution-focused brief therapy: Clinical applications* (pp. 25–63). New York, NY: Haworth.

Cantwell, P., & Holmes, S. (1994). Social construction: A paradigm shift for systemic therapy and training. *The Australian and New Zealand Journal of Family Therapy, 15*, 17–26.

DeJong, P., & Berg, I. K. (2013). *Interviewing for solutions* (4th ed.). Pacific Grove, CA: Brooks/Cole.

de Shazer, S. (1982). *Patterns of brief family therapy: An ecosystemic approach*. New York, NY: Guilford Press.

de Shazer, S. (1984a). *Patterns of brief family therapy: An ecosystemic approach.* New York, NY: W. W. Norton & Company.

de Shazer, S. (1984b). The death of resistance. *Family Process, 23,* 79–93.

de Shazer, S. (1985). *Keys to solution in brief therapy.* New York, NY: W. W. Norton & Company.

de Shazer, S. (1988). *Clues: Investigating solutions in brief therapy.* New York, NY: W. W. Norton & Company.

de Shazer, S. (1991). *Putting difference to work.* New York, NY: W. W. Norton & Company.

de Shazer, S., Berg, I., Lipchik, E., Nunnally, E., Molnar, A., Gingerich, W., & Weiner-Davis M. (1986). Brief therapy: Focused solution development. *Family Process, 25,* 207–222.

de Shazer, S., Dolan, Y., Korman, H., Trepper, T., McCollum, E., & Berg, I. K. (2007). *More than miracles: The state of the art of solution-focused brief therapy.* New York, NY: Haworth.

Dolan, Y. (1992). *Resolving sexual abuse: Solution-focused therapy and Ericksonian hypnosis for adult survivors.* New York, NY: W. W. Norton & Company.

Erickson, M. H., & Rossi, E. (1979). *Hypnotherapy: An exploratory casebook.* New York, NY: Irvington.

Fiske, H. (2008). *Hope in action: Solution-focused conversations about suicide.* New York, NY: Haworth.

Fleuridas, C., Nelson, T. S., & Rosenthal, D. M. (1986). The evolution of circular questions: Training family therapists. *Journal of Marital and Family Therapy, 12*(2), 113–127.

George, E., Iveson, C., & Ratner, H. (1999). *Problem to solution* (2nd ed.). London, UK: BT Press.

Greenberg, L. (2009). *Emotion-focused therapy.* Washington, DC: American Psychological Association.

Greenspan, A. (n.d.). Retrieved May 15, 2018 from https://www.goodreads.com/quotes/204034-i-know-you-think-you-understand-what-you-thought.

Haley, J. (1977). *Problem-solving therapy.* San Francisco, CA: Jossey-Bass.

Haley, J. (1984). *Ordeal therapy: Unusual ways to change behavior.* San Francisco, CA: Jossey-Bass.

Henden, J. (2005). Preventing suicide using a solution-focused approach. *Journal of Primary Care Mental Health, 8*(3), 81–88.

Henggeler, S. W., Schoenwald, S. K., Bourduin, C. M., Rowland, M. D., & Cunningham, P. B. (2009). *Multisystemic therapy for antisocial behavior in children and adolescents* (2nd ed.). New York, NY: Guilford Press.

Johnson, S. M. (2008). Emotionally focused couples therapy. In A. S. Gurman (Ed.), *Clinical handbook of couple therapy* (4th ed., pp. 107–137). New York, NY: Guilford Press.

Kerr, M. E., & Bowen, M. (1988). *Family evaluation: An approach based on Bowen theory.* New York, NY: W. W. Norton & Company.

King, P. (2017). *Tools for effective work with children and families*. New York, NY: Routledge.

Lee, M. Y., Sebold, J., & Uken, A. (2003). *Solution-focused treatment of domestic violence offenders: Accountability for change*. New York, NY: Oxford University Press.

Lerner, H. (1989). *The dance of anger: A woman's guide to changing the patterns of intimate relationships*. New York, NY: Harper/Row.

Liddle, H. (1995). Conceptual and clinical dimensions of a multidimensional, multisystems engagement strategy in family-based adolescent treatment. *Psychotherapy: Theory Research, and Practice, 32*, 39–58.

Lipchik, E. (2002). *Beyond technique in Solution-Focused Therapy: Working with emotions and the therapeutic relationship*. New York, NY: Guilford.

Madanes, C. (1984). *Behind the one-way mirror: Advances in the practice of strategic therapy*. San Francisco, CA: Jossey-Bass.

McGoldrick, M., Gerson, R., & Petry, S. (2008). *Genograms: Assessment and intervention* (3rd ed.). New York, NY: W. W. Norton & Company.

Minuchin, S. (1974). *Families and family therapy*. Cambridge, MA: Harvard University Press.

Minuchin, S., & Fishman, H. (1981). *Family therapy techniques*. Cambridge, MA: Harvard University Press.

Minuchin, S., Montalvo, B., Guerney, B., Rosman, B., & Schumer, F. (1967). *Families of the slums*. New York, NY: Basic Books.

Nelson, T. S. (1994). Do-overs. *Journal of Family Psychotherapy, 5*(4), 71–74.

Nelson, T. S., & Thomas. F. N. (Eds.). (2007). *Handbook of solution-focused brief therapy: Clinical applications*. New York, NY: Haworth

Nylund, D., & Corsiglia, V. (1994). Becoming solution-~~focused~~ forced in brief therapy: Remembering something important we already knew. *Journal of Systemic Therapies, 13*, 5–12.

Palazzoli, M. S., Boscolo, L., Cecchin, G., & Prata, G. (1978). *Paradox and counterparadox: A new model in the therapy of the family in schizophrenic transaction*. New York, NY: Jason Aaronson.

Papp, P. (1983). *The process of change*. New York, NY: Guilford Press.

Sander, F. (2004). Psychoanalytic couples therapy: Classical style. *Psychoanalytic Inquiry, 24*(3), 373–386.

Satir, V. (1967). *Conjoint family therapy*. Palo Alto, CA: Science and Behavior Books.

Scharff, J. S., & Scharff, D. E. (2012). *The primer of object relations*. New York, NY: Jason Aaronson.

Schwartz, R. C. (1995). *Internal family systems therapy*. New York, NY: Guilford Press.

Sexton, T. L., & Alexander, J. F. (2005). Functional family therapy: A mature clinical model for working with at-risk adolescents and their families. In T. I. Sexton, G. R. Weeks, & M. S. Robins (Eds.), *Handbook of family therapy* (pp. 323–348). New York, NY: Brunner/Mazel.

Simon, J. K., & Nelson, T. S. (2007). *Solution-focused brief practice with long-term clients in mental health services: "I'm more than my label."* New York, NY: Haworth.

Solution-Focused Brief Therapy Association (n.d.). *"I'm glad to be alive . . . ." Working with suicidal youth*, DVD. sfbta.org, SKU 00033.

Solution-Focused Brief Therapy Association (n.d.). *I want to want to*. DVD. sfbta.org, SKU 00035.

Thomas, F. N. (2007). Simpler may not be better: A personal journey with and beyond systemic and solution-focused practices. *Journal of the Texas Association for Marriage and Family Therapy, 12*(1), 4–29.

Thomas, F. N., & Nelson, T. S. (2007). Assumptions and practices within the solution-focused brief therapy tradition. In T. S. Nelson & F. N. Thomas (Eds.), *Handbook of solution-focused brief therapy: Clinical applications* (pp. 3–24). New York, NY: Haworth.

Turnell, A., & Edwards, S. (1999). *Signs of Safety: A solution and safety oriented approach to child protection casework*. New York, NY: W. W. Norton & Company.

von Bertalanffy, L. (1968). *General system theory: Foundations, development, applications*. New York, NY: W. W. Norton & Company.

Wampold, B. E. (2015). *The great psychotherapy debate: Models, methods, and findings* (2nd ed.). New York, NY: Routledge.

Watzlawick, P., Bavelas, J. B., & Jackson, D. J. (1967). *Pragmatics of human communication*. New York, NY: W. W. Norton & Company.

Watzlawick, P., & Weakland, J. (1977). *The interactional view*. New York, NY: W. W. Norton & Company.

Watzlawick, P., Weakland, J., & Fisch, R. (1974). *Change: Principles of problem formation and problem resolution*. New York, NY: W. W. Norton & Company.

White, M., & Epston, D. (Eds.). (1990). *Narrative means to therapeutic ends*. New York, NY: W. W. Norton & Company.

Wiener, N. (1948). *Cybernetics, or control and communication in the animal and the machine*. Cambridge, MA: MIT Press.

Bibliography

Systems

Becvar, D. S., & Becvar, R. J. (1999). *Systems theory and family therapy: A primer* (2nd ed.). New York, NY: University Press of America.

Becvar, D. S., & Becvar, R. J. (2012, November/December). *Family therapy: A systemic integration* (8th ed.). New York, NY: Pearson International.

Guttman, H. A. (1991). Systems theory, cybernetics, and epistemology. In A. S. Gurman & D. P. Kniskern (Eds.), *Handbook of family therapy* (Vol. II; pp. 41–62). New York, NY: Brunner/Mazel.

Hanson, B. G. (1995). *General systems theory: Beginning with wholes*. Washington, DC: Taylor & Francis.

Papp, P. (1983). *The process of change*. New York, NY: Guilford Press.

Solution-Focused Brief Therapy

Berg, I. K. (1994). *Family-based services: A solution-focused approach*. New York, NY: W. W. Norton & Company.

Berg, I. K., & de Shazer, S. (n.d.). *A tap on the shoulder: 6 useful questions in building solutions* [CD]. Solution-Focused Brief Therapy Association. http://www.sfbta.org.

Berg, I., & Dolan, Y. (2001). *Tales of solutions: A collection of hope-inspiring stories*. New York, NY: W. W. Norton & Company.

Berg, I., & Miller, S. (1992, June). Working with Asian American clients. *Families in Society: The Journal of Contemporary Human Services*, 356–363.

Berg, I., & Miller, S. (1992). *Working with the problem drinker*. New York, NY: W. W. Norton & Company.

Berg, I. K., & de Shazer, S. (1993). Making numbers talk: Language in therapy. In S. Friedman (ed.), *The new language of change: Constructive collaboration in psychotherapy*. New York, NY: Guilford Press.

Berg, I. K., & Steiner, T. (2003). *Children's solution work*. New York, NY: W. W. Norton & Company.

Berg, I. K., & Jaya, A. (1993). Different and same: Family therapy with Asian-American families. *Journal of Marital and Family Therapy, 19,* 31–38.

de Shazer, S. (1985). *Coming through the ceiling: A solution-focused approach to a difficult case* [Video]. Milwaukee, WI: Brief Family Therapy Center. DVD. sfbta. org.

de Shazer, S. (1985). *Keys to solution in brief therapy*. New York, NY: W. W. Norton & Company.

de Shazer, S. (1991). *Putting difference to work*. New York, NY: W. W. Norton & Company.

de Shazer, S. (1994). *Words were originally magic*. New York, NY: W. W. Norton & Company.

de Shazer, S. (n.d.). *I want to want to* [DVD] (I. K. Berg, & Y. Dolan). Solution-Focused Brief Therapy Association. www.sfbta.org.

de Shazer, S., & Molnar, A. (1984). Four useful interventions in brief family therapy. *Journal of Marital and Family Therapy, 10*(3), 297–304.

Franklin, C., Trepper, T. S., Gingerich, W. J., & McCollum, E. E. (2012). *Solution-focused brief therapy: A handbook of evidence-based practice*. New York, NY: Oxford University Press.

Lipchik, E. (2002). *Beyond technique in Solution-Focused Therapy: Working with emotions and the therapeutic relationship*. New York, NY: Guilford.

Nelson, T. S., & Thomas, F. N. (Eds.). (2007). *Handbook of solution-focused brief therapy: Clinical applications*. New York, NY: Haworth.

Simon, J. (2010). *Solution-focused practice in end-of-life and grief counseling*. New York, NY: Springer.

Simon, J. K., & Nelson, T. S. (2007). *Solution-focused brief practice with long-term clients in mental health services: "I'm more than my label."* New York, NY: Haworth.

Appendix

Major Marriage and Family Therapy Models Charts

Developed by Thorana S. Nelson, PhD and Students[1]

STRUCTURAL FAMILY THERAPY

LEADERS • Salvador Minuchin • Charles Fishman	**ASSUMPTIONS:** • Problems reside within a family structure (although not necessarily caused by the structure) • Changing the structure changes the experience the client has • Don't go from problem to solution, we just move gradually • Children's problems are often related to the boundary between the parents (marital vs. parental subsystem) and the boundary between parents and children

CONCEPTS:
Family structure
• Boundaries
   ○ Rigid
   ○ Clear
   ○ Diffuse
   ○ Disengaged
   ○ Normal range
   ○ Enmeshment
   ○ Roles
   ○ Rules of who interacts with whom, how, when, etc.
• Hierarchy
• Subsystems
• Cross-generational coalitions
• Parentified child
	GOALS OF THERAPY:
	• Structural change
	   ○ Clarify, realign, mark boundaries
	• Individuation of family members
	• Infer the boundaries from the patterns of interaction among family members
	• Change the patterns to realign the boundaries to make them more closed or open

ROLE OF THE THERAPIST: • Perturb the system because the structure is too rigid (chaotic or closed) or too diffuse (enmeshed) • Facilitate the restructuring of the system • Directive, expert—the therapist is the choreographer • See change in therapy session; homework solidifies change • Directive	**ASSESSMENT:** • Assess the nature of the boundaries, roles of family members • Enactment to watch family interaction/ patterns

INTERVENTIONS:	CHANGE:
• Join and accommodate ○ Mimesis • Structural mapping • Highlight and modify interactions • Unbalance • Challenge unproductive assumptions • Raise intensity so that the system must change • Disorganize and reorganize • Shape competence through enactment (therapist acts as coach)	• Raise intensity to upset the system, then help reorganize the system • Change occurs within session and is behavioral; insight is not necessary • Emotions change as individuals' experience of their context changes
TERMINATION:	**SELF OF THE THERAPIST:**
• Problem is gone and the structure has changed (second-order change) • Problem is gone and the structure has *not* changed (first-order change)	• The therapist joins with the system to facilitate the unbalancing of the system • Caution with induction—don't get sucked in to the content areas, usually related to personal hot spots

EVALUATION:
• Strong support for working with psychosomatic children, adult drug addicts, and anorexia nervosa.

RESOURCES:
Minuchin, S. (1974). *Families and family therapy*. Cambridge, MA: Harvard University Press.
Minuchin, S., & Fishman, H. C. (1981). *Family therapy techniques*. Cambridge, MA: Harvard University Press.
Minuchin, S., Rosman, B. L., & Baker, L. (1978). *Psychosomatic families*. Cambridge, MA: Harvard University Press.
Fishman, H. C. (1988). *Treating troubled adolescents: A family therapy approach*. New York, NY: Basic Books.
Fishman, H. C. (1993). *Intensive structural therapy: Treating families in their social context*. New York, NY: Basic Books.

NOTES

STRATEGIC THERAPY (MRI)

LEADERS:	ASSUMPTIONS:
• John Weakland • Don Jackson • Paul Watzlawick • Richard Fisch	• Family members often perpetuate problems by their own actions (attempted solutions)—the problem is the problem maintenance (positive feedback escalations) • Directives tailored to the specific needs of a particular family can sometimes bring about sudden and decisive change • People resist change • You cannot not communicate—people are *always* communicating • All messages have report and command functions—working with content is not helpful, look at the process • Symptoms are messages—symptoms help the system survive (some would say they have a function) • It is only a problem if the family describes it as such • Based on the work of Gregory Bateson and Milton Erickson • Need to perturb system—difference that makes a difference (similar enough to be accepted by system but different enough to make a difference) • Don't need to examine psychodynamics to work on the problem

CONCEPTS:
• Symptoms are messages
• Family homeostasis
• Family rules—unspoken
• Cybernetics
   ∘ Feedback loops
   ∘ Positive feedback
   ∘ Negative feedback
• First-order change
• Second-order change
• Reframing
• Content and process
• Report and command
• Paradox
• Paradoxical injunction
	GOALS OF THERAPY:
	• Help the family define clear, reachable goals
	• Break the pattern; perturb the system
	• First- and second-order change, ideally second-order change (we cannot make this happen—it is spontaneous)

- "Go slow" messages
- Positive feedback escalations
- Double binds
- "One down" position
- Patient position
- Attempted solutions maintain problems and become problems themselves

ROLE OF THE THERAPIST:	ASSESSMENT:
<ul><li>Expert position</li><li>Responsible for creating conditions for change</li><li>Work with resistance of clients to change</li><li>Work with the process, not the content</li><li>Directive</li><li>Skeptical of change</li><li>Take a lot of credit and responsibility for change; however, therapist tells clients that they are responsible for change</li><li>Active</li></ul>	<ul><li>Define the problem clearly and find out what people have done to try to resolve it</li><li>Elicit goals from each family member and then reframe into one, agreed-upon goal</li><li>Assess sequence patterns</li></ul>
INTERVENTIONS:	CHANGE:
<ul><li>Paradox</li><li>Directives<ul><li>Assignments ("homework") that interrupt sequences</li></ul></li><li>Interrupt unhelpful sequences of interaction</li><li>"Go slow" messages</li><li>Prescribe the symptoms</li></ul>	<ul><li>Interrupting the pattern in any way</li><li>Difference that makes a difference</li><li>Change occurs outside of session; in-session change is in viewing; homework changes doing</li><li>Change in viewing (reframe) and/or doing (directives)</li><li>Emotions change and are important, but are inferred and not directly available to the therapist</li></ul>
TERMINATION:	SELF OF THE THERAPIST:
<ul><li>Client decides when to terminate with the help of the therapist</li><li>When pattern is broken and the client reports that the problem no longer exists</li><li>Therapist decides</li></ul>	<ul><li>Therapist needs to be *very* careful with ethics in this model; it can be very manipulative (paradox) and a lot of responsibility is on the therapist as an expert</li></ul>

EVALUATION:
- Very little research done
- Do clients report change? If so, then it is effective

RESOURCES:

Fisch, Richard, John H. Weakland, & Lynn Segal. (1982). *The tactics of change: Doing therapy briefly*. San Francisco, CA: Jossey-Bass.

Lederer, W. J., & Don Jackson. (1968). *The mirages of marriage*. New York, NY: W. W. Norton & Company.

Watzlawick, P., Bavelas, J. B., & Jackson, D. J. (1967). *Pragmatics of human communication*. New York, NY: W. W. Norton & Company.

Watzlawick, P., Weakland, J., & Fisch, R. (1974). *Change: Principles of problem formation and problem resolution*. New York, NY: W. W. Norton & Company.

NOTES

STRATEGIC THERAPY (Haley and Madanes)

LEADERS:	ASSUMPTIONS:
• Jay Haley • Cloé Madanes • Influenced by Minuchin	• Family members often perpetuate problems by their own actions (attempted solutions)—the problem is the problem maintenance (positive feedback escalations) • Directives tailored to the specific needs of a particular family can sometimes bring about sudden and decisive change • People resist change • You cannot not communicate—people are *always* communicating • All messages have report and command functions—working with content is not helpful, look at the process • Communication and messages are metaphorical for family functioning • Symptoms are messages—symptoms help the system survive • It is only a problem if the family describes it as such • Based on work of Gregory Bateson, Milton Erickson, MRI, and Minuchin • Need to perturb system—difference that makes a difference (similar enough to be accepted by system but different enough to make a difference) • Problems develop in skewed hierarchies • Motivation is power (Haley) or love (Madanes)
CONCEPTS: • Symptoms are messages • Family homeostasis • Family rules—unspoken • Intergenerational collusions • First- and second-order change • Metaphors • Reframing • Symptoms serve functions • Content and process	GOALS OF THERAPY: • Help the family define clear, reachable goals • Break the pattern; perturb the system • First- and second-order change, ideally second-order change (we cannot make this happen—it is spontaneous) • Realign hierarchy (Madanes)

- Report and command
- Incongruous hierarchies
- Ordeals (prescribing ordeals)
- Paradox
- Paradoxical injunction
- Pretend techniques (Madanes)
- "Go slow" messages

ROLE OF THE THERAPIST:	ASSESSMENT:
<ul><li>Expert position</li><li>Responsible for creating conditions for change</li><li>Work with resistance of clients to change</li><li>Work with the process, not the content</li><li>Directive</li><li>Skeptical of change</li><li>Take a lot of credit and responsibility for change; however, therapist tells clients that they are responsible for change</li><li>Active</li></ul>	<ul><li>Define the problem clearly and find out what people have done to try to resolve it</li><li>Hypothesize metaphorical nature of the problem</li><li>Elicit goals from each family member and then reframe into one, agreed-upon goal</li><li>Assess sequence patterns</li></ul>
INTERVENTIONS:	**CHANGE:**
<ul><li>Paradox</li><li>Directives<ul><li>Assignments ("homework") that interrupt sequences</li></ul></li><li>Interrupt unhelpful sequences of interaction</li><li>Metaphors, stories</li><li>Ordeals (Haley)</li><li>"Go slow" messages</li><li>Prescribe the symptoms (Haley)</li><li>"Pretend" techniques (Madanes)</li></ul>	<ul><li>Breaking the pattern in any way</li><li>Difference that makes a difference</li><li>Change occurs outside of session; in-session change is in viewing; homework changes doing</li><li>Change in viewing (reframe) and/or doing (directives)</li></ul>
TERMINATION:	**SELF OF THE THERAPIST:**
<ul><li>Client decides when to terminate with the help of the therapist</li><li>When pattern is broken and the client reports that the problem no longer exists</li><li>Therapist decides</li></ul>	<ul><li>Therapist needs to be *very* careful with ethics in this model; it can be very manipulative (paradox) and a lot of responsibility is on the therapist as an expert</li></ul>

EVALUATION:
- Very little research done
- Do clients report change? If so, then it is effective

RESOURCES:

Haley, Jay. (1980). *Leaving home*. New York, NY: McGraw-Hill.

Haley, Jay. (1984). *Ordeal therapy: Unusual ways to change behavior*. San Francisco, CA: Jossey-Bass.

Haley, Jay. (1987). *Problem-solving therapy* (2nd Ed.). San Francisco, CA: Jossey-Bass.

Madanes, Cloé. (1981). *Strategic family therapy*. San Francisco, CA: Jossey-Bass.

Madanes, Cloé. (1984). *Behind the one-way mirror: Advances in the practice of strategic therapy*. San Francisco, CA: Jossey-Bass.

Madanes, Cloé. (1990). *Sex, love, and violence: Strategies for transformation*. New York, NY: W. W. Norton & Company.

Madanes, Cloé. (1995). *The violence of men: New techniques for working with abusive families*. San Francisco, CA: Jossey-Bass.

NOTES

MILAN FAMILY THERAPY

LEADERS:	ASSUMPTIONS:
• Boscolo • Palazzoli • Prata • Cecchin	• Problem is maintained by family's attempts to fix it • Therapy can be brief over a long period of time • Clients resist change

CONCEPTS:	GOALS OF THERAPY:

• Family games (family's patterns that maintain the problem)
  ◦ Dirty games
  ◦ Psychotic games
• There is a nodal point of pathology
• Invariant prescriptions
• Rituals
• Positive connotation
• Difference that makes a difference
• Neutrality
• Hypothesizing
• Therapy team
• Circularity, neutrality
• Incubation period for change; requires long periods of time between sessions
	• Disrupt family games

ROLE OF THERAPIST:	ASSESSMENT:
• Therapist as expert • Neutral to each family member—don't get sucked into the family game • Curious	• Family game • Dysfunctional patterns (patterns that maintain the problem)

INTERVENTIONS:	CHANGE:
• Ritualized prescriptions • Rituals • Circular questions • Counter paradox • Odd/even day • Positive connotation • "Date" • Reflecting team • Letters • Prescribe the system	• Family develops a different game that does not include the symptom (system change) • Requires incubation period

TERMINATION:	EVALUATION:
• Therapist decides, fewer than 10–12 sessions	• Not practiced much, therefore not researched • Follow up contraindicated

RESOURCES:

Campbell, D., Draper, R., & Crutchley, E. (1991). The Milan systemic approach to family therapy. In A. S. Gurman & D. P. Kniskern (Eds.), *Handbook of family therapy (Vol. II)* (pp. 325–362). New York, NY: Brunner/Mazel.

Campbell, D., Draper, R., & Huffington, C. (1989). *Second thoughts on the theory and practice of the Milan approach to family therapy.* New York, NY: Karnac.

Cecchin, G. (1987). Hypothesizing, circularity, and neutrality revisited: An invitation to curiosity. *Family Process, 26*(4), 405–413.

Cecchin, G. (1992). Constructing therapeutic possibilities. In S. McNamee & K. J. Gergen (Eds.), *Therapy as social construction* (pp. 86–95). Newbury Park, CA: Sage.

Palazzoli, M. S., Boscolo, L., Cecchin, G., & Prata, G. (1978). Paradox and counterparadox: A new model in the therapy of the family in schizophrenic transaction. New York, NY: Jason Aaronson.

Palazzoli, M. S., Boscolo, L., Cecchin, G., & Prata, G. (1978). A ritualized prescription in family therapy: Odd days and even days. *Journal of Marriage and Family Counseling, 48*, 3–9.

Palazzoli, M., & Palazzoli, C. (1989). *Family games: General models of psychotic processes in the family.* New York, NY: W. W. Norton & Company.

NOTES

SOLUTION-FOCUSED BRIEF THERAPY

LEADERS:	ASSUMPTIONS:
• Steve de Shazer • Insoo Kim Berg • Yvonne Dolan • Eve Lipchik	• Clients want to change • There's no such thing as resistance (clients are telling us how they cooperate) • Focus on present and future, except for the past in terms of exceptions; not focused on the past in terms of cause of changing the past • Change the way people talk about their problems from problem talk to solution talk • Language creates reality • Therapist and client relationship is key • A philosophy, not a set of techniques or theory • Sense of hope, "cheerleader effect" • Nonpathologizing, not interested in pathology or "dysfunction" • Don't focus on the etiology of the problem: Solutions are not necessarily related to problems • Assume the client has is able to access resources • Only need a small change, which can snowball into a bigger change • The problem is not occurring all the time

CONCEPTS:	GOALS OF THERAPY:
• Problem talk/solution talk • Exceptions • Smallest difference that makes a difference • Well-formed goals (small, concrete, measurable, important to client, doable, beginning of something, not end, presence not absence, hard work) • Solution not necessarily related to the problem • Clients are experts on their lives and their experiences • Therapeutic relationships: customer/therapist, complainant/sympathizer, visitor/host	• Help clients to think or do things differently in order to increase their satisfaction with their lives • Reach clients' goals; "good enough" • Shift the client's language from problem talk to solution talk • Modest goals (clear and specific) • Help translate the goal into something more specific (clarify) • Change language from problem to solution talk

ROLE OF THERAPIST:	**ASSESSMENT:**
• Cheerleader/coach • Offer hope • Nondirective, client-centered	• Assess exceptions—times when problem isn't there • Assess what has worked in the past, not necessarily related to the problem; develop realistic goals • Assess what will be different when the problems are gone (becomes goal that might not be clearly related to the stated problem) • Assess when parts of the miracle are already happening

INTERVENTIONS:
- Help set clear and achievable goals (clarify)
- Help client think about the future and what they want to be different
- Exceptions: Amplify the times they did things that "worked" when they didn't have the problem or it was less severe
- Compliments:
  - "How did you do that?"
  - "Wow! That must have been difficult!"
  - "That sounds like it was helpful; how did you do that?"
  - "I'm impressed with. . ."
  - "You sound like a good. . ."
- Formula first session task: Observe what happens in their life/relationship that they want to continue
- Miracle question:
  - Used when clients are vague about complaints
  - Helps client do things the problem has been obstructing
  - Focus on how having problems gone will make a difference
  - Relational questions
  - Follow up with miracle day questions and scaling questions
  - Pretend to have a miracle day
- Scaling questions
- Midsession break (with or without team) to summarize session, formulate compliments and bridge, and suggest a task (tasks used less in recent years; clients develop own tasks; therapist may make suggestions or suggest "experiments"), sometimes called "feedback" (feeding information back into the therapy with a difference)
- Predict the next day, then see what happens

TERMINATION:	SELF OF THE THERAPIST:
• Client decides	• Accept responsibility for client/ therapist relationship • Expert on therapy conversation, not on client's life or experience of the difficulty

EVALUATION:

Therapy/Research:

• Franklin, C., Trepper, T. S., Gingerich, W. J., & McCollum, E. E. (2012). *Solution-focused brief therapy: A handbook of evidence-based practice.* New York, NY: Oxford University Press.

RESOURCES:

Berg, I. K., & Miller, S. (1992). *Working with the problem drinker.* New York, NY: W. W. Norton & Company.

Berg, I. K. (1994). *Family-based services: A solution-focused approach.* New York, NY: W. W. Norton & Company.

DeJong, P., & Berg, I. K. (2013). *Interviewing for solutions* (4th ed.). Pacific Grove, CA: Brooks/Cole.

de Shazer, S. (1982). *Patterns of brief family therapy: An ecosystemic approach.* New York, NY: Guilford Press.

de Shazer, S., Dolan, Y., Korman, H., Trepper, T., McCollum, E., & Berg, I. K. (2007). *More than miracles: The state of the art of solution-focused brief therapy.* New York, NY: Haworth.

Dolan, Y. (1992). *Resolving sexual abuse.* New York, NY: W. W. Norton & Company.

Lipchik, E. (2002). *Beyond technique in solution-focused therapy.* New York, NY: Guilford Press.

Nelson, T. S., & Thomas, F. N. (Eds.). (2007). *Handbook of solution-focused brief therapy: Clinical applications.* New York, NY: Haworth.

NOTES

NARRATIVE THERAPY

LEADERS:	ASSUMPTIONS:
• Michael White • David Epston • Jill Freedman • Gene Combs	• Personal experience is ambiguous • Reality is shaped by the language used to describe it—language and experience (meaning) are recursive • Reality is socially constructed • Truth may not match historic or another person's truth, but it is true to the client • Focus on effects of the problem, not the cause (how problem impacts family; how family affects problem) • Stories organize our experience and shape our behavior • The problem is the problem; the person is not the problem • People "are" the stories they tell • The stories we tell ourselves are often based on messages received from society or our families (social construction) • People have their own unique filters by which they process messages from society

CONCEPTS:	GOALS OF THERAPY:
• Dominant narrative: beliefs, values, and practices based on dominant social culture • Subjugated narrative: a person's own story that is suppressed by dominant story • Alternative story: the story that's there but not noticed • Deconstruction: take apart problem-saturated story in order to externalize and reauthor it (find missing pieces; "unpacking") • Problem-saturated stories: bog client down, allowing problem to persist (closed, rigid) • Landscape of action: how people do things • Landscape of consciousness: what meaning the problem has (landscape of meaning)	• Change the way the clients view themselves and assist them in re-authoring their story in a positive light; find the alternative but preferred story that is not problem-saturated • Give options for more/ different stories that don't include problems

• Unique outcomes: pieces of deconstructed story that would not have been predicted by dominant story or problem-saturated story; exceptions; sparkling moments	
ROLE OF THERAPIST: • Genuine curious listener • Question their assumptions • Open space to make room for possibilities	**ASSESSMENT:** • Get the family's story, their experiences with their problems, and presumptions about those problems • Assess alternative stories and unique outcomes during deconstruction

INTERVENTIONS:
• Ask questions
  ○ Landscape of action and landscape of meaning
  ○ Meaning questions
  ○ Opening space
  ○ Preference
  ○ Story development
  ○ Deconstruction
  ○ To extend the story into the future
• Externalize problems
• Effects of problem on family; effects of family on problem
• Restorying or reauthoring
  ○ Selfstories
• Letters from the therapist
• Certificates of award
	CHANGE:
	• Occurs by opening space; cognitive
	• Client can see that there are numerous possibilities
	• Expanded sense of self

TERMINATION:	**SELF OF THE THERAPIST:**	**EVALUATION:**
• Client determines	• Therapist's ideas, values, prejudices, etc. need to be open to client, "transparent" • Expert on conversation	• No formal studies

RESOURCES:

Freeman, Jennifer, David Epston, & Dean Lobovits. (1997). *Playful approaches to serious problems: Narrative therapy with children and their families.* New York, NY: W. W. Norton & Company.

Freedman, Jill, & Gene Combs. (1996). *Narrative therapy: The social construction of preferred realities.* New York, NY: W. W. Norton & Company.

White, Michael. (2007). *Maps of narrative practice.* New York, NY: W. W. Norton & Company.

White, Michael, & David Epston (Eds.). (1990). *Narrative means to therapeutic ends.* New York, NY: W. W. Norton & Company.

NOTES

COGNITIVE-BEHAVIORAL FAMILY THERAPY

LEADERS: • Ivan Pavlov • Watson • Thorndike • B. F. Skinner • Bandura • Frank Dattilio	**ASSUMPTIONS:** • Family relationships, cognitions, emotions, and behavior mutually influence one another • Cognitive inferences evoke emotion and behavior • Emotion and behavior influence cognition
CONCEPTS: • Schemas: core beliefs about the world, the acquisition and organization of knowledge • Cognitions: selective attention, perception, memories, self-talk, beliefs, and expectations • Reinforcement: an event that increases the future probability of a specific response • Attribution: explaining the motivation or cause of behavior • Distorted thoughts, generalizations get in way of clear thinking and thus action	**GOALS OF THERAPY:** • To modify specific patterns of thinking and/or behavior to alleviate the presenting symptom
ROLE OF THERAPIST: • Ask a series of question about assumptions, rather than challenge them directly • Teach the family that emotional problems are caused by unrealistic beliefs	**ASSESSMENT:** • Cognitive: distorted thoughts, thought processes • Behavioral: antecedents, consequences, etc.
INTERVENTIONS: • Questions aimed at distorted assumptions (family members interpret and evaluate one another unrealistically) • Behavioral assignments • Parent training • Communication skill building • Training in the model	**CHANGE:** • Behavior will change when the contingencies of reinforcement are altered • Changed cognitions lead to changed affect and behaviors
TERMINATION: • When therapist and client determine	**SELF OF THE THERAPIST:** • Not discussed

EVALUATION:
- Many studies, particularly in terms of marital therapy and parenting

RESOURCES:

Beck, A. T., Reinecke, M. A., & Clark, D. A. (2003). *Cognitive therapy across the lifespan: Evidence and practice.* Cambridge, UK: Cambridge University Press.

Dattilio, F. M. (1998). *Case studies in couple and family therapy: Systemic and cognitive perspectives.* New York, NY: Guilford Press.

Dattilio, F. M. (2001). Cognitive-behavior family therapy: Contemporary myths and misconceptions. *Contemporary Family Therapy, 23*(12), 1–18.

Dattilio, F. M., & Padesky, C. (1990). *Cognitive therapy with couples.* Sarasota, FL: Professional Resource Press.

Epstein, N. B., & Baucom, D. H. (2002). *Enhanced cognitive-behavioral therapy for couples.* Washington, DC: American Psychological Association.

Jacobson, N. S., & Christensen, A. (1998). *Acceptance and change in couple therapy: A therapist's guide to transforming relationships.* New York, NY: W. W. Norton & Company.

Jacobson, N. S., & Margolin, G. (1979). *Marital therapy: Strategies based on social learning and behavior exchange principles.* New York, NY: Brunner/Mazel.

NOTES

CONTEXTUAL FAMILY THERAPY

LEADERS:	ASSUMPTIONS:

• Ivan Boszormenyi-Nagy	• Values and ethics are transmitted across generations
	• Dimensions (all are intertwined and drive people's behaviors and relationships):
	  ○ Facts
	  ○ Psychological
	  ○ Relational
	  ○ Ethical
	• Trustworthiness of a relationship (relational ethics): when relationships are not trustworthy, debts and entitlements that must be paid back pile up; unbalanced ledger gets balanced in ways that are destructive to individuals, relationships, and posterity (e.g., revolving slate, destructive entitlement)

CONCEPTS: • Loyalty: split, invisible • Entitlement (amount of merit a person has based on trustworthiness) • Ledger (accounting) • Legacy (we behave in ways that we have been programmed to behave) • Relational ethics • Destructive entitlement (you were given a bad ledger and it wasn't fair so it's OK to hand it on to the next person—acting out, neglecting important others) • Revolving slate • Posterity (thinking of future generations when working with people) this is the only model that does • Rejunctive and disjunctive efforts	**GOALS OF THERAPY:** • Balanced ledger
ROLE OF THE THERAPIST: • Directive • Expert in terms of assessment	**ASSESSMENT:** • Debts • Entitlements • Invisible loyalties

INTERVENTIONS:	CHANGE:
• Process and relational questions • Multi-directional impartiality: everybody and nobody feel special—all are attended to but none are more special • Exoneration: help people understand how they have been living out legacies and debts-ledgers—exonerate *others* • Coach toward rejunctive efforts	• Cognitive: awareness of legacies, debts, and entitlements • Behavioral: very action oriented—actions must change

TERMINATION:	SELF OF THE THERAPIST:	EVALUATION:
• Never—totally up to the client	• Must understand own legacies, entitlements, process of balancing ledgers, exoneration	• No empirical evaluation

RESOURCES:

Boszormenyi-Nagy, I. (1987). *Foundations of contextual therapy: Collected papers of Ivan Boszormenyi-Nagy*. New York, NY: Brunner/Mazel.

Boszormenyi-Nagy, I., & Krasner, B. (1986). *Between give and take: A clinical guide to contextual therapy*. New York, NY: Brunner/Mazel.

Hargrave, T. D., & Pfitzer, F. (2003). *The new contextual therapy: Guiding the power of give and take*. New York, NY: Brunner/Routledge.

van Heusden, A., & van den Eerenbeemt, E. (1987). *Balance in motion: Ivan Boszormenyi-Nagy and his vision of individual and family*. New York, NY: Brunner/Mazel.

NOTES

BOWEN FAMILY THERAPY

LEADERS:	ASSUMPTIONS:
<ul><li>Murray Bowen</li><li>Michael Kerr (works with natural systems)</li><li>Edwin Friedman</li></ul>	<ul><li>The past is currently influencing the present</li><li>Change can happen—individuals can move along in the process of differentiation</li><li>Differentiation: ability to maintain self in the face of high anxiety (remain autonomous in a highly emotional situation)<ul><li>Change in experience of self in the family system</li><li>Change in relationship between thinking and emotional systems</li></ul></li><li>Differentiation is internal and relational—they are isomorphic and recursive</li><li>Anxiety inhibits change and needs to be reduced to facilitate change</li><li>High intimacy and high autonomy are ideal</li><li>Emotions are a physiological process—feelings are the thoughts that name and mediate emotions, that give them meaning</li><li>Symptoms are indicators of stress, anxiety, lower differentiation</li><li>Anyone can become symptomatic with enough stress; more differentiated people will be able to withstand more stress and, when they do become symptomatic, recover more quickly</li></ul>
CONCEPTS:	GOALS OF THERAPY:
<ul><li>Intimacy</li><li>Autonomy</li><li>Differentiation of self</li><li>Cutoff</li><li>Triangulation</li><li>Sibling position</li><li>Fusion (within individual and within relationships)</li><li>Family projection process</li><li>Multigenerational transmission process</li><li>Nuclear family</li><li>Emotional process</li></ul>	<ul><li>Ultimate: increase differentiation of self (thoughts/emotions; self/others)</li><li>Intermediate: detriangulation, lowering anxiety to respond instead of reacting</li><li>Decrease emotional reactivity, increase thoughtful responses</li><li>Increased intimacy one-on-one with important others</li></ul>

- Four sub-concepts (ways people manage anxiety; none of these is bad by itself—it's when one is used to exclusion of others or excessively that it can become problematic for a system):
  - Conflict
  - Dysfunction in person
  - Triangulation
  - Distance
- Societal emotional process
- Undifferentiated family ego mass

ROLE OF THERAPIST: • Coach (objective) • Educator • Therapist is part of the system (nonanxious and differentiated) • Expert—not a collaborator	**ASSESSMENT:** • Emotional reactivity • Degree of differentiation of self • Ways that people manage anxiety/family themes • Triangles • Repeating intergenerational patterns • Genogram (assessment tool)
INTERVENTIONS: • Genogram (both assessment and change tool) • Plan for intense situations (when things get hot, what are we going to do—thinking; process questions) • Process questions—thinking questions: "what do you think about this?" and "how does that work?" • Detriangulating one-on-one relationships, one person with the other two in the triangle • Educating clients about the concepts of the model • Decrease emotional reactivity—increase thoughtful responses • Therapist as a calm self and calm part of a triangle with the clients • Coaching for changing own patterns in family of origin	**CHANGE:** • Reduced anxiety through separation of thoughts and emotions—cognitive • Reduced anxiety leads to responsive thoughts and actions, changed affect, changed relationships • When we think (respond), change occurs (planning thinking)—when you know how you would like to behave in a certain emotional situation, you plan it, it makes it easier to carry through with different consequences

TERMINATION:	SELF OF THE THERAPIST:	EVALUATION:
• Ongoing—we are never fully differentiated	• Important with this model; differentiated, calm therapist is the main tool • We don't need to join the system • We must be highly differentiated so we can recognize and reduce reactivity • Our clients can only become as differentiated as we are; we need coaching to increase our own differentiation of self	• Research suggesting validity: not much, not a lot of outcome • Did not specify symptom reduction • Client reports of different thoughts, actions, responses from others, affect is evidence of change

RESOURCES:

Bowen, M. (1978). *Family therapy in clinical practice*. New York, NY: Jason Aaronson.

Friedman, E. (1987). *Generation to generation: Family process in church and synagogue*. New York, NY: Guilford Press.

Kerr, M. E., & Bowen, M. (1988). *Family evaluation: An approach based on Bowen theory*. New York, NY: W. W. Norton & Company.

NOTES

PSYCHODYNAMIC FAMILY THERAPY (OBJECT RELATIONS)

LEADERS:	ASSUMPTIONS:
• Freud • Erik Erikson • Nathan Ackerman • Several others who were trained, but their models were not primarily psychodynamic: Bowen, Whitaker, etc. • Object relations: Scharff and Scharff • Attachment theory: Bowlby	• Sexual and aggressive drives are at the heart of human nature • Every human being wants to be appreciated • Symptoms are attempts to cope with unconscious conflicts over sex and aggression • Internalized objects become projected onto important others; we then evoke responses from them that fit that object, they comply, and we react to the projection rather than the real person • Early experiences affect later relationships • Internalized objects affect inner experience and outer relationships
CONCEPTS:	GOALS OF THERAPY:
• Internal objects: mental images of self and others built from experience and expectation • Attachment: connection with important others • Separation-individuation: the gradual process of a child separating from the mother • Mirroring: when parents show understanding and acceptance • Transference: attributing qualities of someone else to another person • Countertransference: therapist's attributing qualities of self onto others • Family myths: unspoken rules and beliefs that drive behavior, based on beliefs, not full images of others • Fixation and regression: when families become stuck they revert back to lower levels of functioning • Invisible loyalties: unconscious commitments to the family that are detrimental to the individual	• To free family members of unconscious constraints so that they can interact as healthy individuals • Separation-individuation • Differentiation

ROLE OF THERAPIST:	ASSESSMENT:
• Listener • Expert position • Interpret	• Attachment bonds • Projections (unrealistic attributions)
INTERVENTIONS:	**CHANGE:**
• Listening • Showing empathy • Interpretations (especially projections) • Family of origin sessions (Framo) • Make a safe holding environment	• Change occurs when family members expand their insight to realize that psychological lives are larger than conscious experience and come to accept repressed parts of their personalities • Change also occurs when more, full, real aspects of others are revealed in therapy so that projections fade

TERMINATION:
Not sure how therapy is terminated

EVALUATION:

RESOURCES:
Sander, F. (2004). Psychoanalytic couples therapy: Classical style. In Feld, B. & Livingston, M. (Eds.), *Psychoanalytic inquiry issue on psychoanalytic treatment of couples* (Vol. 24, pp. 373–386).
Scharff, J. (Ed.). (1989). *Foundations of object relations family therapy.* Northvale, NJ: Jason Aronson.
Slipp, S. (1984). *Object relations: A dynamic bridge between individual and family treatment.* Northvale, NJ: Jason Aronson.

NOTES

EXPERIENTIAL FAMILY THERAPY

LEADERS:	ASSUMPTIONS:
• Carl Whitaker • Virginia Satir	• Family problems are rooted in suppression of feelings, rigidity, denial of impulses, lack of awareness, emotional deadness, and overuse of defense mechanisms • Families must get in touch with their *real* feelings • Therapy works from the inside (emotion) out (behavior) • Expanding the individual's experience opens them up to their experiences and helps to improve the functioning of the family group • Commitment to emotional well being

CONCEPTS:	GOALS OF THERAPY:
• Honest emotion • Suppress repression • Family myths • Mystification • Blaming • Placating • Being irrelevant/irreverent • Being super reasonable • Battle for structure • Battle for initiative	• Promote growth, change, creativity, flexibility, spontaneity, and playfulness • Make the covert overt • Increase the emotional closeness of spouses and disrupt rigidity • Unlock defenses, enhance self-esteem, and recover potential for experiencing • Enhance individuation

ROLE OF THE THERAPIST:	ASSESSMENT:
• Uses their own personality • Must be open and spontaneous, empathic, sensitive, and demonstrate caring and acceptance • Be willing to share and risk, be genuine, and increase stress within the family • Teach family effective communication skills in order to convey their feelings • Active and directive	• Assess individual self-expression and levels of defensiveness • Assess family interactions that promote or stifle individuation and healthy interaction

INTERVENTIONS:	CHANGE:
• Sculpting • Choreography • Conjoint family drawing • Role playing • Use of humor • Puppet interviews • Reconstruction	• Increasing stress among the family members leads to increased emotional expression and honest, open communication • Changing experience changes affect; need to get out of head into emotions; active interventions change experience, emotions

- Sharing feelings and creating an emotionally intense atmosphere
- Modeling and teaching clear communication skills (Use of "I" messages)
- Challenge "stances" (Satir)
- Use of self

TERMINATION:	SELF OF THE THERAPIST:
<ul><li>Defenses of family members are broken down</li><li>Family communicating openly</li><li>Family members more in touch with their feelings</li><li>Members relate to each other in a more honest way</li><li>Openness for individuation of family members</li></ul>	<ul><li>Through the use of humor, spontaneity, and personality, the therapist is able to unbalance the family and bring about change</li><li>The personality of the therapist is key to bringing about change</li></ul>

EVALUATION:
- This model fell out of favor in the 1980s and 1990s due to its focus on the emotional experience of the individual while ignoring the role of family structure and communication in the regulation of emotion
- Emotionally Focused Couples Therapy (Sue Johnson) and Internal Family Systems Therapy (Richard Schwartz) are the current trend
- Need to assess in-therapy outcomes as a measure of success due the fact that they often result in deeper emotional experiences (and successful sessions) that have the potential to generalize outside of therapy

RESOURCES:
Satir, V. (1967). *Conjoint family therapy*. Palo Alto, CA: Science and Behavior Books.
Satir, V. (1972). *Peoplemaking*. Palo Alto, CA: Science and Behavior Books.
Napier, A. Y., & Whitaker, C. A. (1978). *The family crucible*. New York, NY: Harper/Row.

NOTES

EMOTIONALLY FOCUSED THERAPY

LEADERS:	ASSUMPTIONS:
• Susan Johnson • Les Greenberg	• "The inner construction of experience evokes interactional responses that organize the world in a particular way. These patterns of interaction then reflect, and in turn, shape inner experience" (Johnson, 2008, p. 109) • Individual identity can be formed and transformed by relationships and interactions with others • New experiences in therapy can help clients expand their view and make sense of the world in a new way • Nonpathologizing, not interested in pathology or "dysfunction" • Past is relevant only in how it affects the present • Emotion is a target and agent of change • Primary emotions generally draw partners closer; secondary emotions push partners away • Distressed couples get caught in negative repetitive sequences of interaction where partners express secondary emotions rather than primary emotions

CONCEPTS:	GOALS OF THERAPY:
• Attachment needs exist throughout the lifespan • Negative interactional patterns • Primary and secondary emotions • Empathic attunement • Cycle de-escalation • Blamer softening • Withdrawer re-engagement	• Identify and break negative interactional patterns • Increase emotional engagement between couple • Identify primary and secondary emotions in the context of negative interactional pattern • Access, expand, and reorganize key emotional responses • Create a shift in partners' interactional positions. • Foster the creation of a secure bond between partners through the creation of new interactional events that redefine the relationship

ROLE OF THERAPIST:	ASSESSMENT:

• Client-centered, collaborative
• Process consultant
• Choreographer of relationship dance
	• Assess relationship factors such as:
	  ○ Their cycle
	  ○ Action tendencies (behaviors)
	  ○ Perceptions
	  ○ Secondary emotions
	  ○ Primary emotions
	  ○ Attachment needs

- Relationship history, key events
- Brief personal attachment history
- Interaction style
- Violence/abuse/drug usage
- Sexual relationship
- Prognostic indicators:
  - Degree of reactivity and escalation; intensity of negative cycle
  - Strength of attachment/ commitment
  - Openness, response to therapist, engagement
  - Trust/faith of the female partner (does she believe he cares about her)

INTERVENTIONS
- Reflection
- Validation
- Evocative questions and empathic conjecture
  - Self-disclosure
  - Tracking, reflecting, and replaying interactions
  - Reframe in an attachment frame
  - Enactments
  - Softening
  - Heightening and expanding emotional experiences

TERMINATION:
Therapy ends when the therapist and clients collaboratively decide that the following changes have occurred:
- Negative affect has lessened and is regulated differently
- Partners are more accessible and responsive to each other
- Partners perceive each other as people who want to be close, not as enemies
- Negative cycles are contained and positive cycles are enacted

SELF OF THE THERAPIST:
- Accept responsibility for client/ therapist relationship
- Expert on process of therapy, not on client's life or experience of the difficulty
- Collaborator who must sometimes lead and sometimes follow

EVALUATION:	CHANGE:
Therapy/research:	• Change happens as couples have a new corrective emotional experience with one another
• Difficult model to learn	
• When using the emotionally focused therapy model, it is important to move slowly down the process of therapy; this can be difficult to do	• When couples are able to experience their own emotions, needs, and fears and express them to one another and experience the other partner responding to those emotions, needs, and fears in an accessible, responsive way
• Learning to stay with deepened emotions can sometimes be overwhelming, but the therapist must continue to reflect and validate	
• Empirically validated, more than 20 years of research to back up	

RESOURCES:

Johnson, S. M. (2004). *The practice of emotionally focused couple therapy* (2nd ed.). New York, NY: Brunner/Routledge.

Johnson, S. M. (2008). Emotionally focused couple therapy. In A. S. Gurman (Ed.), *Clinical handbook of couple therapy* (4th ed., pp. 107–137). New York, NY: Guilford Press.

Johnson, S. M., Bradley, B., Furrow, J., Lee, A., Palmer, G., Tilley, D., & Woolley, S. (2005). *Becoming an emotionally focused couple therapist: The workbook.* New York, NY: Routledge.

Johnson, S. M., & Greenberg, L. S. (1994). *The heart of the matter: Perspectives on emotion in marital therapy.* New York, NY: Brunner/Mazel.

NOTES

GOTTMAN METHOD COUPLE THERAPY

LEADERS:	ASSUMPTIONS:
• John Gottman • Julie Gottman	• Therapy is primarily dyadic • Couples need to be in emotional states to learn how to cope with and change them • Therapy should be primarily a positive affective experience • Positive sentiment override and friendship base are needed for communication and affect change
CONCEPTS: • Negative interactions (four horsemen) decrease acceptance of repair attempts • Most couples present in therapy with low positive affect • Sound marital house • Softened startup • Love maps	**GOALS OF THERAPY:** • Empower the couple • Problem-solving skills • Positive affect • Creating shared meaning
ROLE OF THE THERAPIST: • Coach • Provide the tools that the couple can use with one another and make their own	**ASSESSMENT:** • Four horsemen are present and repair is ineffective • Absence of positive affect • Sound marital house
INTERVENTIONS: • Sound marital house • Dreams-within-conflict • Label destructive patterns • Enhance the marital friendship • Sentiment override	**CHANGE:** • Accepting influence • Decrease negative interactions • Increase positive affect
TERMINATION: • When couples can consistently develop their own interventions that work reasonably well	**SELF OF THE THERAPIST:** • Not discussed
EVALUATION: • Theory is based on Gottman's research	

> **RESOURCES:**
> Gottman, J. M. (1999). *The marriage clinic*. New York, NY: W. W. Norton & Company. www.gottman.com

NOTES

Note

1 May be used in workshops, courses, and for other use as appropriate. Please give © credit to Thorana Nelson and students. ©Thorana Nelson and Students

Index

Ackerman Institute 80
adaptation means change 100
anxiety 45–49, 101, 164–165, 169, 172
attachment: needs 51; styles 51
axioms of communication 22

Bateson, G. xiii, 17, 35, 53, 66, 151
Bertalanffy von, L. xiii, 1, 85
best friend question 106
best hopes 72, 84, 112
boundaries 4–11, 14, 29–34; balanced 34; clear 34; diffuse 31–34; enmeshed 31; permeable 7; rigid 7, 31; roles and rules 31–32; and rules 31–32; semipermeable 7
Bowen Family Therapy 44–50, 163–172; anxiety 45, 49; assumptions and concepts 45–48; autonomy 47, 49; detriangling 49, 164; differentiation is both internal and external 45; emotional cutoff 46, 164, 166; emotional intimacy 47, 49; emotionality 44, 47; emotional system 45; emotions 165; emotions, separate from thinking 45; family emotionality 45; fusion 46, 164, 166; managing stress 164; multigenerational family transition 45, 165; practices 49–50; process questions 49, 165; reactivity 45; symptoms 45; therapist as nonanxious third part of a triangle 49; triangles 164–65; triangling 45, 46
Brief Family Therapy Center 54, 80
Brief Therapy Center 53, 80, 152

can't not communicate 22
circular causality 15
circularity 15–16, 19–22, 51, 67, 85, 87, 92, 136, 170
circular questions 106
client as expert 85, 101–103, 145
co-construct 62, 80, 87, 95, 103
co-construction 57, 61
Cognitive Behavioral Therapy 51
communication: command 22; content and relationship 22; digital and analogic 24; formulation 61, 113; report 22; theory 22–28
compliments 68–69
constructivism 153
coping questions 70, 75, 79
culture 8, 20, 33, 73, 109
cultural view 7
cybernetics 14–21

detriangling 49, 154
development of Solution-Focused Brief Therapy 53–54
diagnoses as descriptions 87
differentiation of self 44, 45–49, 164–165; internal and external 45

EARS 82
Emotionally Focused Therapy 51; emotion as agent of change 51
emotion attachment 51
enactment: assessment 33, 147, 149; intervention 34, 148
equifinality 11, 84, 92
Erickson, Milton 53, 57
executive subsystem 32
experiments 81

feedback 14, 19, 36, 170; negative 17, 36, 103
feedback loops 19
first- and second- order change 5, 19–21
Functional Family Therapy 50
future talk 61

genograms 49, 165–167
Georgetown University 44
go slowly 41, 153

harm 18, 56, 60, 154
homeostasis 11, 17, 35
homeostatic resistance 30

identified patient 30
integrative approaches 50–52
interactional patterns 21, 41, 54, 152
Internal Family Systems Therapy 99
interrupting sequences 152
isomorphism 13–14, 25, 133, 158, 170

joining 34, 112, 147

leading from behind 62, 105
linear 15, 16, 21, 67, 83, 94, 115

Menninger Foundation 44
Mental Research Institute 36, 53
metaphor 39, 41, 159
metarules 4–5, 9, 18, 21, 31; second-order change 21
MFT model charts 145, 179
Milan approach 80
Minuchin 29, 30, 32, 34, 41, 46, 50
miracle day 64, 70, 74
miracle question 73–75
morphogenesis 9, 17, 19, 35
motivator: control or power 158; love 158
MRI Strategic Therapy 35–41, 151–157
Multidimensional Family Therapy 50
Multisystemic Therapy 50

Narrative Approach 80
National Institute of Mental 44
nonanxious third part of a triangle 49
not-knowing 86

object relations 51
Ockham's Razor 57
ordeal 42, 159
oxbow in a river 88

Palo Alto, CA 36
paradox 39–41, 152–154, 158–159
parentified child 7, 32
parents as team 32
past: cannot be changed 59; exceptions 65; influencing present 45
pattern and sequence 19–20
positive reframe 156
preferred future 62, 64, 67, 69, 70–75, 78, 84, 86, 106–107, 143
pretend intervention 161
primary emotion 52
problem phobic 66, 115

problems as embedded in structures 34
problems in context 6
process 12–13, 18, 24, 37–38, 104,
    132, 137, 144; vs. content 12–13
punctuation 20, 23, 38

raising intensity 50, 147, 149
reciprocity 15
recursion 15, 16, 19, 51
reframe 34, 38, 152, 158; positive 159
relational questions 66–67
resistance 136–137; client 58; death of
    58; homeostatic 30; from others 89

scaling: ability 78; confidence 78;
    courage 78; hope 81; miracle day
    75; motivation 78; preferred future
    75
secondary emotions 52
second-order change 5
Signs of Safety 138
Simplify 57
slow to know 55
Solution-Focused Brief Therapy:
    assumptions 57–62; with Bowen
    Family Systems Therapy 163–72;
    change is constant and inevitable
    57; changes in the approach 83–84;
    client as expert 61; clients have
    resources 58; couples 139–43;
    emotions 83; exceptions 57, 65, 68,
    71–72; experiments 58; families
    108–39; focus on what is possible
    60; future perfect 74; general
    practices 62–70; homework 58, 81;
    identifying resources 58; if it ain't
    broke. . . 57; instances (of miracle
    day) 99; leading from behind 62;
    miracle set 74; relationship between
    problem and solution 58–60;
    resource-based 56; situations vs.
    problems 70; small changes lead to
    bigger changes 60; with Strategic

Family Therapy (Haley and Madanes
    157–63; with Strategic Family
    Therapy (Mental Research Institute)
    151–57; with Structural Family
    Therapy 146–51; therapy is
    co-constructed 61; well-formed
    goals 72
Solution-Focused Brief Therapy
    integration with family therapy:
    change is constant and inevitable
    88–90; clients are experts 101;
    clients have resources 94; client-
    therapist relationship 104; co-
    construct 103; curious questions
    105; do something different
    93; focus on future and change
    100–101; if it ain't broke. . . 91;
    miracle question 106; once you
    know what works 91–92; preferred
    future 106; relationship between
    problems and solutions 94–100;
    relationship questions 105; small
    change leads to bigger change
    101; stance 55–56; Therapy Is Co-
    Constructed 103–4; well-formed
    goals 104–5
Solution-Focused Brief Therapy
    practices: breaks 80; client-therapist
    relationship 62–63; compliments
    79, 84; coping 79; coping questions
    75; details 67–68; directives, tasks,
    and signs 81; exceptions 74, 81;
    instances of miracle or solution
    72; interviews about harm 79; not
    solution-forced 69; preferred future
    72–73; pre-session change 71;
    previous solutions questions 71;
    questions 65; relationship questions
    75; scaling 75–78; second and
    further sessions 82; situations 79;
    strength-based 56; suppositional
    frame 69; tap on shoulder 62; timing
    69–70; well-formed goals 63–65;

what else? 70, 76, 141; what was helpful 82

Solution-Focused Brief Therapy stance 55–56; client competence 56; collaborative 88; curious 55; non-normative and nonpathologizing 56; preferred future 86; respectful 55; tentative 55

Strategic Family Therapy (Haley and Madanes) 41–44, 157–163; metaphor 41; motivation 41; ordeal 42, 159; pretend 42

Strategic Family Therapy (Mental Research Institute) 35–41; assumptions 57–62; direct interventions 39; indirect interventions 39–41; metaphor 39; practices 41; reframe 43; role of therapist 41; symptoms are messages in the system 41; symptoms as metaphor 42; tasks 41

Structural Family Therapy 29–35; goals 32–33; practices 34–35; problems as embedded in structures 34; raising intensity 35; Role of the Therapist 33; rules and roles 8–9; tasks 34; unbalancing 35

subsystems 30
suggestions 65
system concepts 3–14
Systemic thinking as worldview or lens 1
systems 30
systems therapy 24–27

tasks 34, 54, 84; ordeal 42, 159; pretend 42
therapy team 158
Timing 69–70
Titanic 66
triangulation 47

utilization 57

vague (de Shazer) 80
vague responses Solution-Focused Brief Therapy 65
violence 27
Virgin Suicides 6

Wampold 93
Watzlawick 22, 36, 53, 85
Weakland 36, 53, 54
wholeness 2–4, 85